Andrew Seth Pringle-Pattison, Andrew Seth Pringle-Pattison

Man's Place in the Cosmos: and other Essays

Andrew Seth Pringle-Pattison, Andrew Seth Pringle-Pattison

Man's Place in the Cosmos: and other Essays

ISBN/EAN: 9783743358737

Manufactured in Europe, USA, Canada, Australia, Japa

Cover: Foto ©Thomas Meinert / pixelio.de

Manufactured and distributed by brebook publishing software (www.brebook.com)

Andrew Seth Pringle-Pattison, Andrew Seth Pringle-Pattison

Man's Place in the Cosmos: and other Essays

MAN'S PLACE IN THE COSMOS

" Nach ewigen, ehrnen,
Grossen Gesetzen
Müssen wir alle
Unseres Daseins
Kreise vollenden.

Nur allein der Mensch
Vermag das Unmögliche;
Er unterscheidet,
Wählet und richtet;
Er kann dem Augenblick
Dauer verleihen.

Er allein darf
Den Guten lohnen,
Den Bösen strafen,
Heilen und retten ;
Alles Irrende, Schweifende
Nützlich verbinden."

—GOETHE, *" Das Göttliche."*

MAN'S PLACE IN THE COSMOS

AND

OTHER ESSAYS

BY

ANDREW SETH, M.A., LL.D.

PROFESSOR OF LOGIC AND METAPHYSICS IN
THE UNIVERSITY OF EDINBURGH

WILLIAM BLACKWOOD AND SONS
EDINBURGH AND LONDON
MDCCCXCVII

PREFACE.

THE title of this volume may seem disproportioned to its contents. A systematic discussion of "man's place in the cosmos" would obviously involve the whole range of science and of metaphysics. These essays make no pretence to be such a discussion. Nevertheless it is not unadvisedly that the title of the first paper has been extended to the volume as a whole, and thus used to indicate the general character of its contents. The papers of which it is composed were written within the last six years, and are, in the first instance, a criticism of some of the more significant contributions to philosophy which have appeared during that period. They cannot, therefore, be taken as a series, in which there is a systematic progress from the earlier essays to those which follow.

But it will be found that they are all, at bottom, treatments of the same theme, man's relation to the forces of nature and to the absolute ground of things, or, in the words of the title, man's place in the cosmos. The books or pamphlets criticised were originally selected for criticism because of their bearing upon this fundamental question, in which all vital interest in philosophy centres. And whatever the starting-point of the discussion may be, the main concern of every essay is to enforce the same view of the world and of man.

That view I have described in one of the papers as humanism, in opposition to naturalism; in another reference, it might be described as ethicism, in opposition to a too narrow intellectualism. Man as rational, and, in virtue of self-conscious reason, the free shaper of his own destiny, furnishes us, I contend, with our only indefeasible standard of value, and our clearest light as to the nature of the divine. He does what science, occupied only with the laws of events, and speculative metaphysics, when it surrenders itself to the exclusive guidance of the intellect, alike find unintelligible, and are fain to pronounce impossible—he acts. As Goethe puts it in a seeming paradox, *Man alone achieves the impossible.* But inexplicable, in a sense, as man's **personal agency** is—nay, the **one** perpetual miracle—it is nevertheless **our** surest datum and our **only clue to the mystery of existence.**

This position is maintained in several of the essays against the lower **monism of the naturalistic** systems. In the long **essay** entitled **"A New Theory of the** Absolute," it is defended against the Spinozism which permeates **Mr Bradley's** statement **of metaphysical** monism. This **essay** emphasises, on **the** one hand, **the** necessary **limitations of** human insight and, on the other hand, the validity **or** practical truth **of our** human rendering of the divine. **Such a view of the** cosmos **must** rest ultimately, I think, upon **a conviction of the absolute** value of the ethical life. **For there is no such thing as a philosophy without** assumptions. **Every idealistic** theory **of the** world has for its ultimate **premiss** a logically unsupported judgment **of value — a** judgment which affirms an **end of** intrinsic worth, and accepts thereby a standard of unconditional obligation.

On account **of this** unity of contention, the essays have been brought together, in **the** hope that they may serve a useful purpose. The paper **on** Professor Huxley's "Evolution and Ethics" **appeared in 'Blackwood's** Magazine,' **three of the** others in the 'Contemporary

Review,' and the short paper on "The Use of the Term 'Naturalism,'" in the 'Philosophical Review.' To the editors and proprietors of these Reviews I am indebted for their courtesy in sanctioning this republication. The essays are republished without substantial alteration, but I have availed myself of the opportunity of revision, and have also reinserted a few passages which had been omitted, in order to bring the treatment within the ordinary compass of review-articles. The second part of the essay on "The 'New' Psychology and Automatism," though written in 1892 as an integral part of the discussion, is now printed for the first time. It gives the question a wider range, and will be found, I hope, to make the treatment more complete. Mechanism in physiology, "presentationism" in psychology, materialism and sheer pantheism in philosophy, may be regarded as different aspects of the same preconception—the denial of the presence of a real cause at any point in the sequence of events.

I desire in conclusion to express my thanks to my colleague, M. Charles Sarolea, for his kindness in reading the proofs and making many helpful suggestions.

University of Edinburgh, *February* 1897.

CONTENTS.

MAN'S PLACE IN THE COSMOS.

PROFESSOR HUXLEY ON NATURE AND MAN.

PROFESSOR HUXLEY'S Romanes Lecture on
"Evolution and Ethics" deservedly attracted a
large amount of attention on its appearance. That
attention was due not only to the importance of the
subject handled and the reputation of the lecturer,
but quite as much to the breadth and scope of the
treatment, to the nobility of tone and the deep human
feeling which characterised a singularly impressive
utterance. Popular interest was also excited by the
nature of the conclusion reached, which, in the mouth
of the pioneer and prophet of evolution, had the air
of being something like a palinode. Criticisms of the
lecture appeared at the time by Mr Leslie Stephen
in the 'Contemporary Review,' and by Mr Herbert

A

Spencer in a letter to the 'Athenæum';[1] and many discussions appeared in theological quarters. But the subject as a whole was perhaps dismissed from public attention before its significance had been exhausted, or indeed properly grasped. Professor Huxley's argument and the criticisms it called forth illuminate most instructively some deep-seated ambiguities of philosophical terminology, and at the same time bring into sharp relief the fundamental difference of standpoint which divides philosophical thinkers. The questions at issue, moreover, are not merely speculative; already they cast their shadow upon literature and life. The opportunity of elucidation is therefore in the best sense timely, and no apology seems needed for an attempt to recall attention to the points in dispute and to accentuate their significance.

The outstanding feature of Professor Huxley's argument is the sharp contrast drawn between nature and ethical man, and the sweeping indictment of "the cosmic process" at the bar of morality. The problem of suffering and the almost complete absence of any

[1] The Romanes Lecture was delivered on the 18th May 1893, and published shortly thereafter. Mr Spencer's letter appeared in the 'Athenæum' of August 5, and Mr Leslie Stephen's article in the 'Contemporary Review' of August 1893. The present paper was published in 'Blackwood's Magazine,' December 1893.

relation between suffering and moral desert is the theme from which he starts, and to which he continually returns. "The dread problem of evil," "the moral indifference of nature," "the unfathomable injustice of the nature of things"—this is the aspect of the world which has burned itself deeply into the writer's soul, and which speaks in moving eloquence from his pages. The Buddhistic and the Stoic attempts to grapple with the problem are considered, and are found to end alike in absolute renunciation. "By the Tiber, as by the Ganges, ethical man admits that the cosmos is too strong for him; and, destroying every bond which ties him to it by ascetic discipline, he seeks salvation in absolute renunciation" (p. 29). Is the antagonism, then, final and hopeless, or can modern science and philosophy offer any better reconciliation of ethical man with the nature to which as an animal he belongs, and to whose vast unconscious forces he lies open on every side? As Professor Huxley puts the question himself in his opening pages—Is there or is there not "a sanction for morality in the ways of the cosmos"? Man has built up "an artificial world within the cosmos": has human society its roots and its justification in the underlying nature of the cosmos, or is it in

very truth an " artificial " world, which is at odds
with that nature and must be in perpetual conflict
with it ? The Stoic rule which places virtue in "following nature" is easily shown to be a phrase of
many meanings, and to demand qualification by reference, first, to the specific nature of man, and then to
a higher nature or guiding faculty within the mind of
man himself. But the modern ethics of evolution
apparently claim to have bridged the gulf and to have
made the ethical process continuous with the cosmic
process of organic nature,—they claim, in short, to
exhibit the ethical life as only a continuation, on
another plane, of the struggle for existence. If this
claim is well founded, and the two worlds are really
continuous, then the maxim, " Follow nature," will
have been proved to be, after all, the sum and substance of virtue.

It is against this naturalisation of ethics that Professor Huxley protests in the strongest terms. He
readily allows that the ethical evolutionists may be
right in their natural history of the moral sentiments.
But " as the immoral sentiments have no less been
evolved, there is, so far, as much natural sanction for
the one as the other. . . . Cosmic evolution may teach
us how the good and the evil tendencies of man may

have come about; but, in itself, it is incompetent to furnish any better reason why what we call good is preferable to what we call evil, than we had before" (p. 31). That is to say, the **origin** of a belief and the validity of a belief, or the origin **of a** tendency and the ethical quality **of** that tendency, **are logically two dis-** tinct questions. But the evolutionist is apt **to** make the **answer to the first do duty** as an answer to the second also, **because** he **has in** reality no standard of appreciation **to** apply to any phenomenon except that of mere existence. "Whatever **is, is** right," **or** at all events, "Whatever is predominant, is right," is the only motto of the consistent evolutionist. This is embodied in the phrase "survival of the **fittest**," which is used—illegitimately, as **we shall** see—to effect **the transition from the merely natural to the ethical world.**

In opposition **to** such theories, **Professor** Huxley con- **tends** that the analogies of the struggle **for existence** throw **no** light on the ethical nature **of** man.

Cosmic nature is no school of virtue, but the headquarters of the enemy of ethical nature (p. 27). Self-assertion, the unscrupulous seizing **upon** all that can be grasped, the tenacious holding **of** all **that can** be kept, . . . constitute the essence of the **struggle for existence.** . . . For his suc- cessful progress as **far as the savage state, man** has been largely indebted to those qualities which he shares with the ape and the tiger (p. 6).

So far is this struggle from explaining morality that

the practice of what is ethically best—what we call goodness or virtue—involves a course of conduct which, in all respects, is opposed to that which leads to success in the cosmic struggle for existence. In place of ruthless self-assertion, it demands self-restraint; in place of thrusting aside, or treading down, all competitors, it requires that the individual shall not merely respect, but shall help, his fellows. . . . It repudiates the gladiatorial theory of existence. . . . Laws and moral precepts are directed to the end of curbing the cosmic process and reminding the individual of his duty to the community, to the protection and influence of which he owes, if not existence itself, at least the life of something better than a brutal savage.

In short, "social progress means a checking of the cosmic process at every step, and the substitution for it of another which may be called the ethical process." This leads up to the characteristic call to arms with which the address concludes: "Let us understand, once for all, that the ethical progress of society depends, not on imitating the cosmic process, still less in running away from it, but in combating it" (pp. 33, 34).

Such is the logical framework of the lecture. It is obvious that the important points of the treat-

ment are : (1) The emphasis laid upon the division
between man and **nature**, which a **reviewer** in the
'Athenæum'[1] called "an approximation to the Paul-
ine dogma **of** nature and grace"; and **(2)** the mood
of militant heroism, not untouched, however, by stoical resignation, which naturally results from contemplation of the unequal struggle between the microcosm
and the macrocosm.

Before proceeding **to** consider the consistency **of**
Professor Huxley's argument and the ultimate ten-
ability **of** his position, I wish to say, in regard to
the first point, how timely, it seems to **me,** is his
insistence on the gulf between man and non-human
nature; how sound **is** the stand **he** takes upon **the**
ethical nature of man **as** that **which is alone of** significance and worth in the "transitory adjustment of
contending forces," **which** otherwise **constitutes the**
cosmos. Whether the **breach is to** be taken as **abso-**
lute **or not, it** is at least apparent that if **man with**
his virtues and vices be included *simpliciter* and without more ado in **a** merely natural order of facts, we
inevitably tend **to** lose sight of that nature within na-
ture which makes man what he **is.** **The** tendency **so**
to include man has become a settled habit in much of

[1] July 22, 1893.

our current literature. I need not speak of the documents of so-called Naturalism, with their never-ending analysis of *la bête humaine*—analysis from which one would be slow to gather that any such qualities as justice, purity, or disinterested affection had ever disturbed the brutish annals of force and lust. But in other quarters, even where the picture is not so dark, the fashion still is to treat man *as a natural product,* —not as the responsible shaper of his destiny, but, void of spiritual struggles and ideal hopes, as the unresisting channel of the impulses which sway him hither and thither, and issue now in one course of action, now in another. This literature is inartistic, even on its own terms, for, blinded by its materialistic fatalism, it does not even give us things as they are. The higher literature never forgets that man, as Pascal put it, is nobler than the universe; and freedom (in some sense of that ambiguous term) must be held to be a postulate of true art no less than of morality. But besides being bad art, literature of this sort has a subtly corrosive influence upon the ethical temper. For the power of will, as Lamennais said, is that in us which is most quickly used up: "Ce qui s'use le plus vite en nous, c'est la volonté." Hence the insidious force of the sugges-

tion that we **do not will at all,** but are merely **the**
instruments of **our desires.   For this is** to justify,
or at least to excuse, every **passion on the** ground
of its "natural" origin.   This temper of mind is
found invading even more serious writers, and it **is**
traceable **ultimately to** the **same** confusion between
the **laws of human** conduct **and the workings of**
nature **in the** irresponsible creatures of **the field.**
M. Renan, it will be remembered, delicately excuses
himself in his **'Souvenirs'** — **rallies** himself, as **we**
may say—on **his** continued **practice of** chastity :—

I continued to live **in** Paris as I had lived in the semi-
nary.   Later, I saw very well the vanity of that virtue as
of all the rest.   I recognised **in** particular that nature cares
not at all whether man **is** chaste **or not.**   I cannot rid **my-**
self [he says elsewhere in **the** same volume] **of the** idea that
after all it is perhaps the libertine who is right, **and** who
practises **the true philosophy** of life.

Many will remember, too, how Matthew Arnold
took **up** this parable **when** he discoursed in America
on the cult **of the great** goddess Lubricity, to which,
as he said, contemporary France seemed more and
more to be **devoting** herself.   After much delicate
banter and much direct plain-speaking, Mr Arnold
turns upon M. Renan **and** cuts to the root **of the**
fallacy in a single sentence. "**Instead** of saying that

nature cares nothing about chastity, let us say that human nature, *our* nature, cares about it a great deal." And when we meet the same fallacy invading our own literature, the same answer will suffice. I think it may be worth pointing out a notable instance in a novel widely read and highly praised within the last few years. Mr Hardy's 'Tess of the D'Urbervilles' is unquestionably a powerful work, but it suffers, in my opinion, both artistically and ethically, from this tendency to assimilate the moral and the natural. To smack of the soil is in many senses a term of praise; but even rustic men and women are not altogether products of the soil, and Mr Hardy is in danger of so regarding them. What I wish, however, to point out here is the pernicious fallacy which underlies a statement like the following. Tess, after she has fallen from her innocence, is wont to wander alone in the woods, a prey to her own reflections, "terrified without reason," says the author, by "a cloud of moral hobgoblins."

It was they [he continues] that were out of harmony with the actual world, not she. Walking among the sleeping birds in the hedges, watching the skipping rabbits on a moonlit warren, or standing under a pheasant-laden bough, she looked upon herself as a figure of guilt intruding into the haunts of innocence. But all the while she was making a distinction where there was no difference. Feeling herself in antagonism, she was quite in accord. She had been made to break an accepted social law, but no law known to the environment in which she fancied herself such an anomaly.

The implication of such a passage is that the "accepted social law" is a mere convention, and that the deeper truth, "the actual world," is to be found in the hedgerows and the warrens. To satisfy an animal prompting without scruple or hesitation, and without the qualms of a fantastical remorse, is only to fulfil the law of nature, and to put one's self in harmony with one's surroundings. The shallowness of such revolt against "accepted social laws" is too apparent to need further exposure. A convention truly, in one sense, the moral law in question is; but upon this convention the fabric of human society and all the sanctities of the family rest. He must be strangely blinded by a word who deems this sanction insufficient, or who would pit in such a case a "natural" impulse against a "social" law.

In view of pervasive misconceptions and fallacies like these, it is eminently salutary, I repeat, to have our attention so impressively recalled by Professor Huxley to the idea of human life as an *imperium*

in imperio — a realm which, though it rises out of
nature, and remains exposed to the shock of natural
forces, requires for its laws no foreign sanction, but
bases them solely on the perfection of human nature
itself.   For, even though Professor Huxley's way of
stating the opposition should prove ultimately untenable, the breach between ethical man and pre-human
nature constitutes without exception the most important fact which the universe has to show; and for
a true understanding of the world it is far more vital
to grasp the significance of this breach than to be
misled by a cheap desire for unity and system into
minimising, or even denying, the fact.

It is time, however, to examine Professor Huxley's
position and arguments more closely.   His critics have
not been slow to remark upon the ambiguity lurking
in the phrase "cosmic process," which occurs so often
throughout the lecture, in antithesis to the ethical
process—to the moral and social life of man.   And
they point with one accord to Note 19 as containing, in
effect, a retractation of his own doctrine by Professor
Huxley himself.   "Of course, strictly speaking," we
read in the note, "social life and the ethical process, in
virtue of which it advances towards perfection, are part
and parcel of the general process of evolution."   As Mr

Spencer pointedly asks, "If the ethical man is not a product of the cosmic process, what is he a product of?" Or as Shakespeare expressed it in the often-quoted lines—

> "Nature is made better by no means
> But nature makes that means : so, o'er that art,
> Which you say adds to nature, is an art
> That nature makes."

If the cosmic process be understood in the full latitude of the phrase, this is, indeed, so obvious, and the critic's victory so easy, that it is hard to believe Professor Huxley's position rests altogether on a foundation so weak. The term "nature," and still more an expression like "the cosmic process," may be taken in an all-inclusive sense as equivalent to the universe as a whole or the nature of things; and if so, it is obvious that human nature with its ethical characteristics is embraced within the larger whole. The unity of the cosmos—in some sense—is not so much a conclusion to be proved as an inevitable assumption. Professor Huxley apparently denies this unity in the text of his lecture, and is naturally obliged to reassert it in his note. This constitutes the weakness of his position. The part must be somehow included in the process of the whole; there is no extra-cosmic source from which a revolt against the principles of the cosmos could draw inspiration or support.

Now the strength of the evolutionary theory of ethics lies in its frank recognition of the unity of the cosmos; and in this it is, so far, at one with the philosophical doctrine of Idealism to which it is otherwise so much opposed—the doctrine which finds the ultimate reality of the universe in mind or spirit, and its End in the perfecting of spiritual life. But each of these theories exhibits the unity of the world in its own way. The way taken by the ethical evolutionists is to naturalise morality, to assimilate ethical experience to nature, in the lower or narrower sense in which it is used to denote all that happens in the known world *except* the responsible activities of human beings. And it is against this removing of landmarks that Professor Huxley, rightly, as it seems to me, protests. For though Mr Spencer and Mr Leslie Stephen may be technically in the right, inasmuch as human nature is unquestionably part of the nature of things, it is the inherent tendency of their theories to substitute for this wider nature the laws and processes of that narrower, non-human world, to which the term nature is on the whole restricted by current usage.

This tendency is inherent in every system which

takes as its sole principle of explanation the carrying back of facts or **events to their** antecedent conditions. And, as it happens, this is explicitly formulated by Mr Stephen, **in his article in** the 'Contemporary Review,' as the only permissible meaning of **explanation: "To** 'explain' a fact is to assign its causes—that is, give the preceding **set** of facts out **of which it arose."** But **surely, I** may be asked, you do not intend to challenge a principle which underlies all scientific procedure, and **w**hich may **even** claim to be self-evident? I certainly do not propose to deny the formal correctness of the principle, but I maintain most strongly that the current application of it covers a subtle and very serious fallacy, for *the true nature of the cause only becomes apparent in the effect.* Now, if we explain a **fact by giving** "the preceding set of facts out of which **it** arose," **we** practically resolve the fact into these antecedents—that is to say, we identify it with them. When we are dealing with some limited sphere of phenomena, within which the facts are all of one order—say, the laws of moving bodies as treated in mechanics—there **may** be no practical disadvantage from this limited interpretation of causation. But when we pass from one order of facts to another—say, from the inorganic to the organic, or, still more, from animal **life** to the self-conscious life of man—the inadequacy of such explanation stares us in the face. For "the preceding set of facts," which we treat as the cause or sufficient explanation of the phenomenon in question, is *ex hypothesi* different from the phenomenon it is said to explain; and the difference is, that it consists of simpler elements. To explain, according to this view, is to reduce to simpler conditions. But if the elements are really simpler, there is the fact of their combination into a more complex product to be explained, and the fact of their combination in such a way as to produce precisely the result in question. And if we choose to take the antecedent conditions, as they appear in themselves, apart from the all-important circumstance of the production of this effect, we have, no doubt, a "preceding set of facts," but we certainly have not, in any true sense, the *cause* of the phenomenon. We have eliminated the very characteristic we set out to explain— namely, the difference of the new phenomenon from the antecedents out of which it appears to have been evolved. Hence it is that, in the sense indicated, all explanation of the higher by the lower is philosophically a hysteron proteron. The antecedents assigned are not the causes of the consequents; for by antecedents the naturalistic theories mean the *antecedents in abstraction from their consequents*—the antecedents taken as they appear in themselves, or as we might suppose them to be if no such consequents had **ever** issued from them. So conceived, however, the antecedents (matter and energy, for example) have no real existence—they are mere *entia rationis*, abstract aspects of the one concrete fact which we call the universe. **The true** nature of the antecedents **is only** learned by reference **to the** consequents **which** follow; **or, as I** put it before, **the** true nature of the cause **only becomes** apparent in the effect. **All** ultimate **or philosophical** explanation must look to the end. **Hence** the futility of all attempts to explain human **life in terms of the** merely animal, to explain **life in terms of the inorganic,** and ultimately to **find a** sufficient formula for the **cosmic process** in terms **of** the redistribution of matter **and** motion. **If we are in earnest** with the doctrine **that the universe is one, we have to read** back the **nature of the latest consequent** into **the** remotest antecedent. Only then **is** the **one, in any true** sense, the cause of the other.

Applying this to **the present** question, we may say that, just as within the limits **of the** organic world there **may** be exhibited **an** intelligible evolution of living **forms,** so within **the** moral world we may

certainly have an evolution of the moral sentiments
and of the institutions which subserve ethical conduct.
But as, in the one case, we must start with the fact of
life—that is to say, with the characteristic ways of
behaving which are found in living matter and which
are not found in dead matter—so, in the other case,
we must carry with us from the outset the characteristics or postulates of moral experience—namely,
self-consciousness, with the sense of responsibility, and
the capacity for sympathy which is based on the
ability to represent to one's self the life and feelings
of another. Such an evolution within the moral sphere
does not justify us in presenting morality as an "evolution" from non-moral conditions—that is, in resolving
morality into non-moral elements. And this Mr Leslie
Stephen seems to admit in an important passage of the
article already referred to. "Morality proper," he says,
"begins when sympathy begins; when we really desire
the happiness of others, or, as Kant says, when we
treat other men as an end, and not simply as a means.
Undoubtedly this involves a new principle no less than
the essential principle of all true morality." I cannot
but regard this as an important admission, but at the
same time I am bound to say that, till I met this
unexpected sentence of Mr Stephen's, I had supposed

that the admission **of** "a new principle" was precisely what the evolutionists were, of all things, most anxious to avoid.

It seems **to** me, therefore, that though Professor Huxley may have put himself technically in the wrong by **speaking of** "the cosmical **process,**" **his** contention is far from **being so** inept as **a** verbal criticism would make it appear. **It is** really directed against the submergence of ethical man in the processes of non-ethical and non-human **nature; and if** any justification **is to be** sought for the use of the phrase, we may find it in the tendency inherent in the evolutionary method of explanation—the tendency already explained to substantiate antecedents in abstraction from their consequents, and thus practically to identify the cosmos **with** its lowest aspects. **If** the evolutionists do not make this identification in their own minds, they are at least singularly successful in producing that impression upon their readers.

On another important point connected with, and indeed involved **in,** the foregoing, Professor Huxley, **by** an unguarded statement, **laid** himself open to a **pretty** obvious and apparently conclusive rejoinder. "**The** cosmic process," he says **in** one place, "has no sort of relation to moral ends." But "the moral indifference of nature," even in the restricted sense of the term, cannot be maintained so absolutely. Nature undoubtedly puts a premium upon certain virtues, and punishes certain modes of excess and defect by decrease of vitality and positive pain. As Mr Stephen says: "That chastity, temperance, truthfulness, and energy are on the whole advantages both to the individual and the race does not, I fancy, require elaborate proof, nor need I argue at length that the races in which they are common will therefore have inevitable advantages in the struggle for existence." But if so, then it would seem that cosmic nature is not, as it was represented, "the headquarters of the enemy of ethical nature"; to a certain extent it may even be regarded as a "school of virtue." The sphere, however, in which this holds true is a comparatively limited one, being substantially restricted to temperance, in the Greek sense of the word—that is to say, moderation in the indulgence of the animal appetites, to which may, no doubt, be added, with Mr Stephen, energy. But nature, as distinct from that human nature which organises itself into societies and adds its own sanctions to the moral ideal which it is continually widening and deepening—non-human nature seems to have no sanctions even for such fundamental virtues as truthfulness, justice, and beneficence, still less for the finer shades and higher nobilities of character in which human nature flowers. And even in regard to the list of virtues cited, it might be argued that cosmic nature sanctions and furthers them only when we deliberately restrict our survey to the present stage of the evolutionary process — the stage during which man has grown to be what he is on this planet. Within this limited period nature, through the struggle for existence, may be said to have favoured the evolution of the morally best. But it is no intrinsic quality of the struggle to produce this result. Here, it appears to me, we strike upon the deeper truth which prompted Professor Huxley's somewhat unguarded statement, and we are under an important obligation to him for the exposure of what he appropriately calls " the fallacy of the fittest."

Fittest [he writes] has a connotation of "best"; and about best there hangs a moral flavour. In cosmic nature, however, what is "fittest" depends upon the conditions. Long since, I ventured to point out that if our hemisphere were to cool again, the survival of the fittest might bring about, in the vegetable kingdom, a population of more and more stunted and humbler and humbler organisms, until the "fittest" that survived might be nothing but lichens, diatoms, and such microscopic organisms as those which give red snow its colour; while, if it became hotter, the pleasant valleys of the Thames and Isis might be uninhabitable by any animated beings save those that flourish in a tropical jungle. They, as the fittest, the best adapted to the changed conditions, would survive (p. 32).

Mr Spencer has been forward to emphasise his agreement with this position, and has recalled attention to an essay of his own, twenty years old, in which he makes the same distinction:—

The law is not the survival of the "better" or the "stronger," if we give to these words anything like their ordinary meanings. It is the survival of those which are constitutionally fittest to thrive under the conditions in which they are placed; and very often that which, humanly speaking, is inferiority, causes the survival. Superiority, whether in size, strength, activity, or sagacity, is, other things equal, at the cost of diminished fertility; and where the life led by a species does not demand these higher attributes, the species profits by decrease of them, and accompanying increase of fertility. This is the reason why there occur so many cases of retrograde metamorphosis. . . . When it is remembered that these cases outnumber all others, it will be seen that the expression "survivorship of the better" is wholly inappropriate.[1]

Out of the mouth of two such witnesses this point may be taken as established. But if so, I entirely fail to see where, on naturalistic principles, we get our standard of higher and lower, of better and worse.

[1] Essays, vol. i. p. 379, "Mr Martineau on Evolution."

If changed conditions of life were to lead to the de-
humanising of the race, to the dropping one by one
of the ethical qualities which we are accustomed to
commend, whence the justification for pronouncing
this process a "retrograde metamorphosis"?   There
can be no other sense of better or worse, on the theory,
than more or less successful adaptation to the conditions of the environment, and what survives is best
just because it survives.   The latest stage of the process
must necessarily, therefore, be better than all that went
before, from the mere fact that it has maintained itself.
Mere existence is the only test we have to apply, and
at every stage it would seem that we are bound to
say, Whatever is, is right.   But this is tantamount to
saying that, when the theory of evolution is taken in
its widest scope, it is not really legitimate to say that
nature abets or sanctions morality; since the result
of further evolution—or, to speak more properly, of
further cosmical changes—might be to dethrone our
present ethical conduct from its temporary position
as the fittest, and to leave no scope for what we
now regard as virtue.   The type of conduct which
would then succeed, and which would so far have
the sanction of nature on its side, we should be con-
strained, it seems to me, to pronounce superior to

the conduct which, from our present point of view, seems to us better; because the latter, if adopted, would in the altered circumstances set us at variance with our surroundings, and so fail. Failure or success in the struggle for existence must, on the theory, be the sole moral standard. Good is what survives; evil is what once was fittest, but is so no longer. Thus, our present good may become—nay, is inevitably becoming—evil, and that not, as might be contended, in the sense of merging in a higher good. We have no guarantee that the movement of change, miscalled evolution, must continue in the line of past progress : it may gradually, and as it were imperceptibly, assume another direction—a direction which our present moral ideas would condemn as retrograde. Yet, none the less, the mere fact of change would be sufficient to convert our present good into evil.

Such, I must insist, is the only logical position of a naturalistic ethics. But an important outcome of the recent discussion has been to show that the most prominent upholders of the theory do not hold it in its logical form. Mr Spencer, as we have seen, has strongly insisted that survival of the fittest does not mean survival of the better, or even of the stronger; and Mr Stephen tells us that the struggle for existence, instead of being the explanation of morality, "belongs to an underlying order of facts to which moral epithets cannot properly be applied. It denotes a condition of which the moralist has to take account, and to which morality has to be adapted, but which, just because it is a 'cosmic process,' cannot be altered, however much we may alter the conduct which it dictates." Surely this comes very near to admitting Professor Huxley's contention, that our moral standard is not derived from the struggle for existence, but rather implies its reversal, substituting for selfishness sympathy for others, and, in Mr Stephen's own words, "the sense of duty which each man owes to society at large." Mr Spencer speaks of an "ethical check" upon the struggle for existence: it is our duty, he says, "to mitigate the evils" which it entails in the social state. "The use of morality," says Mr Stephen, "is to humanise the struggle, to minimise the sufferings of those who lose the game, and to offer the prizes to the qualities which are advantageous to all, rather than to those which serve to intensify the bitterness of the conflict." But this is neither more nor less than to say that, as soon as man becomes social and moral, he has to act counter to the leading characteristics of the struggle for existence. He becomes animated by

other ideals, or, to speak more strictly, he then first becomes capable of an ideal, of a sense of duty, instead of
obeying without question the routine of animal impulse.

But if this is so, I still ask the evolutionist who
has no other basis than the struggle for existence, how
he accounts for the intrusion of these moral ideas and
standards which presume to interfere with the cosmic
process, and sit in judgment upon its results? This
question cannot be answered so long as we regard
morality merely as an incidental result, a by-product,
as it were, of the cosmical system. It is impossible
on such a hypothesis to understand the magisterial
assertion by itself of the part against the whole, its
demands upon the universe, its unwavering condemnation of the universe, if these demands are not met
by the nature of things. All this would be an incongruous, and even a ludicrous, spectacle if we had
here to do with a natural phenomenon like any other.
The moral and spiritual life remains, in short, unintelligible, unless on the supposition that it is in reality
the key to the world's meaning, the fact in the light
of which all other phenomena must be read. We must
be in earnest, I have already said, with the unity of the
world, but we must not forget that, if regarded merely
as a system of forces, the world possesses no such

unity. It acquires it only when **regarded in the light of** an End of absolute worth or value which is realised or attained in it. Such an End-in-itself, as Kant called it, **we find only in** the self-conscious life of man, in the world of Truth, **Beauty, and Goodness which he** builds up for himself, and **of which** he constitutes himself **a** citizen. **If** it were possible **to consider the** system **of** physical nature apart from the intelligent activities and emotions of rational beings, those **worlds on worlds,**

" Rolling ever
From creation to decay,"

would possess **in** themselves **no spark of the** value, **the intrinsic** worth, which we **unhesitatingly assert** to belong, at least in possibility, **to the meanest human life.** The endless redistribution **of matter and motion in** stupendous cycles of evolution and dissolution would be **a world** without **any** justification **to offer for its** existence—a world which **might just as well** not have been.[1] **But if we are honest with ourselves, I** do **not**

---

[1] Without encumbering **the main argument by inopportune** discussion, one may perhaps ask in a note in what sense even existence could **be** attributed to a system **of** unconscious forces—a material world *per se.* **We** cannot perform the abstraction required of us in conceiving **such a** system. Nature refuses to be divorced from the thoughts and **feelings of** her children and her **lords, and** we need not be subjective idealists to hold the literal truth of **the poet's** words that "in our life **alone does** Nature live."

think we can embrace the conclusion that the cosmos is a mere brute fact of this description. The demand for an End-in-itself — that is, for a fact of such a nature that its existence justifies itself—is as much a necessity of reason as the necessity which impels us to refund any phenomenon into its antecedent conditions. And further, unless we sophisticate ourselves, we cannot doubt that we possess within ourselves— in our moral experience most conspicuously—an instance and a standard of what we mean by such intrinsic value. As Carlyle has put it in one of his finest passages,—

What, then, is man! What, then, is man! He endures but for an hour, and is crushed before the moth. Yet in the being and in the working of a faithful man is there already (as all faith, from the beginning, gives assurance) a something that pertains not to this wild death-element of Time ; that triumphs over Time, and *is*, and will be, when Time shall be no more.

This conviction of the infinite significance and value of the ethical life is the only view-point from which, in Professor Huxley's words, we can "make existence intelligible and bring the order of things into harmony with the moral sense of man." And it is impossible to do the one of these things without the other. To understand the world is not merely to unravel the sequence of an intricate set of facts. So long as we cannot "bring the order of things into harmony with the moral sense of man," we cannot truly be said to have made existence intelligible: the world still remains for us, in Hume's words, "a riddle, an enigma, an inexplicable mystery."

What, then, is Professor Huxley's final attitude? The lecture breathes throughout the loftiest temper of ethical idealism. It is the writer's keen sense of the superiority of ethical man to non-ethical nature that prompts him to pit Pascal's "thinking reed" in unequal struggle against the cosmic forces that envelop him; and the noble words at the close stir the spirit by their impressive insistence on the imperishable worth of human effort inspired by duty. Yet this unflinching conviction does not lead Professor Huxley to what seems the legitimate conclusion from it—namely, that here only, in the life of ethical endeavour, is the end and secret of the universe to be found. It serves but to accentuate the stern pathos of his view of human fate. His ultimate attitude is, theoretically, one of Agnosticism; personally and practically, one of Stoical heroism. Substantially the same attitude, it appears to me, is exemplified in the Religion of Humanity—the same despair, I mean, of harmonising human ideals with the course of the universe. The Religion of Humanity rightly finds in man alone any qualities which call for adoration or worship ; but it inconsistently supposes man to develop these qualities in a fundamentally non-ethical cosmos, and so fails to furnish a solution that can be accounted either metaphysically satisfying or ethically supporting. But we must bear in mind, I repeat, the principle of the unity of the world. The attitude of the Agnostic and the Positivist is due to the separation which they unconsciously insist on keeping up between nature and man. The temptation to do so is intelligible, for we have found that nature, taken in philosophical language as a thing in itself — nature conceived as an independent system of causes—cannot explain the ethical life of man, and we rightly refuse to blur and distort the characteristic features of moral experience by submerging it in the merely natural. We easily, therefore, continue to think of the system of natural causes as a world going its own way, existing quite independently of the ethical beings who draw their breath within it. Man with his ideal standards and his infinite aspirations appears consequently upon the scene as an alien without rights in a world that knows him not. His life is an unex-

plained intrusion in a world organised on other **prin-**
ciples, and no **way** adapted as a habitation for **so**
disturbing and pretentious a guest. And the consequence is that he dashes his spirit against the steep
crags of necessity, finds his ideals thwarted, his aspirations mocked, his tenderest affections **turned to instru-**
ments **of** agony, and is driven, if not into **passionate**
revolt or nerveless despair, then at **best** into stoical
resolve. Some such mood as this appears also in much
of Matthew **Arnold's poetry, and is to** my mind the
explanation **of its insistent note** of sadness.

> "No, we are strangers here, the world is from of **old,** . . .
> To tunes we did not call, our being must keep **chime."**

It is powerfully expressed **in the** famous **monologue**
or chant in "Empedocles on **Etna,"** with its deliberate
renunciation of what **the poet deems man's "**boundless
hopes" **and** "intemperate prayers." It inspires the
fine lines **to** Fausta on "Resignation," and reappears
more incidentally in all his verse. But calm, as he
himself reminds **us,** is not life's crown, though calm
is well; and the poet's "calm lucidity of soul" covers
in this case the baffled retreat of the thinker. We
have, in truth, no **right** to suppose an independent
non-spiritual world on **which** human experience is in-

congruously superinduced. If we are really in earnest,
at once with the unity of the world and with the
necessity of an intrinsically worthy end by reference
to which existence may be explained, we must take
our courage in both hands and carry our convictions
to their legitimate conclusion. We must conclude that
the end which we recognise as alone worthy of attainment is also the end of existence as such—the open
secret of the universe. No man writes more pessi-
mistically than Kant of man's relation to the course
of nature, so long as man is regarded merely as a
sentient creature, susceptible to pleasure and pain.
But man, as the subject of duty, and the heir of
immortal hopes, is restored by Kant to that central
position in the universe from which, as a merely
physical being, Copernicus had degraded him.

To a certain extent this conclusion must remain a
conviction rather than a demonstration, for we cannot
emerge altogether from the obscurities of our middle
state, and there is much that may rightly disquiet
and perplex our minds. But if it is in the needs of
the moral life that we find our deepest principle of
explanation, then it may be argued with some reason
that this belongs to the nature of the case; for a
scientific demonstration would not serve the purposes

of that life. The truly good man must choose goodness on its own account; he must be ready to serve God for naught, without being invaded by M. Renan's doubts. As it has been finely put, he must possess "that rude old Norse nobility of soul, which saw virtue and vice alike go unrewarded, and was yet not shaken in its faith."[1] This old Norse nobility speaks to us again, in accents of the nineteenth century, in Professor Huxley's lecture. But because such is the temper of true virtue, it by no means follows that such virtue will not be rewarded with "the wages of going on, and not to die."

[1] R. L. Stevenson, Preface to 'Familiar Studies of Men and Books.'

THE PRESENT POSITION OF THE PHILOSOPHICAL SCIENCES.[1]

YOU will not find it wonderful if my feelings are deeply stirred in appearing before you to-day for the first time in my new capacity. There is no honour

[1] An Inaugural Lecture on assuming the duties of the Chair of Logic and Metaphysics in the University of Edinburgh, October 26, 1891.

The Lecture is printed exactly as it was delivered, and the nature of the occasion will perhaps be held to excuse the personal references with which it opens. The general survey of the philosophical field which it undertakes, and the philosophical point of view indicated in the concluding pages, seem to give it a useful place in the present volume. But to prevent misconception, it may be well to append here the Prefatory Note which accompanied it on its original appearance: "The title of this Lecture may seem to promise too much. The Lecture does not profess to deal with the circle of the philosophical sciences, but only with the subjects traditionally associated with a Chair of Logic and Metaphysics in Scotland. Moreover, as the occasion demanded, it is addressed not so much to the expert as to the large general public interested in philosophy."

or privilege which I could possibly esteem higher than to teach philosophy in my own *alma mater*, and in the capital of my native land—to teach, moreover, in the Chair which, through the lustre of its occupants for half a century, is, in the mind of the country (I think I may say it without offence) in some respects the most famous of Scottish philosophical Chairs. All this is deeply gratifying. But it also lays a heavy responsibility upon him who succeeds to such great traditions. He who did not feel diffident at stepping into the place of these eminent men would be unworthy of the trust committed to him. I am deeply sensible of my own deficiencies, but I hope, if it is granted me, to live and learn.

It is also a very gratifying experience to join as a colleague those who were the guides of one's youth. All are not here; but of the seven Professors of the Arts curriculum in my time only two have been removed by death. One, the genial and universally beloved Kelland, passed away in the ripeness of his years. The other leaves an untimely gap, which speaks of recent loss and a common sorrow. One whose welcome to-day would have sounded with peculiar pleasantness in my ears, the generous and high-souled Sellar, has gone from us too soon; and to those who knew him, his loss seems not less but greater as the days go by.

All the more is it matter of heartfelt satisfaction to me that no such painful gap exists in connection with my own Chair—that I succeed my honoured and beloved teacher while he is yet among us in full health and in the unimpaired vigour of his powers. Long may he live to counsel us wisely and inspire us by his example, and to embody in literary form the ripe results of a life's reflection. In these circumstances, and in his presence, it is not for me to pronounce any eulogy upon his thirty-five years of strenuous and fruitful work in this university, or to attempt to sum up his happily unfinished achievement. But I will at least record a little of what I personally owe to him. He taught me to think; and in the things of the mind that is the greatest gift for which one man can be indebted to another. Seventeen years ago I entered the Junior Logic class of this university, with a mind opening perhaps to literature, but still substantially with a schoolboy's views of existence ; and there, in the admirably stimulating lectures to which I listened, a new world seemed to open before me. What the student most needs at such a period is to be intellectually awakened. The crust of custom has to be broken, and the sense of wonder and mystery stirred within him. He should not be crammed with ready-made solutions of difficulties he has never been made to feel. Rather should he be sent "voyaging through strange seas of thought alone." He has to be induced to ask himself the world-old questions, and to ponder the possible answers. Above all, the listener should be made to feel that the questions of which the Professor speaks are not merely information which he communicates—that they are to him the most real things in the world, the recurring subjects of his deepest meditation. All this his students found realised in Professor Fraser's teaching. His sympathetic exposition enabled us to catch the spirit of the most diverse systems, while his searching criticism prevented us from resting in any of those facile solutions which owe their simplicity to the convenient elimination of intractable elements. The sense of mystery and complexity in things, which he brought so vividly home to us, inspired a wise distrust of extreme positions and of systems all too perfect for our mortal vision. This union of dialectical subtlety with a never-failing reverence for all that makes man man, and elevates him above himself, lives in the memory of many a pupil as no unworthy realisation of the ideal spirit of philosophy. I shall count myself happy if, with his mantle, some portion of his spirit shall be found to have descended upon his successor. I hope that, in the days to come, the dingy but famous class-room will be distinguished as of old by searching intellectual criticism and impartial debate, not divorced from that spirit of reverence and humility which alone can lead us into truth.

That reminds me that you will expect to hear from a new Professor some indication of the view he takes of his subject, and of the present outlook in connection with it. Anything that can be said on an occasion like the present must necessarily be of a very general character, but even so it may have a certain interest and usefulness.

The discipline of the Chair, then, seems to me to be of a threefold character — logical, psychological, and metaphysical or philosophical in the strict sense. That is to say, we study, in the first place, the nature of the reasoning process, or, to be more accurate, the nature of proof or evidence—the conditions to which valid reasoning must conform. In the second place, we study, introspectively and otherwise, the phenomena of consciousness. We bring observation and experiment to bear upon those internal facts which are for each of us the only facts immediately present to us, the facts through which we know all other facts. We try to analyse and lay bare the inmost nature of those functions of knowing, feeling, and willing which lie "closer to us than breathing, nearer than hands or feet,"—which constitute, in fact, our very life, the expression of the self in time. In the third place, we study, under the title of philosophy proper, the twofold question of Knowing and Being. On the one hand, we investigate human knowledge as to its constitutive notions and its scope or validity; we discuss the question of the possibility of knowledge, as it is called, or the relation of knowledge to reality. This is what is termed Epistemology or Theory of Knowledge. On the other hand, so far as the discussion has not been already anticipated, we approach those questions as to the ultimate nature, the origin and destiny, of all that is, which have occupied the speculative intellect of mankind from the dawn of history, and will occupy it till its close. These may be embraced under the special title of Metaphysics, both Epistemology and Metaphysics falling under the wider designation of Philosophy.

These three lines of training—the logical, the psychological, and the philosophical — are cognate, and the

first two are in a measure introductory or propædeutic
to the third.   Both logic and psychology, at all events,
if we go beneath the surface, lead us into the very
heart of philosophical difficulties ; and most treatments
of either subject involve a tissue of metaphysical assumptions, of which the writer is, in all probability,
either quite unconscious or only half aware.   But
though the subjects are thus cognate and continuous,
and so fitly combined under one Chair, the discipline
they afford has in each case a character of its own.
Logic gives a training almost purely abstract or formal,
comparable in some respects with the mental discipline
of mathematics—a training in clearness of thinking, in
accuracy of definition, in appreciation of what is meant
by demonstration or proof.   Psychology brings us face
to face with a concrete subject-matter—the actual facts
of mental life.   It views these facts, partly in themselves, but largely in their connection with material conditions and accompaniments.   So far as it approaches
these facts by the ordinary methods of observation
and experiment, classifying them and endeavouring to resolve complex phenomena into their simplest
constituents or causes,—so far it affords a scientific
discipline comparable to that gained, say, in the study
of one of the natural sciences.   And if it often lacks

the exactness of the sciences of external nature, it has the advantage, as compared with them, of cultivating fresh powers of mind through the attitude of " reflection " or introspection which it is forced to take up. Self-observation or introspection is by no means so easy as the observation of a foreign object. We can more easily analyse a substance in a phial before us than we can analyse the exact nature of what passes at any moment in our own mind. Hence Psychology, which incessantly calls for the exercise of this faculty, and sharpens and perfects it by constant use, was justly praised by Hamilton as one of the best gymnastics of the mind. Philosophy carries us into a more difficult region; for here we deal not with any particular department of fact, but with the ultimate principles of knowledge and the ultimate constitution or meaning of the cosmos as such, including the prior question whether we are justified in speaking of a cosmos or orderly unity at all. These are questions of supreme and intimate concern to us all, seeing that they embrace the question of man's place and destiny in relation to the system of things. He to whom they have no voice must be either less or more than man. And I fail to see how any one can lay claim to a liberal education who is ignorant of what has been thought by the great minds of the past upon these subjects, or who is unacquainted with the elements of the problems as they face us to-day. The rudiments of such a knowledge are necessary, were it for nothing else, to enable any one to take an intelligent part in the incessant discussion and conflict of opinion which is so marked a feature of the present time.

This threefold discipline may be justified, therefore, in a liberal curriculum, whether we look at it, from the formal side, as a discipline of mental powers otherwise untrained—as the cultivation of one whole side of human nature—or, on the concrete side, as a communication of knowledge of singular importance and interest. And its permanent value seems to me so high and unimpeachable, in both these respects, that it needs no defence at my hands. A defence is generally a confession of weakness. In offering such for philosophy, "we do it wrong, being so majestical."

I turn, therefore, by preference, to say a little about the present outlook in the three departments to which reference has been made, and the way in which it seems to me that a philosophical Professor should shape his work at the present time. Logic I will pass over lightly—almost with a word—because, of the three, its discussions are most technical in character.

It appeals, therefore, least to a general audience. Moreover, if we penetrate beneath the surface and examine the foundations on which it rests, we are immediately involved in difficult questions of general philosophy; and it becomes impossible to maintain a rigid distinction between Logic and Epistemology and Metaphysics. For that reason the very conception or definition of the science has long been matter of keen debate, and at present the aspect of things is confessedly chaotic. The activity, however, in the higher theory of logic has of late been great both in this country and in Germany. I need only refer to the important treatises of Lotze, Sigwart, and Wundt in Germany, and of Bradley and Bosanquet in this country, not to speak of the more distinctively English work of Jevons, Venn, and others. The chaos, moreover, if at first bewildering, is not of the kind which should be disheartening to the serious student. It is of the kind which portends and accompanies growth, and bears in it the promise of future order. Evidently, however, such discussions do not lend themselves to exoteric exposition; they belong to the labours of an advanced class of metaphysics.

The other aspect of Logic is the elementary doctrine which has so long formed part of the curriculum of educated Europe—the ordinary formal logic, originally based upon Aristotle, to which has come to be added some discussion of the theory of scientific method and the conditions of inductive proof. It has been the fashion of late with many philosophers to sneer at the logic of the schools; but this is only justifiable, as it seems to me, when extravagant claims are made on its behalf. No doubt the ordinary logic depends on many uncriticised assumptions; its analysis of the process of thought is often superficial; it cannot stand as a coherent philosophical doctrine. All this is granted. The whole discipline is essentially of an elementary and propædeutic character; it is a continuation, in a more abstract form, of the grammatical training received at school. But just this circumstance, that it continues and attaches itself to the studies of the school, gives it a peculiar claim to stand as the gateway of the philosophical sciences; whilst, on the other hand, the very defects and ambiguities which discussion reveals in many of its conceptions form an excellent stimulus to the opening mind, and introduce the student insensibly to important psychological and metaphysical problems. The formal mechanism may certainly, in great part, be relegated with advantage to text-book work and tutorial instruction. But even this is not to be despised; I have always found it an admirable test in picking out the really clear-headed members of a class. Here there are no cloudy phrases in which to take refuge; the issue is as clear and definite as in a mathematical proposition, and inaccuracy of mind is tracked remorselessly down. In view of these merits, which the study undoubtedly possesses, I cannot share the contempt frequently expressed for the logic of the schools. Its names and distinctions, moreover, have entered so largely into the thought, and even the familiar language, of the civilised races, that a certain acquaintance with its forms and processes may well be demanded in the interests of historical culture.

It is not so long since a somewhat similar contempt for Psychology was current in the leading idealistic school of this country. The horror of the true-blue experientialist for what he calls "metaphysics" was amply repaid by the tone of condescension and indifference which the idealists adopted towards "empirical psychology." Misled by a name, they visited upon the head of an unoffending science the inadequacies of Empiricism as a philosophical theory. Because the chief cultivators of psychology in England had been of the Empiricist persuasion, and had fre-

quently confounded the limits of psychology and metaphysics, the transcendentalists tabooed the science as
beneath the notice of a philosopher. Hence a state
of unnatural division and mutual distrust—a distrust
rooted in both cases largely in ignorance. To-day the
situation is greatly changed. Psychology has become
more scientific, and has thereby become more conscious of her own aims, and, at the same time, of
her necessary limitations. Ceasing to put herself
forward as philosophy, she has entered upon a new
period of development as science; and in doing so
she has disarmed the jealousy, and is even fast con-
quering the indifference, of the transcendental philosopher. For whatever be the bearing of these
psychological investigations upon philosophy — be
their importance in that connection great, or be it
small—it is at least certain that in the near future
no philosopher will speak with authority, or will
deserve so to speak, who does not show a competent
acquaintance with the best work in psychology.

The marvellous activity displayed just at present
in the department of psychology constitutes, indeed,
to an expert perhaps the most notable feature in the
state of the philosophical sciences. In Germany and
France, in America, and now in England, there may

almost be said to be a "boom" in that direction. In Britain the study of psychology is a native growth, and it had long flourished in the hands of the Associationists, such as Hartley, James and John Mill, and Professor Bain. But before such a school was heard of by name, the works of Hobbes, Locke, Berkeley, and Hume had brilliantly exemplified the national genius in that direction. As already indicated, however, the British thinkers of the past were far from keeping their psychology unadulterated. Betraying frequently an insular ignorance of the great metaphysical systems of ancient Greece and modern Europe, they gave us, in general, psychology and philosophy inextricably intermingled. The impulse towards a differentiation of provinces came from Germany, where the clearer formulation of aims and methods may be regarded as one beneficial result of the training which the German intellect has enjoyed at the hands of Kant and succeeding thinkers. But the influence of Germany upon psychological investigation has not been limited to this formal or methodic stimulus. There has been much good work done there in psychology since the time of Kant. The psychology of Herbart and his followers is in many respects the more elaborate counterpart of English Associationism; and artificial as his constructions often seem, it is acute and able work, which no modern student of the subject can afford to neglect. The names of Lotze and Wundt represent work at once brilliant and patient on independent lines, and bring before us also the close connection between psychology and physiology, which is the distinguishing mark of most recent investigation in this department. Some of Lotze's most characteristic work was contained in the book he called 'Medical Psychology;' and 'Physiological Psychology' is the name Wundt gives to his important treatise. Psychology, physiology, and physics meet in the great works of Helmholtz on 'Sensations of Tone' and 'Physiological Optics.' Another mark of recent investigation is the potent influence exerted on psychology, as on all other departments of knowledge, by the conception of evolution. Wherever life is met with, there the psychologist now finds material for illustrating and enlarging his science. The old meaning of ψυχή has been revived, and the beginnings of a comparative psychology have come into being. The observation of abnormal mental developments, such as insanity, hysteria, the hypnotic state, and similar phenomena, forms another field assiduously cultivated by modern observers, especially in France, where, no less than in Germany and America, there is a large amount of psychological activity among the younger men.

All these influences may be said to meet and come to fruition in the best English work of the last few years—such work, I mean, as Mr Ward's masterly treatise in the 'Encyclopædia Britannica,' and the rich and stimulating volumes published a year ago[1] by Professor James of Harvard. Such work may not unreasonably be taken as marking the new departure that has been achieved in psychology — the critical maintenance of a purely psychological standpoint, the wider range of material, the more minute and experimental analysis.

For one of the most striking results of the rapprochement between psychology and physiology just referred to has been the attempt to introduce experiment into psychological science. Starting from the experiments of Weber and the more extended psychophysical researches of Fechner, but taking a wider scope, there has sprung up a new line of inquiry, which, under the name of Experimental Psychology, sometimes aspires to the dignity of a separate dis-

[1] In 1890.

D

cipline, and looks back with no little condescension upon the observational and descriptive science with which we are familiar. Wundt has been the leader of this movement, and Leipzig its great centre; but it is now widely spread in Germany, and has been enthusiastically taken up in America, where every well-equipped college aims at the establishment of a psychological or psycho-physical laboratory. England shows some disposition to follow in the wake. At least the University of Cambridge has voted a small sum for the same purpose, and the younger generation of Oxonians are found deserting the philosophy of Green to work in the laboratories of Freiburg, Leipzig, and Berlin.

Let me say at once, to prevent misconception, that I think the experimental psychologists magnify their office overmuch. The field of experiment is necessarily limited; it is limited to those cases where we are able to manipulate the physical and physiological processes which condition mental facts. The facts of sensation, the phenomena of movement, and the time occupied by the simpler mental processes, constitute, therefore, practically the whole accessible area. Within these limits, moreover, the results are often so contradictory as to leave everything in doubt; where definite results are obtainable, their value is often not apparent. Finally, many of the results are of a purely physiological nature, and are only by courtesy included in psychological science. These are the serious deductions which I think require to be made by a dispassionate observer of all this eager work. But the appetite for facts is a healthy symptom, and the whole movement is one which every student of psychology must take note of. We need not look for light from this quarter upon the problems of philosophy and the deeper mysteries of being; but it is impossible that so much patient ingenuity should be devoted to analysing the substructure of our mental life without ultimately important effects upon our knowledge of the psychological mechanism.

A collateral effect of this scientific development of psychology has been an immense increase of detail-work. Already it is becoming more and more the practice for psychologists to publish elaborate monographs on special phenomena, or on comparatively small departments of the subject. The number of psychological journals has also largely increased. One result of this is obvious. As psychology becomes increasingly scientific in character, and as the literature of the subject becomes more and more voluminous, the severance between philosophy and psychology must necessarily become more pronounced—for it will become impossible for the same man to do original work in both departments. From the point of view of philosophy there might seem to be a certain advantage in this, as effectually preventing any further confusion between the two spheres and sets of problems. But this advantage is more apparent than real. For psychology, as the science of mental life, must always stand to philosophy in a more intimate relation than any of the other sciences can. If the divorce, then, be carried so far that the philosopher and psychologist are no longer on speaking terms, the old evils will recur; for a critical severance of provinces can be effected and maintained only by one who is familiar with both departments, even though his original work should lie only in one. It is to be hoped, therefore, that the psychologists of the future will all be trained in philosophy, and the philosophers in psychology. With this view, and in the present situation of affairs, I cannot help adding that it seems to me extremely desirable, in a great university like this, that there should be a third man connected with the philosophical department—a Lecturer or Assistant-Professor—specially charged with the teaching of psychology in its most recent developments. Such work would lie, of course, largely with Honours students; for psychological detail could not profitably replace to the Passman that introduction to the problems of philosophy and the history of thought which the retention of the Chair in a liberal curriculum is meant to ensure.

To Philosophy, then, we come in the last place. It is by philosophy that this Chair and others like it in the Scottish universities must ultimately justify their existence; and it is to the inbred Scottish bent towards philosophy that the public interest felt in them is due. The outlook here is not discouraging. Within the present century, as is well known, Comte promulgated his law of the three stages, representing metaphysics as a disease of childhood, like measles, which the race was in the act of outgrowing. And since then, Comtian and other influences have undoubtedly produced in many quarters a positivistic or agnostic attitude of mind, which gives itself great airs of finality from time to time in our newspapers and reviews. But metaphysics shows no inclination to die, by way of obliging these prophets of her decease. It is sufficient answer to their vaticinations to point to the marked revival of interest in philosophical discussion within recent years. There was a period, perhaps, when philosophical interest languished ; but there has seldom been a time when people were more anxious than they are at present to listen to any one who has anything to say. For indifferentism here, as Kant says, can be, in the nature of the case, no more than a temporary phase of feeling. " It is in reality vain to profess indifference in regard to such inquiries, the object of which cannot be indifferent to humanity."

Apart from indifference, there was a time when the vast strides made by science—more especially by the natural sciences in the third quarter of the present century—fascinated men's attention, and diverted it from the problems which lie beneath and behind all science. But the very progress of science has brought men face to face once more with ultimate questions, and has revealed the impotence of science to deal with its own conditions and presuppositions. The needs of science itself call for a critical doctrine of knowledge as the basis of an ultimate theory of things. The idea entertained in some quarters that all difficulties would be solved by a scientific conception like that of evolution, has been found illusory, inasmuch as that conception itself requires a philosophical interpretation before it can throw any light at all upon the metaphysical question. History is not philosophy, and nothing is

explained merely **by** being **thrown** back **in** time.
Evolution notwithstanding, the old questions all **re-**
appear in a slightly altered form. They are brought to
light again **by** the very success **of** science **in dealing**
with **her own** problems.

Philosophy is first, then, at the present day, a doctrine
of knowledge ; and as such the critic of scientific categories, to purge us of bad metaphysics. For the sweeping away of bad metaphysics is not the least important
part of **the** philosophical task, and **there is** no metaphysics **so** bad as the metaphysics of the physicist or
biologist when, in the **strength** of his own right arm,
he makes a raid into philosophical territory. This
critical **office of** Philosophy must also **be** extended to
the metaphysical systems **of** the past. And in this
connection we have one **of** the richest parts **of the**
training afforded by a philosophical Chair ; for here the
teacher must constitute himself the historian of thought,
and, with a wise admixture of sympathy and criticism,
introduce his hearers **to the** typical thinkers of the
world—

> " The dead but sceptred sovrans who still rule
> Our spirits from their urns."

But this critical, and to **a** certain extent **negative,**
work is not all. Philosophy must finally endeavour to

be itself critically constructive, or, if that is a contradiction in terms, it must endeavour to be constructive
without forgetting its own critical strictures. The
criticism of past philosophies, therefore, should not
be purely negative. Truly light-giving and helpful
criticism should seek to lead the learner, through the
very consciousness of defects and inconsistencies in the
systems examined, to a truer statement of the problem,
and a more adequate solution. In this way, the systems
of the past become so many stepping-stones on which
we rise to fuller and clearer insight. And if, at the
end, a completed system should still prove beyond our
reach, the philosophical teacher will at least seek to
indicate the general lines upon which an ultimately
satisfactory theory must move.

I have only time here to mention one or two points
on which I think that a true philosophy should lay
stress, and on which it should lay special stress at
the present time. The first is the necessity of a
teleological view of the universe. Trendelenburg, the
eminent German Aristotelian, devotes one of the most
interesting of his essays to illustrating what he calls
the fundamental difference or antithesis between philosophical systems,—the difference, namely, between the
teleological and the mechanical point of view. Whether

an exhaustive classification of systems is possible on this basis or not, I believe with him that the antithesis he signalises is fundamental for philosophy; and there is nothing of which I am more profoundly convinced than that philosophical truth lies, in this case, altogether with the teleological point of view. Any system which abandons this point of view lapses thereby from philosophy to science.

The word teleology acts upon some people like a red rag upon a bull, from its association with certain old-fashioned arguments which explained particular phenomena from their supposed adaptation to external ends, more especially from their adaptation to the requirements and conveniences of man. This paltry mechanical teleology was never at any time convincing to strong and sincere thinkers, and after being riddled by modern science, it may be held as finally beaten off the field. Its unsatisfactory character arose in great part from its taking facts in isolation, and then endeavouring artificially to fit them together in the relation of means and end. The philosophical teleology of which I speak concerns itself only with the End of the whole evolution. It concentrates itself upon the proof that there *is* an End, that there is an organic unity or purpose binding the whole process into one and making it intelligible—in one word, that there *is* evolution and not merely aimless change. For it is only when contemplated in the light of a realised idea that any one speaks of a series of changes as steps in an evolution. A speculation which does not see that evolution spells purpose has not made clear to itself the difference between progress and aimless variation. Such speculation rests ultimately on a purely mechanical view of the universe.

Let us try, therefore, in a sentence or two, to illuminate by contrast these two opposite points of view. The mechanical view explains the universe as a collocation of mere facts—so many real existences which just happen to be there. They are not there to express any idea, meaning, or purpose: they have no further significance; they simply are. Every change in these facts is completely determined by its immediate antecedents, acting as a blind *vis a tergo*. A cause may thus be assigned for every change, but a reason can be given for none; for where there is no question of realising any idea or purpose, all change must be entirely motiveless. One collocation of facts is just as good as another. The mechanical explanation of things is thus a constant looking backward; the teleological or philosophical explanation, a looking forward to the end or ultimate purpose which is **being** realised —to the *reason* **of the whole development,** which **is** also in **the deepest** sense **its cause.**

The mechanical explanation of any phenomenon is not false **in** itself. Nor need **there be any** quarrel between the causal and the teleological view of things, for they **move upon** different **planes.** The mechanically causal view only **becomes false,** when it professes to be a complete explanation **of any** phenomenon, and therefore, by implication, **a** philosophy of the universe. True, under certain limitations, as science, it is false **when it** puts itself forward as philosophy. Mechanical **explanation is a** *progressus in infinitum,* **which** can ultimately explain nothing. In the last resort, *causæ efficientes pendent a finalibus;* the complete explanation of anything **is only** reached when we are able to view it in the **light of a purpose, of** which it forms an integral **part or** element. Philosophy, therefore, stands **or** falls with the possibility of discovering a reasonable meaning or end **in** the universe. Every true philosophy is in this sense an attempted theodicy — the vindication of a divine purpose in **things.**

The antithesis of teleology and mechanism is, as you perceive, substantially the old opposition of Idealism **and** Materialism more strictly expressed. And it is equally obvious that while the mechanical view, through looking ever backward, finds an explanation of things in reducing them to their lowest terms, and presents us, for example, with matter and motion as philosophical ultimates, the teleological or idealistic view seeks the true explanation of the lower in the higher, of which it is the germ. For *if* the lower carries in it the promise and potency of the higher, then it must involve no less than a falsification of the facts to substantiate the lowest terms as independent self-existent facts, out of relation to the ultimate term in which we read the meaning of the whole development. That, however, is precisely what is done by all materialistic and quasi-materialistic systems.

If philosophy, then, is the indication of an end, meaning, or purpose in the universe, what has philosophy to say, finally, as to the nature of the End? Here again, it seems to me that philosophy has to wage unsparing battle against certain tendencies of our time. As it defends the truth of teleology in spite of former abuses of the principle, so it has to champion the truth underlying the old view which made man the centre of the universe. In a material aspect, man is but an atom or a point in the system of things, and we smile when we read in Cicero of

the heavenly ædile who nightly lights the **candles
of** the sky for **our mortal comfort and convenience.
But** the Copernican view of **the universe is pressed**
too far when **we are** invited, on the strength **of it,**
to efface ourselves before the immensities of external
nature.   Much current thought is *naturalistic* at heart
—that is to **say, it makes human nature only a part**
of nature **in general, and seeks, therefore, to explain**
away the most fundamental characteristics **of intelli-**
gence and moral life.   **As against this** naturalistic
tendency, philosophy must be unflinchingly *human-*
istic, anthropocentric.

   Not to man as **a** creature specially located **upon**
this earth, **but** to man and all creatures **like him
who are sharers in the life** of thought, and **called
thereby to be authors** of their **own perfection — to**
man **as rational all things** are **relative.   To him the**
creation looks; **for him all** things are made.   This is
the imperishable **grandeur of** Hegel's system that he
has given such **sonorous** utterance to this view, and
expressed it with such magnificent confidence.   **I cannot** always emulate his confidence, nor **can I adopt
as perfectly** satisfactory his universalistic mode of
expression. The achievements of the **world-**spirit
do not move me to unqualified admiration, and I

cannot accept the abstraction of the race in place of
the living children of men. Even if the enormous
spiral of human history is destined to wind itself at
last to a point which may be called achievement, what,
I ask, of the multitudes that perished by the way?
"These all died, not having received the promises."
What if there *are* no promises *to them?* To me the
old idea of the world as the training-ground of individual character seems to offer a much more human,
and, I will add, a much more divine, solution than this
pitiless procession of the car of progress. Happily,
however, the one view does not necessarily exclude
the other : we may rejoice in the progress of the race,
and also believe in the future of the individual.
Nature's profusion and nature's waste will doubtless
be urged against us, when we plead for the rights
of the individual life. But these are objections which
every theodicy has to meet. I do not wish to minimise
them : on the contrary, they appeal to me with painful
force. But the possibility of any theodicy depends on
our being able to show that nature and nature's ways
of working are not the last word of creation. Nature
is non-moral, indifferent, and pitiless; but man is
pitiful, and human nature flowers in love and self-

denial, in purity and stainless **honour**. **If these have no root** in the **nature** of **things, then** indeed

> " The pillared firmament is rottenness,
> And earth's base built on stubble."

But we do well, as Goethe teaches in one **of his** finest **poems, to** recognise **in** such attributes of human-kind **our nearest** glimpse **into the** nature of the divine. The part **is** not greater than the whole; and we may rest **assured** that whatever **of wisdom** and goodness **there is in us** was not born **out of** nothing, but has **its fount,** somewhere and **somehow, in a more** perfect Goodness **and** Truth.

THE "NEW" PSYCHOLOGY AND AUTOMATISM.[1]

I.

ALL who take an intelligent interest in the movement of contemporary thought—whether it be philosophy more strictly so called, or the advance of science—are aware of the great activity which has been shown of late years in the department of psychology. Till within the last half century or thereabouts, psychology had been an appanage of the philosophers; and it cannot be said that they neglected this province of their dominion. In this country in particular—in England and Scotland—psychology has formed the bulk of our philosophic treatises; and Hobbes, Locke, Berkeley, Hume, Hartley, Dr Thomas Brown, and the Mills,

[1] An Address to the Edinburgh University Philosophical Society, November 9, 1892.

Reid, Stewart, and Hamilton, must always remain among the classics of the science. But it may be admitted that their work often shows a crossing of interests and of points of view. Questions of logic and theory of knowledge were mixed up with the more properly psychological inquiry. And, at other times, the investigation was subordinate to the establishment of some metaphysical theory. The distinguishing note of most recent psychology has therefore been insistence on the separation of psychology from philosophy, and on the maintenance of a purely psychological standpoint. In psychology, it is argued, we have a realm of phenomena, a moving world of causes and effects, which it is our business to investigate in the ordinary scientific way, with all the resources of observation and experiment. Imitating the example of physics, we have to reduce this world of complex phenomena to its ultimate constituents and the laws of their interaction, and we have to do this without any *arrière pensée* as to the bearing of our results on the ultimate problems of philosophy.

No advice could be more excellent; disinterestedness is the very watchword of science. But it seems to me that a good many of those who talk most loudly of "the new psychology" are exposed to the usual danger of reaction. The rise of this "scientific" psychology, as it also calls itself, is connected with the great development of science, especially of the natural sciences, which has marked the present century. The growth of biology and physiology has naturally reacted powerfully upon the whole conception and method of psychological investigation. And it is worth observing that the general scientific movement referred to coincided, especially in Germany, with a revulsion against the idealistic speculation which marked the beginning of the century. Probably the two were partly connected as cause and effect, the hunger for hard facts and patient detail-work being a healthy protest of the human spirit against over-hasty and over-confident attempts at universal synthesis. Any way, the new psychology, as I have said, has its roots in this movement. And therefore its absorbing concern was and is to keep itself clear of metaphysics, and of every hypothesis which it imagines to savour of that region of mysteries. To a large class of scientific and would-be scientific thinkers, metaphysics is what clericalism is to the French Liberal: it is the enemy, to be fought at all points. These two characteristics of this militant psychology—its renunciation of metaphysics and its affiliation to biology—are concisely put by Ribot, one of its standard-bearers: "The new psychology differs from the old in its spirit—it is not metaphysical. It differs in its aim—it only studies phenomena. It differs in its methods—it borrows them as far as possible **from** the biological sciences. Consequently the sphere of psychology specifies itself; **it** has for its subject nervous phenomena accompanied by consciousness." [1]

I am far **from** asserting that this **distrust is without** historical justification. **Natural** explanations — *i.e.*, regulated **sequences and** coexistences of phenomena — **are** what **every science has to** seek in **its own** sphere; and, accordingly, science justly regards as suspect **the** explanation **of any** phenomenon by the immediate causality of a metaphysical agent. The interjection of such a causality into the empirical connections which she seeks to unravel, she treats **as** a form of *ignava ratio*. "It makes the investigation **of causes a** very easy task," says Kant, "**if we refer** such and **such** phenomena immediately **to** the unsearchable will **and counsel of the Supreme Wisdom,** whereas we ought to investigate their causes in the general mechanism **of matter. This is to** consider the labour of reason as ended, **when** we have **merely** dispensed

---

[1] '**La** Psychologie Allemande,' Introduction. Ribot's deliverance dates from **1879, but** precisely the same position is formulated in the opening **and closing** sentences of one of the most recent manuals on the subject, **Ziehen's** 'Introduction to the Study of Physiological Psychology.' If the polemic against metaphysics is not always so marked, **it** is because **the** enemy is supposed **to have been beaten** off the field.

with its employment."[1]   In the old psychology, this otiose method of explanation, by means of the soul and its faculties, was no doubt often resorted to. Hence, in shaking the dust of metaphysics off their feet, the new psychologists accepted from Lange[2] as their badge the somewhat paradoxical motto " Psychology without a soul."   As Ribot puts it triumphantly : " The soul and its faculties, the great entity and the little entities, disappear ; and we have to do only with internal events, — events which, like sensations and images, are translations (so to speak) of physical events, or which, like ideas, movements, volitions, and desires, translate themselves into physical events."

In this respect, however, the new psychology was not so original as it perhaps imagined.   The attempt to dispense with a soul had been systematically made by Hume and the Associationists long before the second half of the nineteenth century.   It was not simply the determination to discard the soul that stamped the new movement ; the second and more characteristic feature was the affiliation of psychology to physiology and to general biological science — the study of the facts of consciousness consistently and exclusively in correla-

---

[1] Werke, vol. iii. p. 468 (ed. Hartenstein).

[2] Geschichte des Materialismus, vol. ii. p. 381.

tion with the organic facts of nerve and brain.   This
method of explanation was declined, as we know, by
Locke and Hume; and it has been made matter of
reproach against a modern associationist like Mill, that
he held by the old psychological method and went on
" exactly as he might have gone on if he had lived in
the days of Aristotle, . . . at a time when a new method
highly fertile in fact and of more fruitful promise was
available." [1]   The physiological method, in short, is the
distinguishing mark, and "physiological psychology" is
the term very generally given to the recent developments of "psychology as a natural science."   It is to be
noted also that in speaking of the conditions of mental
states (and it is agreed that the discovery of conditions
constitutes scientific explanation) writers of this way of
thinking have exclusively physiological conditions in
view.   Professor James tells us, for example, that he
has "treated our passing thoughts as integers, and regarded the mere laws of their coexistence with brain-
states as the ultimate laws for our science;" [2] and Mr
Shadworth Hodgson defines psychology as "that positive and special science which takes its stand upon the
results of physiology and biology, and studies the phen-

---

[1] Maudsley, **Physiology of Mind**, p. 76.
[2] Principles of **Psychology**, Preface.

omena of sentience and consciousness in connection
with their proximate conditions in individual living
organisms."[1]

Let me say at once that it is far from my intention
to object to this intimate linking of the psychological
and the biological. It may be taken as a postulate
generally admitted, that our mental life is at every
point physiologically conditioned; and the physiological method of study does indeed promise, as its vot-
aries say, to be most fruitful in its application. It
alone furnishes the basis for introducing experiment
into mental science; and though it can only lay siege,
as it were, to the outworks of the mental citadel, to the
phenomena of sense-perception and movement and a
few of the simpler aspects of the mental processes, yet
the amount of patient detail-work accumulated in these
departments, and the light thrown on other departments
by the scientific study of abnormal mental states in
their physiological relations, are already enriching the
science in no ordinary degree, and transforming the very
look of our psychological text-books. The philosopher
would be singularly cross-grained who did not welcome
this accumulation of material, and who did not congrat-
ulate himself that all this detail-work was taken out of

[1] Mind, vol. xi. p. 489 (October 1886).

his hands by those who, from their training and aptitudes, can do it so much better.   But he will reserve
to himself, as philosopher, the ultimate verdict on the
validity and sufficiency of the theory on which physiological psychology proceeds.   **For it is the most in-**
defeasible function of philosophy to act as critic of the
sciences.   The philosopher **has to examine the concep-**
tions which each science accepts without criticism, **and**
on which it proceeds in working out its results ; he has
to point out the limits **or** conditions within which the
conception or theory holds true.   In other words, he
has to restrain the ardour of the specialist who would
build upon his results a philosophic theory of the universe, by showing that the results which the investigation **seems** to establish are really involved **in the**
conceptions or standpoint from which it started, and
are therefore in no sense to be accepted as an independent proof **of the theory.**   I propose to show that this
is pre-eminently the case with the main thesis of the
" new " psychology—at least in the hands of its most
advanced representatives.   In abjuring the soul and
limiting itself to the concomitance of physical and
psychical events, it is really dominated by a very
definite theory **which** dictates the character of its
results beforehand.

The result supposed to be proved, it had best be stated at once, is the complete parallelism of the bodily and the mental — the denial, therefore, of any real causality to consciousness, which remains the inert accompaniment of a succession of physical changes over which it has no control.   In a word, the result is the doctrine of human automatism.   The doctrine of conscious automatism has been ventilated a good deal since 1870, or even earlier, by Mr Shadworth Hodgson, Professor Huxley, Professor Clifford, and others; but, though no doubt definitely embraced by a few, it is safe to say that by the most it has been rather talked about, and toyed with, than fully conceived, much less believed.   The doctrine has, however, been recently expressed with great clearness and force by Dr Münsterberg, who is perhaps the ablest and most stirring of the younger generation of physiological psychologists, and one whose theories have attracted considerable attention both in England and on the Continent.   He teaches in the most unequivocal fashion that consciousness is simply, as he calls it, a "Begleiterscheinung," a concomitant phenomenon, or inactive accompaniment of a series of mechanical changes.

Münsterberg's work, which has appeared in a suc-

cession of pamphlets since the year 1888, takes largely
the form of a polemic against Wundt's doctrine of
Apperception. Wundt's 'Physiologische Psychologie,'
first published in 1874, still remains, in its later
editions, the most authoritative work on the subject ;
and the psychological laboratory established by him
in Leipzig in 1879, as the first of its kind, is still
probably the chief centre of experimental work.
But, although he may thus fairly be called the father
of the whole movement, inasmuch as he has organised
experimental psychology and induced the world to
accept it as a new science, Wundt has never lent his
countenance to the automatist conclusions which the
young bloods are now drawing from their experimental
labours.   His doctrine of Apperception is far from
clear, and its precise meaning has given rise to considerable controversy, but it seems to imply a function
of subjective selection or central initiative analogous
to what Dr Ward calls Attention ; and this is apparently
in harmony with the general philosophical position
which the author has elaborated in his recently published 'System of Philosophy.' But, be that as it may,
it is at any rate certain that Wundt has been attacked
by the upholders of thorough-going mechanism as an
inconsistent and retrograde thinker for attributing

activity to the Subject. So much by way of explanation was necessary for the right understanding of Münsterberg's work. His first pamphlet in this controversy was 'Die Willenshandlung,' an analysis of the act of will, published early in 1888. This was followed in 1889-90 by three instalments of 'Contributions to Experimental Psychology,' in which, after an elucidation of principles, he endeavoured, by a series of carefully devised experiments, to assimilate the apperceptive process to the type of reflex action and thus reduce the whole conscious action to a play of association. In 1891 he published an introduction to the study of psychology,[1] in the course of which we get a re-statement of his own position. The standpoint does not vary throughout the different expositions, and therefore, though illustrating freely from all, so far as they throw light upon my points, I will draw chiefly from the first and fullest statement—that contained in his very acute analysis of the act of will.

The 'Willenshandlung' is divided into three parts, the first treating of the voluntary act as "movement-process" (*Bewegungsvorgang*); the second treating of it

---

[1] 'Ueber Aufgaben und Methoden der Psychologie,' 1891. A fourth instalment of the 'Contributions to Experimental Psychology' has since appeared.

as a phenomenon or appearance in consciousness (*Bewusstseinserscheinung*); and the third, which is intended to combine the results of the preceding parts, considering the act of will in its totality as "conscious movement" (*bewusste Bewegung*). Münsterberg makes a start from the well-known saying of Kant: "That my will moves my arm is no whit more intelligible to me than if any one were to tell me that it could hold back the moon in its orbit." He accepts the problem as thus indicated: How does my will move my arm? The first part of his treatise deals with the voluntary act exclusively from the physiological side, and analyses it into a series of movements. We may say analyses it *necessarily* into a series of movements, for the succession of bodily movements, whether visible movements of the limbs or molecular movements of the nerves and brain, are all of the process that could by any possibility be *seen ;* and reduction to processes which are intelligible in the sense of being pictorially presentable, is the postulate of explanation which he lays down.[1] There is not much that is peculiar to Münsterberg in this first section ; the same has been vividly put by many writers,[2] and in a sense this purely physical explana-

---

[1] **Zurückführung** auf anschaulich verständliche Vorgänge, p. **10.**

[2] Never better perhaps than by Lange, ' Geschichte des Materialismus,'

tion is true from the physiological side, though I think
it is possible to show that, even from the physiological
standpoint, it is not the whole truth.   Meanwhile it is

vol. ii. p. 370.   The passage has been often quoted, but may do duty
again : "A merchant is sitting comfortably in his easy-chair, and
would find it hard to say with what the greater part of his Ego is
occupied — whether with smoking, sleeping, reading the newspaper,
or digestion.   Suddenly the servant enters with a telegram which
runs—'Antwerp, Jonas and Company failed.' 'Tell James to put
the horses to.'   The servant flies.   The master has sprung to his feet,
completely sobered; some dozen paces through the room, down to his
office, instructions given to the confidential clerk, letters dictated,
telegrams despatched, then into the carriage.   The horses pant ; he
visits the bank, the exchange, his business friends.   Before an hour
is over, he throws himself again into his easy-chair with the sigh,
'Thank heaven, I have secured myself against the worst : now let
me consider further.'   A splendid occasion for a picture of the soul.
Terror, hope, feeling, calculation—ruin and victory compressed into
one moment.   And that all aroused by a single idea !   What does
not the human consciousness comprise !

"Softly, let us look at our man as an object in the material world.   He
springs up, why ?   His muscles contract in the appropriate way.   Why
so ?   They were moved by an impulse of nervous force which discharged
the stored-up stock of elasticity.   Whence this impulse ?   From the
centre of the nervous system.   How did it arise there ?   Through the
. . . soul.   The curtain falls,—the salto mortale is made from science
to mythology."   On the contrary, Lange proceeds, "we must trace back
the physical series of causes through the brain to the first occasion of
the whole sudden movement without taking any account whatever of
the so-called consciousness.   Or let us take it in the opposite direction.
What came into the man ?   The picture of certain strokes with blue
pencil upon a white ground.   Certain rays of light fell upon the retina,
rays which in themselves do not develop more vital force in their vibra-
tions than other light-rays.   The vital force for the propagation of the
impact is ready in the nerve as that for muscular contraction in the

enough to note the **purely mechanical point of view and** the explicit reduction **of** all physiological facts to physico-chemical processes.   **Passing to the** more char-

muscles : it **can be discharged by** the infinitely weak impact of the **light-wave only as** the elastic forces of the powder-cask are **set free by the glimmering spark.   But** how comes it, then, **that** just *these* **lines** pro-duce in *this* **man** just this effect ?   **Every answer which falls back here upon ideas and the like is** as good as no answer **at all.   I wish to see** *the channels, the paths of the vital force,* the extent, **the mode** of propa-**gation, and** the sources of *the physical and chemical processes* from which **the nervous impulses proceed which call into activity, and** that precisely **in** the manner **required for** springing to **one's feet,** first the *musculus psoas,* then the **rectus femoris,** the *vasti,* and **all** the co-operating com-**pany.** I wish to see the far **more** important nervous streams which dis-tribute themselves to the organs of speech, the muscles of breathing, producing command, word, and call, and which, by way of sound-waves **and** the auditory nerves of other individuals, renew tenfold the **same performance.   I** will, **in a word,** make a present for the time being of the so-called psychical action **to** the **pedants of the schools, and will have** the physical **action which I** see **explained** *by physical causes.***   In like manner, Münsterberg concludes that, " from the physiological stand-point there **must correspond to every centrally initiated movement a** complex **of** centripetal stimuli ; and in these stimuli acting from with-out, taken **together** with the **existing** structure and condition of the nervous mechanism, **must lie** the absolutely sufficient causes for the necessary **occurrence of the definite act of will."** Innumerable past stimuli in the life **of the individual and the race are stored** up as poten-**tial** energy **in the nervous mechanism.** Hence the sound-waves of a spoken word (on which, as in the case put by Lange, action follows) may **represent** "scarcely a millionth part of the joint-causes which bring **about that** particular movement in the hearer." But the mechanical **determination** by the joint-causes is as absolute here as in the case of **the simplest reflex (pp.** 17-20).   It is, indeed, the avowed " postulate " **of the whole investigation** that the act of will shall be explained " als **Mechanik der Atome "** (p. 9).

acteristic psychological analysis, contained in the second part of the treatise, we find that Münsterberg is at some pains at the outset to define the problem he sets himself. It is purely a problem of empirical psychology, and does not raise the metaphysical question as to the ultimate ground of phenomena or as to how consciousness exists at all.   In that connection, Münsterberg seems to indicate that he regards Will, conceived as Schopenhauer conceived it, to be the most probable metaphysical hypothesis.   His present investigation, however, has to do only with Will as a conscious fact; it seeks " only to establish the conscious phenomena which are peculiar to the act of will" (p. 56).   " Wherein consists the content of our inner experience, empirically given to each of us, which we designate will " (p. 60).   Or, again, " For our investigation, limited as it is to facts, the will is a phenomenon like other phenomena ; and accordingly we have only to ask in what it consists, what regularly precedes it in consciousness, and what follows it " (p. 61). This strictly empirical character of the inquiry has one important consequence.

It is well known [he proceeds] that modern psychology designates as sensations the ultimate irreducible constituents into which the content of consciousness (*Bewusstseinsinhalt*) may be analysed ; ascribing to sensations a quality, an intensity, and a tone of feeling which expresses their relations to consciousness.   But, if sensation is the element of all psychical phenomena, and if, on the other hand, the will, so far as we are concerned with it, is only a phenomenon of consciousness (*Bewusstseinserscheinung*), it follows necessarily *that the will too is only a complex of sensations.*[1]

Having thus marked out his goal beforehand, Münsterberg proceeds to the actual analysis of the facts. He analyses first what he calls the inward activity of will—*i.e.*, the voluntary guidance of the train of thoughts in the form of attention; and secondly, the outward activity of will in bringing about muscular contractions. Under the first head, then, the question is, "Wherein consists the inner activity in the direction of the current of our ideas? or, more precisely, what must be the nature of the feelings present in consciousness, if they are to produce in us the feeling of inward freedom, of active will?" This more precise way of putting the question, it will be observed, is not without significance for the nature of the answer which it is to elicit. Let us get to the details, however. Four cases of the inward directive activity of will are analysed by

---

[1] Page 62. The italics are Münsterberg's own. It need hardly be pointed out that this astonishing invocation of "modern psychology" begs everything which is afterwards put forward as proved. Wundt criticises the assumption, 'Philosophische Studien,' vol. vi. p. 382 *et seq.* We shall return to it in discussing the theory as a whole.

Münsterberg: (*a*) the case of voluntary recollection or trying to remember; (*b*) the exercise of choice between different ideas presented, the concentration of attention upon one of these and its retention in the field of consciousness to the exclusion of the others; (*c*) the case of logical thinking or reasoning, in which we pass along a definite and apparently self-directed path from premisses to conclusion; and (*d*) the case of simple attention to an idea or percept which presents itself in consciousness.

The analysis is most ingenious in the case of voluntary recollection and logical thinking. How is voluntary recollection distinguished from involuntary reminiscence? If a fact *a* has been connected in experience with *b*, and the appearance of *b* calls up in consciousness the idea of *a*, I do not attribute to myself any voluntary action in the matter; I take it as an instance of the ordinary play of association.

On the other hand, when I cannot remember *a*, when I seek it in my memory, recall to myself the place where I saw it, the connection in which I heard it, and when at last *a* actually emerges in consciousness, then it was plainly my will (we say) which dragged to light the object of my search (p. 64).

How does the case stand, however, when more closely analysed?

If I try to remember a, if I seek it in my memory, a is of course not itself present in consciousness, but what I do perceive does unquestionably correspond in content with a. So long as I have not found a, I feel, it is true, only an x, but I feel this x in a series of relations, such that x can be only a and nothing else. I try to remember a word. In doing so, I see in memory the passage where I read the word, I remember the moment at which I heard it, I know exactly, too, the meaning of the word; but the word itself is not present to me. At last it rises in consciousness. Can it be denied that that word was already given in its full content (*vollinhaltlich gegeben*) in the series of ideational relations which I remembered? No doubt it was represented in consciousness by entirely different qualities; it was given in its relations to other things, whereas it is afterwards distinguished by its own characteristics. But the two states of consciousness coincided with one another as to their inner meaning (p. 67).

The only peculiarity, accordingly, which Münsterberg is prepared to admit in this process as contrasted with a case of involuntary association is that " the clear consciousness of the idea a was preceded by another state of consciousness which, in respect of its content, already contained the idea a." He italicises this as the standing mark of voluntary control of our ideas. Reasoning is distinguished, he argues, by the same characteristic. The premisses already contain the conclusion, or, to put it more pointedly, the whole process of thought is determined from the outset by the idea

F

of the end to be reached.   In the second case mentioned
above, where several ideas are presented, and we pur-
posely retain one of them, *a*, the same thing manifestly
holds.   "Here," says Münsterberg, "there is no need
to prove that this *a* was in consciousness beforehand.
The reasons why just *a* and not *b* remained in consciousness are admittedly only the occasions or motives
of the voluntary act; they are left therefore unnoticed
here,—the remaining behind is itself the achievement
of the will (*das Zurückbleiben selbst ist die Willens-
leistung*)."   The same line of argument explains his
fourth case, the case of simple attention to any idea
presented in consciousness.   "In the first moment in
which a sensation emerges in us, the perception appears
involuntary, because the *a* was till then preceded by a
not-a; in the second moment, however, it appears to us
as intentionally retained, just because we were already
conscious of it in the preceding first moment."

The solemnity with which this is propounded as a
serious account of the facts in question would be too
impudent if it stood alone; but Münsterberg hastens
to supplement it by reference to the bodily sensations
which usually accompany acts like attention and selection or efforts of thought and memory.   He cites the
admitted fact that there are feelings of innervation in

the sense-organ, when ideas of that particular sense are present in consciousness for any length of time. Whenever there is a strain of attention, other sensations are usually present, such, for example, as feelings of tension in the skin of the head and the knitting of the brow in trying to remember or in thoughtful consideration. Nor are such feelings confined to the head; they may be traced all over the trunk, and even in the extremities. Münsterberg does not hold, however, that such feelings of innervation necessarily accompany all voluntary activity. In reasonings or calculations that proceed without any particular difficulty, for example, they are not observable; but just in these processes, he hastens to add, we are not specially conscious of our voluntary activity. It is only in subsequent reflection that we class them as acts of will, and in so doing, we fall back upon the criterion already signalised—namely, the pre-existence of the idea in the preceding moment of consciousness. He concludes the first part of his psychological investigation thus :—

The inner will has thus shown itself on analysis to be a very complicated group of ideas (ein sehr mannigfaltiges Vorstellungsgebilde), composed of certain definite series of ideas plus feelings of innervation. Nothing unknown, nothing which stands over against the ideas as something heterogeneous, has been found, as we saw, in the first group of ideas or sensations; it only remains, therefore, to ask whether any mysterious element is concealed in these innervation processes. Should these also be found to be a mere complex of sensations, the inner will would then be reduced to a series of sensations, each one of which is of the same order as blue, hard, sweet, or warm (p. 73).

The consideration of the feelings of innervation cannot, however, be conveniently separated from the external action of the will upon the body, and so we pass to the second head of this psychological investigation. The stock example will suffice — I lift an object with my hand.

But the result of this experiment is usually a very poor one: the feeling of will which I seek (*die gesuchte Willens-empfindung*) I cannot discover in myself. I perceive just a slight feeling of tension in the head. For the rest, I am only conscious that I actually execute the movement —viz., bending the joints of the elbow and hand. I feel no special impulse to the movement, lying in time between the theoretical intention and the practical execution of it. It is quite different, however [he proceeds], when I do not simply have the intention of lifting an object, and carry this out, but slowly analyse the movement for myself, and direct my attention to the individual parts of the bendings. Now I really perceive more than the actually executed move-ments; the bending in the elbow is now preceded by the feeling of a peculiar impulse. It is not a general feeling

of exertion, but a quite specific impulse, which is different
for every movement, and plainly stands in relation to the
special performance intended.

What, then, has analysis to say of these feelings of
innervation which immediately precede the movement,
and seem to be its cause? Münsterberg turns round
triumphantly to apply his former criterion. What we
call impulse in the case of muscular contraction is
simply the circumstance that the idea of the effect to
be produced precedes the effect as actually produced.
The feeling of innervation is just the memory-idea of
the movement anticipating the movement itself.

There has been much discussion as to the precise
nature of the so-called feelings of innervation; but,
as Wundt, who had formerly held an opposite theory,
has explicitly accepted this view of them as the one
most consonant with the present state of our knowledge
of the subject, there is no need to reproduce here the
arguments which go to establish the position. It
commends itself by its naturalness and simplicity.
When we are on the point, say, of making a stroke
at a ball, we have a premonitory feeling of the energy
which we are about to expend; it seems to flow forth
toward the limb which we are about to use. One
theory, formerly a good deal in evidence, explained

this feeling as due to an immediate consciousness of outgoing energy; but the physiological difficulties in the way of such a conception are great. It is not necessary here to decide whether an immediate consciousness of effort is or is not possible; but, in any case, this theory leaves unexplained the specific character of the feeling in question. For it is to be observed that it is a premonitory feeling of the exertion of *that* limb, not merely a general consciousness of virtue going out from us. This is satisfactorily explained by supposing, as Münsterberg does, that it is due to the reproduction in memory of previous movements of the same nature.

Plainly, however, Münsterberg's theory of the feelings of innervation may be accepted, without admitting that this sequence of memory-image and actual perception constitutes, as he contends, the differentia and sufficient explanation of the voluntary act. But it will be observed how ingeniously Münsterberg has reduced all cases of voluntary action—internal and external— to examples of the same phenomenon, namely, to cases of an idea or perception A preceded by *a*—the same idea in a different form. "The feeling of innervation," as he puts it, "is an anticipated idea of the actual movement" (p. 88). Exactly the same analysis applies to those voluntary actions **which do not end in a muscular** contraction but aim at the production of some effect in the external **world.**

When **I move** my finger, **not in** order to practise **the** different **movements,** but to write something down; **when I** contract the muscles **of my organs of** speech, **in order to** make a communication to **somebody; when I bend my arm in order to** greet a **passer-by,—in all these cases I perceive in the** first stadium **the more** or **less** distinct, **more or less** clearly represented, **idea of** the end; and in **the second** stadium **I have a sensation of** (*ich empfinde*) the **end as** attained. **That alone is the type of the** external **act** of will (p. **89).**

However complicated the action is, extending possibly over a longer period of time (a journey, the erection **of a building),** it may always be resolved into the ultimate end **in** view and the subordinate actions which have to be performed in order to attain **that end.** In the process **of execution, the ultimate** end falls temporarily into the **background, and the** subordinate actions or means become, each in turn, in **a** definite series, the proximate end before the mind. And, step by step, the same analysis holds good : the end **is first** present as idea, then as a perception of accomplished fact. Münsterberg **goes on** courageously **to apply** his analysis **to the usually received distinction between** desire and will. "In order that the desire of an attainable object pass into the corresponding act of will, neither more nor less requires to be added than just the carrying out of the desire, *so that the idea of the end may be completed by the perception of its attainment.*" "The liveliest feeling of practical freedom cannot alter the fact that the will itself is nothing more than the perception (frequently accompanied by associated sensations of tension in the muscles of the head) of an effect attained by the movement of our own body, along with an antecedent idea of the same effect drawn from imagination—*i.e.*, in the last resort from memory; this anticipated idea being given as feeling of innervation, when the effect is itself a bodily movement. "*A theory of the soul does justice, therefore, to the whole field of psychical phenomena, if it assumes, as the only function of the soul, sensation characterised by quality, intensity, and tone of feeling; a definite group of sensations we call will*" (p. 96).[1]

This is the conclusion of the second part of the investigation. The first, or purely physiological, part, reduced the phenomenon to a series of reflex movements; the second, or purely psychological, part, has reduced it to a series of sensations. The third, or

---

[1] The italics are Münsterberg's.

psycho-physical, part, investigates the relation of these two series to one another. We cannot believe that the two series are quite independent, and if we are driven to suppose that the one is conditioned by the other, there can be little hesitation in settling which is the conditioning factor. The psychical series is discontinuous, constantly interrupted by perceptions which are shot inexplicably into its midst, without the possibility of causal explanation from the foregoing train of ideas; there are many bodily functions which, so far as we know, are not represented in consciousness. These and similar considerations make the psychic series unfit to be the explaining factor, and accordingly Münsterberg reaches the conclusion that "the series of conscious phenomena is conditioned by the regular course of material occurrence." This leads to the inquiry, What are the processes in the sensory-motor apparatus which correspond, when inwardly contemplated, to the sensational complex called a volition?

Münsterberg's results are reached in the course of an interesting, and in some respects brilliant, discussion as to the localisation of brain-function. It is beyond our interest to follow him in his detailed criticism of different theories. His own positions are mainly two: (1) that there are no specifically motor centres; and

(2) that perception and memory are connected with the same material substratum; or, to put it otherwise, that ideas of sensation and the corresponding ideas of memory are connected, not with different parts of the brain, but with the same set of material processes differently excited. There is much to be said for these conclusions. Whether the will is analysable into sensations and ideas or not, it is at least inseparable from them, and therefore we may reasonably conclude that the centres concerned in voluntary movement cannot be separated physiologically from the sensory regions of the brain. Similarly, it may be argued that in perception and memory the same brain-tracts are excited, the liveliness and strength of the impression being greater when its stimulus proceeds from its peripheral end-organs than when it is conducted by fibres of association from other parts of the cortex.

On the physiological truth of these hypotheses I do not feel competent to decide, nor is it necessary for my purpose to do so. It is with Münsterberg's application of them that we are concerned. "Every ganglion of the cerebral cortex," he resumes, "is thus end-organ of a centripetal path—but every ganglion is also the initial organ of a motor path. Motor centres do not exist, therefore, or, more properly, every centre is sen-

sory and motor at once; every motor impulse has its
source in a sensory stimulus, and every sensory stimulation presses on into a motor path" (pp. 141, 142).
What happens in consciousness, then, when a response
to stimulus takes place? At first, nothing precedes
the movement except the sensation or perception which
causes its discharge. The movement, in other words,
"goes off," in a purely reflex way, through the force of
the incoming stimulus. But as soon as the movement
actually takes place, consciousness has something new
before it—namely, the feeling of movement produced
in the contracted muscle. This feeling of movement
follows, therefore, immediately upon the perception
of the stimulus which discharged the movement; and
the sensory excitation of the central ganglion which
corresponds to this feeling of movement becomes
connected accordingly by an association - path with
the first excitation, which gave the impulse to the
movement.

If, now, this process is several times repeated, the connection becomes so close that the first excitation inevitably
calls forth the second, directly by the path of association,
before it has time to be produced by the actual contraction
of the muscle. Psychologically expressed, that is as much
as to say, *the perception of the stimulus must call forth by
association the memory-idea of the corresponding sensation*

*of movement, before that sensation itself is produced by the
actual execution of the movement.* The former process takes
place by the shorter way of the association-paths in the
hemisphere; the latter requires first to be conducted to the
muscle, the inertia of the muscle has to be overcome, the
contraction to be actually produced, the sensory nerve to be
affected, and the sensory stimulus conducted back to the cortex. All this occupies an appreciable time, and the sensory
stimulus arrives accordingly considerably later. And now
we see clearly why our feeling of innervation precedes the
perception of the actual movement. In it, as the constant
signal of movement, a signal that is also the actual counterpart of the movement, we involuntarily believe that we see
the movement's cause. This is the type of voluntary action,
from which all other forms may be developed (p. 145).

Take, for example, an act of choice. Here we have,
let us say, two stimuli, both alike in strength, but
incapable of combination in a common reaction. At
first no motor reaction can result, but each stimulated
ganglion rouses the centres which are connected with
it by association-paths; and now it is not an opposition
of stimulus against stimulus, but on both sides there
collect the associations won by former experiences.
In the first place, naturally, there is the associated
idea of the movement corresponding to the stimulus.
If this is stronger upon the one side than upon the
other, or if it rouses more pleasurable feelings upon the
one side than upon the other, then the corresponding
movement will result. This is the type of any act

of choice; but there may be indefinite complication, both in the nature of the stimulus and in the mass of associations brought to bear upon it. Still, however great the complication may be, the sensory stimuli with their associated ideas constitute the sufficient and only verifiable cause of the resultant movement; or, as he puts it in another place, "the act of will is the motor discharge of sensory excitation, whether it be the sensation of a single stimulus or a world of internally and externally combined ideas. As soon as the sensory excitation-complex, the conscious content of ideas, is there, the movement is necessarily given too" (p. 156). And thus the only psychical criterion of the will remains what it was found to be at the end of the psychological section—namely, that before the perception of the actual result, the *idea* of the result is present in consciousness.

We have the theory now pretty fully before us, and, as has been indicated, there is much in the physiological analysis that is freshly put and that claims consideration. It seems important to remember, alike in physiology and psychology, that the sensory centre in the brain, the central ending of the sensory nerve, does not constitute a terminus, and, consequently, that there is no such thing as passive sensation, sensation which is simply received without producing further effects. All consciousness is impulsive. If the stimulus received does not find an immediate vent in movement, it irradiates other brain-tracts in the form of association. The phenomena of imitation, suggestion, and many other considerations, reinforce this conception of the dynamic quality which all sensations and ideas possess. Münsterberg, however, has skilfully woven these truths into the texture of a preconceived theory. In the very act of emphasising movement and the dynamic aspect of ideas, he eliminates altogether the notion of action or activity. Ideas "go off" or explode, as it were, in movement of their own accord. There is first the idea of the movement, as in contemplation; and secondly, the perception of the movement, as executed. In other words, there is a series of happenings somehow passing before us, but no real activity, no real actor in the whole affair. In all so-called action, we only seem to act; a sequence of ideas exhausts the phenomena of will. The conscious subject is reduced to an inactive spectator of these psychological happenings, which are themselves the inert accompaniments of certain transformations of matter and energy. There results, in fact, as indicated at the outset, the doctrine of conscious automatism in the most unqualified sense of the words.

Now, I do not hesitate to say that this conclusion is in the strictest sense incredible; no amount of so-called "evidence" in its favour would avail to make it even momentarily believable. But as the theory airs itself **with a great** deal of confidence, and troubles a good **many minds, I will** endeavour to show that such results are **not reached by** any cruel "logic **of** facts," but are all involved in a few erroneous psychological **presuppositions, perhaps I** ought to say one fundamental prejudice, by which the analysis is vitiated from the **outset. This** prejudice may be called Phenomenalism, or perhaps best Presentationism; Wundt calls it **in one** place Intellectualism. **It is the fore-gone** conclusion that the conscious life is analysable without remainder into ideas or presentations. Evidently, **if** phenomena **or** *objects* of consciousness are alone to be accepted **as facts, then** all real activity on the part **of the subject is necessarily** eliminated; the subject **remains only nominally, as** a static impersonal condition of the series of events. If we insist upon phenomenalising **the** act of will, doubtless all the *phenomena* in the case are the ideas that precede and the perceptions that follow, with perhaps some feelings of tension in the head **thrown** in. But does it not **require some effrontery to** offer us these antecedent, concomitant, **and sequent** *ideas* as an account of the *volition* itself. To attempt to analyse a volition into ideas is about as hopeful as trying to reduce miles and furlongs to pounds avoirdupois; there is no common denominator. In the course of such analysis, the real fact of volition is necessarily dropped; it is overlaid by the mass of antecedents, concomitants, and sequents which acute introspection enables us to discover. But, as M. Fouillée says, the physiological psychologists might fill volumes with their analysis of the sensations which accompany the voluntary act, without touching the essence of the act itself.[1]

The result of analysis infected with this phenomenalistic prejudice is necessarily a Panphenomenalism essentially similar to that of Hume. There is the same elimination of all real causality: sequent ideas are all. And if, in deference to a quasi-Kantian theory of Knowledge, the Self or subject is apparently retained, this seeming difference from Hume is only skin-deep. For, as Münsterberg tells us twice over, "the subject in question is entirely impersonal;"[2] it is the static or logical condition of consciousness in general. The individual self is reduced, as with Hume, to groups and sequences of ideas; it is an object in consciousness

---

[1] Revue philosophique, vol. xxxii. p. 238.

[2] Aufgabe der Psychologie, pp. 99 and 130.

—an object, presumably, for this impersonal spectator-subject.

I pointed out in passing how entirely Münsterberg's psychology was dominated by this phenomenalistic point of view.   It appears, incidentally, in the very expressions he uses, as a reference to the passages already quoted abundantly shows.   In his equation of phenomenon with fact, in the constantly repeated use of the term *Inhalt* or content, it is presupposed that objects or presentations *in* consciousness are the only elements that will be allowed to stand as real.   At times, Münsterberg speaks, even more naïvely, of "the sensation of will," of which he is in quest.   This recalls, even verbally, Hume's famous expedition into his own interior, in order to discover the perception of the Self. Show me the impression from which the idea is derived, says Hume, and because no particular impression can be found, the idea is pronounced a fiction; the Self is resolved into a bundle of perceptions.   Show me the sensation to which the word "will" corresponds, says Münsterberg, and finding a number of accompanying sensations, he mistakes these for the act of will itself, and concludes roundly, as we saw before, that "the will is only a complex of sensations."   But this conclusion depends, on Münsterberg's own showing,

upon two all-important "ifs." *If* sensation is the
sole element of all psychical phenomena, and *if* the
will is only a phenomenon in consciousness, then,
and only then, does it follow necessarily that the
will is resolvable into a complex of sensations. In
support of the first "if," Münsterberg, as we have
seen, has nothing to offer but a vague reference to
"modern psychology." Wundt, in criticising his speculation,[1] justly censures this attempt to clothe an assumption with the air of an accepted truth, and to
cover it with the ægis of "modern psychology."
Wundt's own phraseology has wavered in his different
editions, and its looseness may be partly responsible,
as Dr Ward suggests,[2] for the extreme conclusions of
his followers. Perhaps in view of these conclusions,
he now explicitly disavows the resolution of all consciousness, including feeling and will, into sensational
elements. Sensations, he holds, are the ultimate elements of "those conscious contents which we refer to
external objects"—that is to say, of our perceptions or
presentations. Whether this revised statement is un-
exceptionable or not, such a position is at least intelligible; but it contains no warrant for identifying

---

[1] Philosophische Studien, vol. vi. p. 382 *et seq.*
[2] In an article in 'Mind,' January 1893.

feeling and will with any presentation or combination of such.

There is, in fact, no distinction more fundamental to a sound psychology than that between the feeling-directed activity, which, under all its forms, from the simplest act of attention and response to stimulus, may be summarised as Will, and the content or matter with which that activity deals. Doubtless the two cannot be separated; each is an abstraction without the other. But one thing at least is certain, that to resolve the fact of conscious experience into a sequence of presentations or conscious phenomena is to omit the vital characteristic of all consciousness. It is to offer us a machinery without any motor force; and when we mildly point out the omission, we are met by the ready but somewhat brazen retort, that the machinery is *self-acting*. Wundt comments acutely on the way in which this "intellectualistic" psychology substantialises ideas or presentations, treats them as if they were things or entities that could independently exist and interact. Even when it is admitted that presentations have an existence only *in and for* consciousness, so that the unity of consciousness is acknowledged to be their necessary complement or point of reference, the ideas still seem to stand *over against* the conscious-

ness to which they are referred, and to carry on their
evolutions independently. Consciousness, according to
this way of thinking, becomes a mere form inclusive
of a certain matter, but without influence upon it: it
is regarded as purely speculative or contemplative; an
eye (shall we say?) contemplating the movement, or,
to be strict and to avoid metaphor, merely an ideal
point of unity. Metaphor or no metaphor, the result
of this way of looking at things is obvious. The whole
weight is thrown upon the objects—the ideas or phenomena, thus quasi-independently conceived — and the
recognition of the subject becomes an empty acknowledgment. It is entirely denuded of activity, all action
being refunded into the play of presentations.[1]

---

[1] Dr Ward has very aptly called attention ('Mind,' xii. 50) to a current
form of words which favours this habit of thought—viz., the way we
have of speaking of "conscious states" in abstraction from the activity
of the conscious subject whose states they are. We get into the habit
of thinking of the "states"—"phenomena" is another word—as if they
existed separately, as if they interacted and established relations between themselves, evolving in course of time the idea of the subject.
But, in strictness, we have no right to speak of a *state* as conscious ;
in so doing we are making an entity of it, and conferring upon an
abstraction attributes which it can possess only as an element in the
activity of a unitary conscious being. Dr Ward declaims with justifiable warmth against the confusion in which our psychological nomen-
clature is involved. Even the favourite term "states of consciousness,"
of which "conscious states" may be supposed an abbreviation, is open to
a similar objection. Consciousness, as the form of the word proclaims, is

For this assumption, however, there is an entire absence of warrant. A psychology which aims at keeping in touch with fact must strenuously resist this subtle tendency to reduce everything to knowledge. Experience is, in this reference, a wider term than knowledge; and feeling and will are inexpugnable and irreducible features of experience. Knowledge, feeling, and will are three aspects of experience—inseparable aspects, it may be freely admitted—but none of them can be expressed in terms of the others; no one of them can be reduced to simpler elements, no one of them can, properly speaking, be defined or explained otherwise than by pointing to the living experience in which it is exemplified. Münsterberg's position here is rather inconsistent; he denies will as more than a complex of sensations, but he contrives to smuggle in feeling by calling it an attribute which every idea possesses. He follows Wundt in saying that every sensation, in addi-

---

an abstraction; it is the quality or characteristic of a subject or conscious being. States are states of the conscious being, then, not states of consciousness. This is not a mere piece of verbal purism. A great deal of vague thinking—thinking that has not faced an inevitable issue and made up its mind clearly—finds a convenient refuge under the quasi-abstract term consciousness. People make no scruple about admitting or postulating a transcendental unity, a unity of consciousness, who would think their reputation for modernity at stake if they were taxed with upholding a soul or subject as a real being.

tion to its intensity and its quality (as touch or taste, red or blue, and so forth), also possesses a tone of feeling, or, as Professor Bain puts it, an emotional side; and to this third aspect of sensation, curiously enough, he allows that there is no material counterpart.[1]

This statement is curious, not in itself, of course, but as coming from Münsterberg. There can be no material counterpart, in Münsterberg's sense, just because feeling is not itself an object, phenomenon, presentation, or stimulus, but the attitude of the subject towards a given stimulus—the relation of the stimulus to the life of the individual as a whole. This subjective appreciation cannot, in the nature of the case, be represented in objective terms. Feeling, as Dr Ward says after Hamilton, is something subjectively subjective. If we are to be strict, we do not *know* feeling; for knowledge is of objects, of phenomena, and feeling cannot be phenomenalised. We experience feeling, and we know *about* it by its results; but, using the term in this sense, we know only the causes, accompaniments, and consequents of feeling. It may be said that we remember our feelings and emotions, and that we must know them at the time, in order to remember. But we remember feeling only in the sense that, when the ideas which caused or

[1] Willenshandlung, p. 137.

accompanied it are recalled, they are recalled with the same tone of feeling; in other words, we re-experience in a fainter degree the feeling which we then felt. It is this characteristic of feeling that explains its frequent neglect by psychologists. For feeling cannot be recalled or considered, except in connection with its objective causes or accompaniments: in recording the facts, therefore, the psychologist is apt to forget the subjective tinge of the ideas or presentations, and to report upon them in an impersonal way, as, so to speak, ideas-in-themselves. But it was only in virtue of what I have called the subjective tinge that the ideas were *his* ideas at all, and had any relation to his life. As they presented themselves, they were felt to be either a furtherance or a hindrance to the vitality of the subject, to be either relevant to the dominant interests of the individual or discordant. Interest and desire are the result in the one case, indifference or repulsion in the other. And it can hardly be too strongly emphasised that the dynamic efficacy of ideas is entirely excited through the feeling subject. Ideas have hands and feet, as Hegel finely said, and how often are we told that ideas move the world. It is true, or at least we hope so. But every one must acknowledge that to speak in that way is to use a vivid

metaphorical shorthand.   *Ideas entertained* tend to pass
into action; a plan conceived and cherished tends to
execute itself; but, as Fichte long ago said, the real
force is not in the ideas, but in the will of the person
who adopts them as his.   So, when psychologists like
Münsterberg attribute the whole march of the conscious
life to the dynamic influence of idea upon idea, it is
well to remember again that this is at best a convenient shorthand.   Ideas in themselves are pale and in-
effective as the shades of Homeric mythology ; they are
dynamic only as they pass through the needle's eye of
the subject.   It is the subject which acts upon its
appreciation of the stimulus, and the emotional attitude of welcome or repulse is what is meant by feeling.

In its earliest and simplest forms, such an emotional
wave passes immediately into the appropriate motor
response.   The food is clutched or somehow absorbed,
the disagreeable intrusion is evaded, edged away from,
as far as the powers of the being admits of.   Feeling,
thus conceived, and allied thus closely with action,
forms what may be called the driving-power in all life.
Here we strike upon the roots of individuation, and
when we say that, is it going too far to add, upon the
fundamental characteristic of real existence ?   In this
connection I am confident that, whether we look at the

matter psychologically or physiologically, we are shut up to the conclusion that all action of living beings was originally feeling-prompted, and that what we call reflex action is everywhere a secondary product, a degraded form of purposive action. We know that many actions at first performed voluntarily, actions learned with effort by repeated forth-puttings of concentrated attention, become by degrees habitual, and are performed automatically without attention—*i.e.*, without any need for express volition to come into play at all. Great part of the detail of our daily life is handed over to mechanism in this way, and psychologists and physiologists have not been slow to emphasise the beneficent operation of this fact. It is, indeed, the very condition of progress, that aptitudes once acquired should establish themselves as definite tendencies within our mental and physical organism—definite co-ordinations of stimulus and response which do their work without **our** active superintendence. **The powers** of intelligence and will—the powers **of** personality, **if I** may so speak— are thus set free for new tasks and further achievements, till these in turn are, as it were, built into the **structure of** the Self. Only thus is the spirit fitted **to** advance **upon** its endless path. But mechanism **is** thus, in **every** sense, posterior to intelligence and

will; it is a means created and used by will. In a
strict sense, will creates the reflex mechanism to which
it afterwards deputes its functions.

Mechanism, in fact, here as everywhere, is a means,
something secondary; it is impossible to conceive it as
something primary, existing on its own account, much
less as carrying in it the explanation of the higher conscious and voluntary processes. Intelligent volition is
not reflex action grown complicated, and so become
conscious of itself. That is precisely to invert the
true relation—an inversion that would be ludicrous,
if it were not disastrous. Reflex action is purposive
action grown unconscious or sub-conscious, according
to the economy of nature, because consciousness is
no longer necessary to its proper performance. It
is not to be supposed, of course, that this takes
place within the life-history of the individual human
being, or of any highly developed organism. In such
an organism, many reflex paths, many co-ordinations
of stimulus and response, are doubtless fixed; they
have been established in the long process of race-
evolution, and in virtue of their establishment that
evolution has proceeded. But follow the process as
far back as we may, all analogy points to the same
conclusion — namely, that feeling - prompted action,

i.e., action which is germinally purposive, germinally voluntary, is the πρότερον φύσει, the first in the order of nature. In the lowest organisms, the reaction upon stimulus may be so simple and uniform as to wear to an **observer the** appearance of a mere mechanical reflex. But this **is, if I** may so speak, to make the creature *a mere outside;* it forgets, as this mechanical psychology is constantly forgetting, that wherever there is life, there is unity. Every organism is a unity, and resumes itself as **a** unity. Feeling is the inward expression of this unity; and, to my mind, it is not doubtful that the movement of attraction or repulsion, which, *to us* and from the outside, may seem a simple reflex, is **to** be interpreted rather as the total response of a ger**minal** consciousness, **as** the expression of the being's **likes and** dislikes.

Physiology, **so long as it** remains *pure* physiology, **is** perhaps debarred from taking account of feeling or consciousness **as such. The psychical in all** its forms lies outside the **scope of** physiological methods. But the self-preservative, recuperative, self-adaptive ten**dencies** of organisms **and** organic tissue are **the** physiological way of expressing the same fact. Such a **mode of** expression is imperfect and mythological, perhaps, **and** one can understand that many physiologists, *supposing it to be put forward as an ex-planation of the facts,* grow impatient and fall back upon a purely mechanical theory of vital function. But these expressions are in no sense explanations, as science uses that term; they are rather *finger-posts to the unexplained;* they merely name or indicate the fundamental characteristic of life as such, which differentiates it from mechanism or what seems to us to be mechanism. Life is the presupposition of physiology, the fact on which its existence is based, a fact which it has simply to accept, as all the other sciences have to accept their own presuppositions. Its explanations move within the fact of life, and cannot be used to explain that fact itself, or, in other words, to explain it away. Yet that is, in substance, what a purely mechanical physiology tries to do.

Physiology, for the last fifty years, has been dominated by a reaction against what is called vitalism. The older investigators were in the habit of calling in "vital force" as a *deus ex machina* to account for any phenomena which baffled their powers of natural explanation. Vital force, conceived as extraneously interfering with otherwise mechanical processes, was evidently a hypostatised entity of the worst type, and it was accordingly discarded by scientific physiology as part of the baneful legacy of metaphysics. Mechanical explanation, or, in other words, the resolution of physiology into physics, became the watchword and ideal of the best workers. But they did not observe that they were in danger of throwing away the child with the bath, as the Germans say. After all, physiology is not physics; living matter behaves differently from dead matter. What is the difference and the basis of the difference? In rendering mechanically intelligible the inter - relation and interaction of this and the other part of the bodily structure, physiologists tend to forget that all such mechanical arrangements are arrangements *in the service of life*, arrangements perfected in the living being (in all probability) by the responsive and self-adaptive action of its living ancestors in the course of ages. *Purposiveness* is the notion upon which physiology is built, and it is worked into the whole theory of development; yet it is a notion entirely alien to the blind *vis a tergo* of mechanism as such. The more clearly a physiologist realises what pure mechanism means, and the more fully he grasps the import of the facts he has to deal with, the more ready will be his acknowledgment that to call them mechanical is at best an analogy. They belong to a different order of facts; life and purpose govern them from one end to the other.   A self-acting and self-regulating machine is only by an abuse of language spoken of as a machine at all.

It is in vain therefore that many psychologists at the present time outdo the physiologists in the glibness with which they talk of nervous currents and explosions of nervous energy and paths of least resistance. The appearance of explanation conveyed by the use of the expression "path of least resistance" is in the last degree illusory.   We are transferring an expression which has a perfectly definite and intelligible meaning in physics or mechanics to a sphere where the conditions are quite different, and where we are, moreover, almost quite ignorant as to the nature of what actually takes place.   Path of least resistance means, in such a case, simply the particular reaction which we find the stimulus, as a matter of fact, to produce.   We have no right to go further than this.   The use of the physical phrase implies, however, that what takes place is precisely the same as the selection of a channel made by a rill of water trickling down a hillside.   This is to make the living being simply a network of pathways through which the energy of external nature takes its course—soaks in, and oozes out again.   But this is not a true account even of the humblest organism.   Such a representation totally ignores the unitary character of the organic and sentient being. We are misled, in short, by words like currents, and energy, and least resistance. What do we mean by nerve currents? Nerve currents cannot be treated in this isolated fashion, as if they took place *in vacuo*, or in an indifferent medium; they take place in a living individual, and apart from the unity of that individual they are mere abstractions. A nerve current is a physiological process, which, originally and normally, means central stimulation and appropriate central reaction. You cannot separate either the appreciation of the stimulus or the reaction upon it from the organism as a whole. To speak psychologically, it is the living being, as a unity, that is aware of the sensation and responds to it. There is no need here to revive any hypothesis as to the specific seat of the soul, or to conceive any point of convergence in the brain for the multitudinous nerves of sensation and motion. However the nervous system acts, the unity of consciousness, as we experience it every moment, is proof sufficient of the fact that it does act as a unity. Every living being is a similar individuate unity. Abnormalities, as when the removal of the higher centres gives rise to the establishment of independent unities (in the spinal cord, for example), are no arguments against what is here contended for ; they rather go to prove that even the mutilated organism, so long as it lives at all, reconstitutes itself into a kind of unity.

A living being, then, is, at the very least, a centre of sensation and reaction ; and when sensation is so used, it means not only intellectual awareness of some presence, but also a subjective drawing to, or away from, the intruder.   This second element of feeling proper is the condition in virtue of which the sensation as knowledge calls forth the reaction as will.   The appetitive is the first phase of consciousness.   And however the growth of the intellectual life and of volitional self-control may emancipate us from the promptings of the moment, it is to the end through feeling that the whole process of our life goes on.   It is in feeling that we assert our individuality, give expression to our preferences and distastes.   Feeling leads each of us to select from the infinite of the knowable and do-able, that little world of interests and habits which differentiates us one from another, and gives to each his peculiar point of outlook upon the universe.

The necessity of taking feeling first has led us in appearance away from our specific theme.   But it is only in appearance, for it was impossible to separate the treatment of feeling and will, and what has been said of the one applies *mutatis mutandis* to the other. The presentationists endeavoured to make feeling a relation between ideas, instead of the relation of ideas to the subject of them.   If the subject has identified itself, as we say, with certain ideas or interests, then any idea which conflicts with these ideas will result in pain or displeasure to the subject.   But here, as always, it is not the relations of ideas as such—relations, as it were, in the phenomenal plane—but relation to a subject, that constitutes the fact of feeling. Similarly with volition.   Volition is the action of a subject, and as such, it cannot be phenomenalised. But this is just what the phenomenalists, from Hume to Münsterberg, insist on doing.   They resolve volition into a sequence of presentations; first, an idea, then a perception (as we have seen Münsterberg put it), but no intervening fiat, no power, no real action, nothing corresponding to what we mean by volition— just the one first, and the other second.   The answer to be made to this ingenious theorem has been indicated already.   To ask to know the will as a presentation is to ask to know it *as it is not.*   The phenomena which Münsterberg offers us are very likely all the phenomena in the case, or if there are more, the others are like unto

H

them. But his whole investigation is a *petitio principii*. The heading of the psychological section of his treatise runs, "The Will as a Phenomenon in Consciousness"; and that we may be in no doubt as to his meaning, he says in his preface: "It might also run—The Will as Idea *(der Wille als Vorstellung)." The will as idea—* that is the whole theory in a nutshell. No enemy could have put the case more conclusively against Münsterberg than he has done himself in these words, which are, nevertheless, the key‑note of his whole inquiry.

II.

But this Presentationism or Phenomenalism, as has been already hinted, is not a new doctrine. It is a motive which has been widely influential in the history of philosophy. Let us generalise our conclusions, there‑ fore, and enforce them by historic example. Activity, as Berkeley long ago said, is not an idea, or anything like an idea, though doubtless activity is involved in the existence of any idea, seeing that ideas exist only for a subject, or, to be more exact, seeing that ideas, from the psychological point of view, are in every case just activities of some subject. But because, in the nature of the case, action cannot be made a presentation of, cannot be held up as an object in the mental field of view, this theory proposes to efface activity altogether. In saying this, we are not attributing to the Presentationists a conclusion which they disclaim. All real action, all real causality, is eliminated from their account of the universe as known. Causality is reduced, as with Hume, to mere sequence. We ourselves do not act—we only seem to ourselves to act; in reality, we merely look on at happenings. Münsterberg suggests that the real agent in all these sequences, including the events which we mistakenly attribute to our own agency, may be, as Schopenhauer conceived, a unitary unconscious will. To this extent, therefore, he differs from Hume: he does not leave us with a purely sceptical phenomenalism. He is prepared to admit will or force, in this sense, as ultimate metaphysical reality and sole cause. But such an admission has no bearing on our contention, so long as the psychological reality of the individual Will is denied.

It must be admitted unreservedly that, if to know means to have a presentation before us, then we do not and cannot *know* the fact of our volitional activity. In this sense, we can only know the motives which led to it and the changes which followed upon it in the

phenomenal field.   I am not advocating this usage, for
I admit that it sounds absurd to say that we do not
know our own activity, our own existence.   All I would
urge is that, if the associations of "knowledge" with the
objective, the presentable, the phenomenal, are incradi-
cable, then we shall be obliged to fall back upon some
other term to express the acquaintance which the subject has with his own activity.   This is exactly the
position which Berkeley took up, when he corrected
his first impulse to resolve the Self into a procession
of ideas.   In his suggestive distinction between "ideas"
and "notions," he anticipates and combats the Panphenomenalism of Hume and of such theories as we
have been considering.

There can be no *idea* formed [he says] of a soul or spirit;
for all ideas whatever being passive and inert, cannot represent unto us by way of image or likeness that which
acts.   A little attention will make it plain to any one that
to have an idea which shall be *like* that active principle of
motion and change of ideas is absolutely impossible.   Such
is the nature of Spirit or that which acts, that it cannot be
of itself perceived, but only by the effects which it produceth. . . .   So far as I can see, the words *will*, *soul*,
spirit, do not stand for different ideas, or in truth for any
idea at all, but for something which is very different from
ideas, and which, being an Agent, cannot be like unto or represented by any idea whatsoever, though it must be owned

at the same time that we have some *notion* of soul, spirit, and the operations of the mind, such as willing, loving, hating—inasmuch as we know or understand the meaning of the words.[1]

In a later section he formally repeats the distinction in the same terms[2] and adds: "I will not say that the terms idea and notion may not be used convertibly, if the world will have it so; but yet it conduceth to clearness and propriety that we distinguish things very different by different names." And with his accustomed fine - edged irony, he remarks that "much scepticism about the nature of the soul" has arisen "from the opinion that spirits are to be known after the manner of an idea or sensation." "It is even probable that this opinion may have produced a doubt in some, whether they had any soul at all distinct from their body, since, upon inquiry, they could not find they had an idea of it."[3] The modern doctrine of automatism lends fresh point to this shaft of sarcasm.

---

[1] Principles of Human Knowledge, section 27.

[2] Section 142. "We may not, I think, strictly be said to have an *idea* of an active being or of an action, although we may be said to have a *notion* of any mind and its acts about ideas—inasmuch as I know or understand what is meant by these words. What I know, that I have some notion of."

[3] Section 137. The preceding section is also so aptly expressed, especially with reference to the subsequent argument of Hume, that I

Berkeley's proposed use of idea in this restricted or specific sense is equivalent to that of the modern terms presentation, phenomenon, or object; and it will be observed how he expressly defines mind and spirit as "that which acts." It must be for ever impossible to phenomenalise an action; we cannot objectify the subjective function as such. In his own words, that which acts cannot be itself perceived, but only by the effects which it produceth. But are we to conclude, therefore, that there is no activity in the case, that there is no active subject at all? Surely not. On the contrary, it is in activity or the will that we, as it were, lay hold upon reality and have immediate assurance of it. And if, as already said, the associations of "knowledge" are too narrow to permit of its application here, we must even fall back upon some

cannot forbear reproducing it here. "It will perhaps be said that we want a *sense* (as some have imagined) proper to know substances withal, which, if we had, we might know our own soul as we do a triangle. To this I answer that, in case we had a new sense bestowed upon us, we could only receive thereby some new sensations or ideas of sense. But I believe nobody will say that what he means by the terms *soul* and *substance* is only some particular sort of idea or sensation. We may therefore infer that, all things duly considered, it is not more reasonable to think our faculties defective, in that they do not furnish us with an *idea* of spirit or active thinking substance, than it would be if we should blame them for not being able to comprehend a *round square.*"

such phrase as "immediate assurance," "immediate experience," or **"self-feeling."** [1]

There is, after **all, a certain** justification for the narrower use **of the** term knowledge. **For is it not** the case that knowledge, in its very nature, **brings with** it a species of *foreignness?* **Of course we all see clearly** enough that there is another, and, I **admit,** a more important sense, in which knowledge may **truly be said** to be just the overcoming, the banishing, of this strangeness. The knower and his knowledge, **as Aristotle** said, are in a sense one. When we have thoughts, says Hegel, we recognise in nature's inner heart only our own reason, and feel at home there. "Spirit has the certainty which Adam had when **he saw Eve.** 'This is flesh of my flesh, and bone of my bone.'" No one, I say, will question that in this sense knowledge means unity, appropriation, the breaking down of the middle wall of partition. **But that is** without prejudice to the other and more subtle aspect **of the case** which I desire **to** emphasise. Knowledge, in its very nature, implies difference. What we know is an *object,* something held

---

[1] The last phrase is used by Mr Bosanquet (Logic, vol. i. p. 77) in a passage in which he also speaks of "the immediate feeling of my own sentient existence that goes with" any **act of perception.** **"Immediate experience"** **is used** by Mr Stout in contrast to cognition or "discriminative thinking," 'Analytic Psychology,' Bk. I. c. i., and Bk. II. c. i.

as it were at a distance from us, something opposite to
us. What we know is in fact always *something different
from ourselves*. The knower and the known are never
in this sense one, even in the limiting case of psychological introspection. It is often said that here the
observer and the observed are one and the same;
but the statement is not literally true. All introspection, it has been more truly said, is really retro-
spection; it is a *post-mortem* examination. When I
know a state, that state has already ceased to exist
as a living pulse of thought and feeling. It belongs to
the past. I recognise it as *having been mine;* but it is
different from the present psychologically-minded self,
intent upon its examination.[1] The case of introspection has been mentioned, because there, if anywhere,
it might be said that there was an identity of knowing
and being. But, as we have just seen, it is not so.
Knowing and being are not identical; they cannot help
being different. The fact is, we are face to face here
with a constant characteristic of knowledge, and if, as
we are apt to do, we take knowledge as exhaustive of

---

[1] So Professor Sully and Professor James. The latest expression of
this fact is perhaps to be found in Mr Stout's 'Analytic Psychology,'
vol. i. p. 159 : "The immediate experience of any moment is never at
that moment an object of thought."

experience, a far-reaching vista of consequences soon
appears. We may interpret the characteristic in the
relativistic sense which is so popular in agnostic and
positivistic theories. We may say, knowledge never
gives us the real thing; we are always going round
about things, and always baffled with their mere out-
sides. We know only phenomena; reality, whether
of the self or the not-self, is beyond us. **This is one**
line of thought which meets us in certain forms of
Kantianism and Neo-Kantianism, in Hamilton, and
in Spencer. Or, if we do not take this line, we fall
into what I may call an Absolute Phenomenalism. In
this case, we spurn the unknown and unknowable
mystery of the relativists; we see that **it is** absurd
to speak **as if** knowledge were constructed merely to
baulk **us.   So far all** seems well; but we have not
really escaped the consequences of accepting knowledge as **our** ultimate. For we dissolve **the universe**
altogether **into** objects or phenomena; all things and
all finite persons, including ourselves, are merely
objects in experience.   **And thus,** in another way
than the agnostic, we as surely deprive men and things
of reality; for mere objects are not real, they are halves
craving completion. And that completion they **do** not
get from the **addition of a universal** self. That **uni-**

versal self has itself no nerve of reality about it, if it is taken merely as the unifying self of knowledge. It is simply the formal unity of a spectacular process of phenomena. There is no warrant, on the theory, for understanding this self in any other way.

If, then, we are to lay hold upon reality and lift ourselves out of the flux of phenomena, we must do so by a species of assurance different from knowledge, as knowledge has just been analysed and explained. Now, we have no such certainty of any reality, save the reality of self-existence. We know other things and other persons; no sane person at least doubts that we do. But we do not immediately feel or experience their existence; they are *other* beings, and their existence is a hypothesis to explain certain phenomena of our own experience. And though the hypothesis is infinitely probable, it is theoretically open to doubt. Similarly, if we try to build even upon our own existence *as known*, that existence tends to melt away into a dreamlike succession of phenomena passing before an inactive spectator, and the result is, that we fail to find reality anywhere. Existence resolves itself into a magic-lantern march of pictures, but, as Fichte says, without anything of which they are the pictures. It is not in knowledge, then, as such, but in feeling and

action, that reality is given.   In saying this, I do not
for a moment mean to do what I said before was impossible, to divorce any of the three aspects of experience from the others: the being who feels and acts
must also know.   Knowledge may even be said, with
some truth, to be the pre-condition of the other two.
But the immediate certainty of real existence attaches
not to what is known in the knowledge, but to the
accompanying awareness of subjective activity in the
knowing act and the tinge of subjective feeling in
connection with it.   Knowledge is itself from this
point of view an activity of the subject, and, as such,
it will serve perfectly well as a basis of certainty.   It
is when the element of activity in knowledge is left
out of sight, and attention is concentrated on the
content or object of knowledge, that we enter upon
a false path, and end in the self-contradictory notion
of a knowledge which is nobody's knowledge, and a
knowledge of nothing.   But knowing is not a colour-
less or impersonal function — as it were a series of
happenings in vacuo.   Every cognitive act is suffused
with feeling, and in virtue of this suffusion it is felt
by me as mine, by you as yours.   In knowing any
object, therefore, whether a thing in the external world
or a state of his own mind, the knowing subject pos-

sesses, in this element of feeling, an immediate assurance of existence there and then.

This certainty is, in the first instance, in the moment of acting, a pure immediacy, a mere awareness. After action, and to the psychological observer, it must be mediated by knowledge and reflection—*i.e.*, the changes are presented or represented in consciousness, and with them comes the feeling of self-origination, from which remembered conjunction springs the reasoned conviction of our active causality. But the reflective assertion of the psychologist depends entirely upon the immediate feeling—the sense of living, as we might call it—which went with the action originally. I feel the activity, the experience, at the moment, and in virtue of this immediate accompanying feeling, I afterwards acknowledge it as mine.

It was not, therefore, without reason that Fichte[1] eventually returned to this primal certainty, as the sole means of escape from a limitless scepticism. Descartes's *cogito*, though intended to embrace the volitional aspect of consciousness, laid stress, designedly or not, upon the intellectual; and the result was, that the real activity of the subject was discarded by his immediate successors. The content of consciousness

---

[1] The reference is to his treatise on 'The Vocation of Man.'

became everything; the subject a mere empty vessel
or form for the content. And in Spinoza, accordingly,
we get a system or procession of *ideæ*, or modes of
thought, and a parallel procession of *ideata*, the corresponding modes of extension. The identity of intellect and will is one of Spinoza's central doctrines,
and he presents us accordingly with a system in which
real activity, or real causality, has as little place as it
has in Münsterberg's. His parallelism of modes of
thought and modes of extension is, in fact, the very
doctrine of Automatism which we have had under
consideration. And it results from the very same
considerations—from exclusive attention to the intellect, to the knowledge-content of the mind. Scan the
history of philosophy as we may, we shall find the same
cause everywhere producing the same effect, now in a
more materialistic form, now in the guise of Idealism;
but whether the automatism be materially or ideally
conceived, matters practically not one jot. With the
elimination of real causality from the course of things,
the world is emptied of real meaning; it is reduced to
a spectacular sequence of happenings, which have no
raison d'être, seeing that all is absolutely predeter-
mined from the outset. There is no life or reality
in the show which passes before us; for the nerve

of reality is furnished solely by the conviction of our own activity, our own real causality.

And with the conviction of real activity, it is to be noted, goes the belief in an end or aim which the action is to realise. It is upon *purposive*, idea-guided action that Fichte takes his stand as the ultimate certainty. The idea is present to me, he says, not as a *Nachbild* or copy, an after-picture of an independent reality, but as a *Vorbild*, a fore-picture, an ideal or purpose, which does not yet exist, but which I have myself to make real. In the ingenious caricature which Münsterberg offers us, he does not deny that this is the fundamental characteristic of voluntary action; but, in accordance with his presuppositions, he denies the reality of the nexus between the conception and its execution. It is undeniable that the one is before the other, but the first has no influence or efficacy in bringing about the second; for the whole train of happenings, he expressly tells us, is independent of our consciousness.[1] The whole train is driven, in fact, *a tergo* by a Schopenhauerian dynamo-machine in the background.

[1] Die Willenshandlung, p. 3. The bodily and the mental series, he says, are "zwei verschiedene Erscheinungsformen desselben einheitlichen, von unserem Bewusstsein unabhängigen, wirklichen Geschehnisses."

The same line of thought which leads to the elimination of real activity from the course of things, thus leads necessarily to the denial of purpose everywhere. And it is noteworthy, in this connection, that Spinoza is the most embittered opponent of any doctrine of teleology or final causes. To Spinoza, as to Münsterberg, all determination is mechanical, *a tergo* or from the past; the notion of self-determination in view of ideas, determination *a fronte* or by the future, was inconceivable to him. The human being was to Spinoza as completely determined, and determined in the same way, as a stone propelled through the air. We do not know whether there is anywhere such purely mechanical causality as Spinoza took for granted in the case of the stone; but we do know that that is not the mode in which the actions of conscious beings are determined. The causality of the future, or of the ideal, is coterminous at least with the confines of life. All action of living beings, I have argued, is originally purposive—that is to say, in a wide sense, voluntary—directed more or less clearly by the creature towards some aim. Only if this is so, is action in any sense an action of the creature itself, and not, in Münsterberg's language, "a phenomenal phase of the unitary happening" which goes on in the creature irrespective

of its feelings or desires. With the acknowledgment
of purposive action, the whole process of things acquires
a new aspect. It is no longer a motiveless procession
of appearances, or, as Professor James well puts it, the
dull rattling off of a chain forged ages ago. It is an
evolution which is real at every point. And if it has
seemed, in the course of this exposition, that knowledge
and ideas have been depreciated at the expense of the
will, they are here restored to their rightful function
as the necessary conditions of selection or choice, the
springs of all activity, and so the guiding star of all
advance. But ideas in themselves are nothing, and the
analysis of knowledge as knowledge can never give us
reality. If we were to recast Descartes's formula, in
the light of all that has come and gone in philosophy
since his day, not *Cogito ergo sum* but *Ago ergo sum*
is the form his maxim would take.

A NEW THEORY OF THE ABSOLUTE.[1]

I.

THERE can be little doubt among those qualified
to judge, that Mr Bradley's 'Appearance and
Reality' is the most important metaphysical work
which has appeared in England since the publication
of Green's 'Introduction to Hume' in 1874. It is so,
in my opinion, not because its conclusions are likely
to become assured possessions of philosophical thought,
but because of the intrepidity of the treatment and the
singularly stimulating quality which belongs to all that
Mr Bradley writes.

[1] **Appearance and Reality** : a Metaphysical Essay. By F. H. Bradley,
LL.D. (Glasgow), Fellow of Merton **College,** Oxford. London : Swan
Sonnenschein & Co. **1893.** The criticism which follows appeared as
two articles in **the** 'Contemporary Review' of November and December 1894.

I

The author modestly says in his preface that his book does not design to be permanent. It is his contribution to the sceptical discipline of the English mind, from which he is not without hopes of seeing "a rational system of first principles" emerge. And it is true that the book is hardly likely to take its place as a classical treatise in the literature of the subject. The highly abstract character of most of the discussion, suggesting at times a delight in logic for logic's sake, the unadorned dryness (for the most part) of the style, and the seemingly deliberate perversities of manner which mar it at times, forbid such a destiny. But the brilliant dialectic of which the book is full, the thoroughness and sincerity with which it sifts the most vital questions, its ruthless criticism of conventional solutions, ensure for Mr Bradley's latest volume an important influence upon the thought of his contemporaries.

Mr Bradley's courage is also to be commended in publishing a book which throughout deals avowedly and in set terms with "the Absolute." What a shock to the precisians of Agnosticism and the puritans of the empirical tradition! This particular bogy, so potent in the middle of the century, has apparently lost its terror even for the English mind. As soon as men began to reflect a little on what was meant by the term, it became evident that the ultimate object of philosophy always is, and must be, the Absolute. Mr Bradley's remarks, in his short Introduction, on the unavoidableness of metaphysical inquiry, the necessity of a new metaphysic for each fresh generation, and the utility of even an imperfect knowledge of the Absolute, may be commended to the candid reader who is still unconvinced, or perhaps a confirmed sceptic, on those points.

The chapters of destructive criticism, which form the first part of the book, are largely in Hegel's manner, and the influence of Hegel is unquestionably predominant throughout. But in spite of this general indebtedness, the book is distinguished by an independence of style and treatment not usual with followers of this master, or indeed of any master. But Mr Bradley has always insisted on calling his soul his own. Whatever else this volume may be, and whatever criticisms we may have to make upon it, it is certainly no easy reproduction of another man's thoughts: in the sweat of his own brow its author has conceived and executed it.

This independence of treatment will prove of good omen, it may be hoped, for the future of philosophical discussion among those who may be regarded, in a general way, as carrying on the traditions of Green and representing the influence of Hegel, or at least of German Idealism, in British philosophy. In this connection, Mr Bradley's book may be said, perhaps, to mark the close of the period whose beginning was signalised, twenty-three years ago, by the publication of Green's work already mentioned. When we think of the Hamilton - Mill controversy in the sixties, it is obvious that serious study of the Critical Philosophy and German Idealism had yet to begin. Only the outworks of the Kantian scheme had been mastered even by the accredited leaders of British thought, while Hegel, or at least his strangely refracted image, was simply the philosophical "bogy-man," useful to frighten back the unwary wanderer into the fold of Empiricism or the Philosophy of the Conditioned. Yet Hegel was probably the richest mind that had been devoted to philosophy since Aristotle, and, whatever judgment may be passed on his system as a logical whole, had done more than any other man to mould the thought of the century in all the humanistic sciences.

The publication of Dr Hutchison Stirling's ' Secret of Hegel,' in 1865, first removed the reproach of ignorance and indifference, or worse, from British philosophy. It was published in the same year as Mill's 'Examination of Hamilton,' and in the noisy, multitudinous echoes of that controversy, the accents of the new voice were partly drowned. But they penetrated, like tidings of a land that is very far off, to ears fit to receive them. While Mr Spencer's philosophy gradually established itself as the persuasion of the average man, the majority of serious thinkers in England were devoting themselves to the study of Kant and Hegel; and Green's 'Introduction' was the first noteworthy symptom of this new direction of thought at the universities. The movement thus inaugurated has been growing in volume since then, and, as was to be expected, it has somewhat changed its character; and Mr Bradley's book may perhaps be found in this respect to mark the end of the period of absorption or assimilation. During these *Lehrjahre*, English writers have repeated too anxiously, and with too minute exactitude, the formulæ of a foreign master, treating them rather as oracles of truth than as utterances of finite wisdom, and showing too great a reluctance to submit them to legitimate criticism. But of late a calmer and more critical tone has been noticeable, and a more catholic spirit has shown itself.

Other names have claimed attention, such as Lotze on the one hand, and Schopenhauer on the other (to mention only these two). As Mr Bradley puts it in his preface, "the present generation is learning that to gain education a man must study in more than one school." And the result of this wider range can hardly be other than to diminish the somewhat partisan zeal of the so-called neo-Hegelian party for the *ipsissima verba* of Hegel's theory, and to set them upon a more independent handling of the subject itself, in accordance with the genius of their own time and nation. Then the *Lehrjahre* and the *Wanderjahre* will be ended and the *Meisterjahre* will begin. For disciples, as Bacon puts it in a well-known passage, do owe unto masters only a temporary belief and a suspension of their judgment till they be fully instructed, and not an absolute resignation or perpetual captivity Though Germany once possessed the hegemony of Europe in matters philosophical, that time is past, and the fact that it once existed constitutes no reason why we should remain in perpetual tutelage to German masters. "I have a high opinion," says Mr Bradley in his preface, "of the metaphysical powers of the English mind;" and his book is conceived throughout in the spirit of intellectual freedom.

The author describes his work in the preface as "a critical discussion of first principles." "The chief need of English philosophy," he tells us, "is a sceptical study of first principles, and I do not know of any work which seems to meet this need sufficiently." The object of his own work is, therefore, "to stimulate inquiry and doubt"—doubt or scepticism being understood to mean not doubt or disbelief in any particular tenets, but "an attempt to become aware of and to doubt all preconceptions." This is in Mr Bradley's mind—and not without good reason—the first and all-important condition of sound work in metaphysics. The short Introduction puts unanswerably the necessity and the utility of metaphysics. As it is impossible to abstain from thought about the universe, "the question is merely as to the way in which this should be done. . . . Metaphysics takes its stand on this side of human nature, this desire to think about and comprehend reality. And it merely asserts that, if the attempt is to be made, it should be done as thoroughly as our nature permits." On the second count, he maintains, as we have seen, that even a "miserably incomplete" knowledge of the Absolute must have its usefulness. But in a passage of characteristic frankness and force he contends that, even if metaphysics has no positive

results, it would still be highly desirable that it
should continue to be studied:—

There is, so far as I can see, no other way of protecting
ourselves against dogmatic superstition.   Our orthodox
theology on the one hand, and our commonplace materialism on the other (it is natural to take these as prominent
instances) vanish like ghosts before the daylight of free
sceptical inquiry.   I do not mean, of course, to condemn
wholly either of these beliefs; but I am sure that either,
when taken seriously, is the mutilation of our nature.
Neither, as experience has amply shown, can now survive
in the mind which has thought sincerely on first principles.
.   .   .   That is one reason why I think that metaphysics,
even if it end in total scepticism, should be studied by a
certain number of persons.

But, while thus insisting on the indispensable function of metaphysical inquiry, Mr Bradley is not the
man to magnify his office as metaphysician unduly.
And in the Meredithian extracts from his note-book
which conclude the preface, he characteristically turns
the shafts of his irony against his own occupation.
"Metaphysics," it is there written, "is the finding of
bad reasons for what we believe upon instinct, but to
find these reasons is no less an instinct." From the
other glimpses vouchsafed into this note-book, its
aphoristic treasures would appear to be of a highly
various and piquant description.   They cannot but

awaken an unchastened curiosity in the heart of many students, which it is to be hoped the owner of the note-book may take measures to satisfy.

Mr Bradley starts with a threefold general definition of metaphysics. "We may agree, perhaps, to under-stand by metaphysics an attempt to know reality as against mere appearance, or the study of first prin-ciples or ultimate truths, or again the effort to com-prehend the universe, not simply piecemeal or by fragments, but somehow as a whole." These three definitions are plainly intended to be taken as equi-valent, but, though the third is probably the most satisfactory of the three, it is the first which gives the title to Mr Bradley's volume, and it is the con-trast between appearance — or, as he calls it here, "mere appearance" — and reality that explains the two parts into which it falls. The first book, entitled "Appearance," is a sceptical or destructive criticism of the phenomenal world as inherently self-contradictory and incomprehensible, and therefore, in Mr Bradley's use of the word, unreal. The second book, entitled "Reality," though also abounding in negative criticism of obnoxious "preconceptions," is the constructive complement of Book I., intended to describe the nature of the Absolute, in which the contradictions of pheno-

mena must be somehow reconciled or overcome. It
is important at the outset, for the understanding of
Mr Bradley's argument, especially in its negative or
sceptical aspect, to note the equivalence, or at least
interchangeableness, of these different formulations of
the metaphysician's task, even though his procedure
and conclusions should turn out to be unduly dominated
by the first. Reality is used by Mr Bradley throughout in the sense of ultimate reality, so that reality and
the absolute are convertible terms, and he means by
both "the universe" comprehended "somehow as a
whole." Appearance, on the other hand, is applied to
the whole of the phenomenal world. Appearances,
of course, *exist*, as he repeatedly tells us, but they are
not real, in the sense of being independent, self-contained and self-explanatory. We fall into hopeless
contradictions if we attempt to take them so. Every
finite or phenomenal fact betrays its character of
"mere appearance" by the "ragged edges" which
stamp it as a part torn out of its context. The self-
contradiction of the part taken as the whole, the
phenomenal taken as the real, is most obvious in the
infinite progress upon which it launches us—a species
of treadmill exercise, best exemplified in the case of
such notions as time, space, and causation.

The contradictions of the finite are, accordingly, the theme of Mr Bradley's First Book, in which he sets out to criticise the chief "ideas by which we try to understand the universe." Taking up, first, the popular scientific proposal to find the reality of the world in the primary qualities, he has little difficulty in showing that the line of thought which undermines the reality of the secondary qualities can be used with equal effect against the primary. The primary qualities cannot be conceived or presented without the secondary; and, further, we cannot think of extension without thinking at the same time of a "what" that is extended. Extension is, therefore, simply the abstraction of one element from the rest, from which it is in reality inseparable — an abstraction scientifically convenient, but metaphysically indefensible, when it puts itself forward as an ultimate account of things.

The distinction of "substantive and adjective"— the grouping of the world's contents into things and qualities—is next taken up (chap. ii.) and declared to be "a clear makeshift." If we lay stress on the unity of the thing, then the plurality of its attributes is in no way explained; they lie side by side in mere distinctness one from another, as so many independent coexistences.

The whole device is a clear makeshift. It consists in saying to the outside world, " I am the owner of these my adjectives," and to the properties, " I am but a relation, which leaves you your liberty." And to itself and for itself it is the futile pretence to have both characters at once. . . . The thing with its adjectives is a device for enjoying at once both variety and concord. But the distinctions, once made, fall apart from the thing, and away from one another, and our attempt to understand their relations brought us round merely to an unity, which confesses itself a pretence, or else falls back upon the old undivided substance which admits of no distinctions (p. 23).

The next chapter (chap. iii.) analyses the ideas of quality and relation. Qualities depend upon the relation of things to one another; unrelated reals would be qualityless. But, on the other hand, "nothings cannot be related;" "relations must depend upon terms, just as much as terms upon relations." Consequently, all thinking that moves by the machinery of terms and relations is pronounced to be "a makeshift, a device, a mere practical compromise, most necessary, but in the end most indefensible." For there is the same attempt to bring diversity into the unity of the thing, an attempt which proves impossible except by dividing the thing altogether into an endless process of relations. Hence, "our experience when relationed is not true;" and

any one who has grasped the principle of this chapter, **we** are told, "will have condemned, almost without a hearing, **the great** mass of phenomena." Mr Bradley proceeds, however (in the next five chapters), to apply his principle more **in** detail to the **cases of** " space and **time," " motion and** change," "causation " and "activity." **In a time-honoured** and somewhat **well-worn argument,** the aspects of discreteness and continuity in **space are** sceptically opposed to **one** another, and **the** conclusion reached that "space vanishes internally **into** relations between units **which** never can exist." Precisely the same argument holds of time; hence, **both are** not real, but **"contradictory** appearances." The problem of change

points back to the dilemma of the one and the many, the **differences and the** identity, the adjectives and the thing, **the qualities and the relations.** How anything can possibly be anything else was a question which defied our efforts. Change is little beyond **an instance** of this dilemma in principle. . . . **It** asserts two **of** one, and so falls at once under the condemnation of our previous chapters. . . . **Change,** upon any hypothesis, is impossible. **It can** be no **more** than appearance (pp. 45-47).

So with causation. **If you** resolve cause into identity, you eliminate the very fact to be explained — the difference of the effect from its cause. For surely the very problem of causation " consists in the differences and in their sequence in time." In fact,

it is the old puzzle how to justify the attributing to a subject something other than itself, and which the subject is not. If " followed by B " is not the nature of A, then justify your predication. If it is essential to A, then justify, first, your taking A without it; and in the next place show how, with such an incongruous nature, A can succeed in being more than unreal appearance " (p. 57).

Activity is condemned because " nothing can be active without an occasion, and what is active, being made thus by the occasion, is so far passive." Hence, " it is certain that activity implies finitude, and otherwise possesses no meaning." It cannot, therefore, be an ultimate principle of explanation. Chap. viii. deals with " things," but the preceding argument has " undermined and ruined " any meaning we can attach to the term. " The thing is a thing only if its existence goes beyond the now and extends into the past;" but " it does not appear how this relation of sameness can be real." " The identity of a thing lies in the view you take of it." " We seem driven to the conclusion that things are but appearances."

So far, therefore, " our facts have turned out to be illusory," but we have been dealing up to this point with " the inanimate," and in order to complete his argument Mr Bradley goes on in the next two chapters (chaps. ix. and x.) to criticise the claims of the Self to reality. In the first he passes in review different meanings of the self, and in the second he concludes that the self simply presents "the old puzzle as to the connection of diversity with unity." It will be necessary to return upon various points in these important chapters, but we must first have Mr Bradley's main line of thought before us and the conclusion at which he arrives. It is sufficient, therefore, for the present, to note his verdict on the self, and the ground on which the verdict is explicitly based. "The consciousness of personal identity," he curiously says, "may be supposed to have some bearing on the reality of the self." Most people are probably benighted enough to think it has.

But to my mind [proceeds Mr Bradley] it appears to be almost irrelevant. Of course the self, within limits and up to a certain point, is the same. . . . As long as there remains in the self a certain basis of content, ideally the same, so long may the self recall anything once associated with that basis. . . . This, of course, shows that self-sameness exists as a fact, and that hence *somehow* an identical self is real. But, then, the question is *how?* The question is whether we can state the existence and the continuity of a real self in a way which is intelligible, and which is not ruined by the difficulties of previous discussions. Because, otherwise, we may have found an interesting fact, but most assuredly we have not found a tenable view about reality. . . . The end of metaphysics is to understand the universe, to find a way of thinking about facts in general which is free from contradiction. . . . It is this, to repeat it once more, on which everything turns. The diversity and the unity must be brought to the light, and the principle must be seen to comprehend these. But the self is so far from supplying such a principle, that it seems, when not hiding itself in obscurity, a mere bundle of discrepancies. Our search has conducted us again, not to reality, but mere appearance (pp. 113, 120).

The two short chapters on "Phenomenalism" and "Things in Themselves," which conclude the First Book, add nothing to this argument. They are rather of the nature of appendices, which deal effectively with these two phases of philosophic theory, as attempts either to evade the philosophical problem altogether, or to solve it by doubling it. As I am in complete agreement with Mr Bradley's arguments in these pages, there is the less need to dwell upon them here. So I pass at once to the opening chapters of the Second Book, dealing with "The General Nature of Reality," and containing the counter-stroke to the preceding negative polemic.

The first position taken up is at once important, for

it alone enables a start to be made. Phenomena have been condemned as self-contradictory, but what is thus rejected as appearance admittedly still exists. "It cannot bodily be shelved and merely got rid of, and, therefore, since it must fall somewhere, it must belong to reality." Reality, therefore, "must own," and somehow include, appearance; it cannot be less than appearance. But whereas appearances, taken as real, proved self-contradictory, the absolute or ultimate reality must be "such that it does not contradict itself. This is our first criterion—a criterion which has been implicit in all the preceding negative criticism." Accordingly, we may say, concludes Mr Bradley, that

everything which appears is somehow real in such a way as to be self-consistent. . . . Appearance must belong to reality, and it must, therefore, be concordant and other than it seems. The bewildering mass of phenomenal diversity must hence somehow be at unity and self-consistent; for it cannot be elsewhere than in reality, and reality excludes discord. Or again, we may put it so; the real is individual. It is one in the sense that its positive character embraces all deficiencies in an inclusive harmony (p. 140).

In short, "reality must be a single whole"—"a single system." In his second chapter Mr Bradley supplements this "formal and abstract" definition of the Absolute by identifying existence with "experience," laying down the position, almost in Berkeley's language, that existence has no meaning apart from sentient experience. "There is no being or fact outside of that which is commonly called psychical existence." Any supposed fact, other than this, "is a vicious abstraction whose existence is meaningless nonsense, and is not possible." If we combine this with the former position, "our conclusion, so far, will be this, that the Absolute is one system, and that its contents are nothing but sentient experience. It will, hence, be a single and all-inclusive experience, which embraces every partial diversity in concord." Finally, Mr Bradley proceeds to ask whether we really have a positive idea of an Absolute, thus defined as "one comprehensive sentience;" and he answers that, while we cannot fully realise its existence, its main features are drawn from our own experience, and we have also a suggestion there of the unity of a whole embracing distinctions within itself. This we have in "mere feeling or immediate presentation," where we experience as an undifferentiated whole, what we afterwards proceed, in the exercise of relational thought, to analyse into the known world of self and not-self, with all its manifold objects and distinctions. Combining this primitive experience of felt unity with the later experience of known diversity, **we** can recognise the **latter** as a transitional stage, and **reach** the idea of a higher experience **in** which thought shall, as **it** were, **return** to the immediacy of feeling. " We **can** form the general idea of an absolute intuition in which phenomenal distinctions **are merged**; a whole become immediate at a higher stage without losing any richness." This view **of the** Absolute is developed and **enforced in the immediately** following chapter on "Thought **and Reality**" (chap. xv.) which, in various aspects, is one of the most important in the book. As such, it will claim our attention in the **sequel; but it** is enough, in the meantime, to note a little more fully the nature of the results arrived **at. The position** reached **is** simply this, that "the relational form **is a** compromise on which thought stands and which it develops. **It is an attempt to unite** differences **which** have broken **out of** the felt totality" **(p.** 180). It is essentially an attempt **to pass** beyond itself and to recapture this immediate unity. But, both **in** theory **and in** practice, the attempt proves unsuccessful on **the** basis of thought **or** relation; it resolves **itself** into **the** infinite progress. Thought's own ideal, therefore, **can be** reached only by passing beyond thought. **For us "this** completion of thought beyond thought"

necessarily "remains for ever an other." Still " thought
can form the idea of an apprehension, something like
feeling in directness, which contains all the character
sought by its relational efforts "—"a total experience
where will and thought and feeling may all once more
be one," and where consequently the distinction between
thought and its object—between subject and predicate
—is likewise transcended.[1]

We have now before us one complete phase of Mr
Bradley's position and argumentation, and it is time,
therefore, to investigate critically the legitimacy of the
method and the value of the conclusion. Mr Bradley
started, as we saw, with two somewhat different definitions of the Absolute ; and, in like manner, his criticism
throughout the First Book seems to rest upon two somewhat different principles. The one condemns phenomena because they are fragmentary ; no object of
experience is by itself a *res completa*, an independent
and self-contained individual, strong in solid singleness,
self-explaining, harmonious and all-inclusive. Whatever fact we take proves to be infected by external
relations, and so carries us beyond itself, and ultimately
brings in the whole context of the universe. Thus

[1] See pp. 160, 172, 179, 181.

activity transforms **itself into** passivity, because **we
cannot** think of activity as (so to speak) **a mere** bolt
from the blue—an unconditioned fiat out of a blank
eternity. The beginning of the activity **of** anything
depends, **for our** thinking, upon a stimulus from beyond
the nature of the thing **itself; and the** thing, therefore,
is quite as much **passive as active. This argument may
be applied all round.** Thought cannot rest in any finite
individual, but **is carried** beyond **it in an** infinite pro-
gress. So with any portion of space **or** time in which
we arbitrarily and momentarily rest; **so** with things, so
last of all with the finite self. For I do not imagine
that those who insist most strongly on the reality **of the**
self, and hold that "it provides us with **a** type by the
aid **of which we** may **go on to comprehend** the world,"
are at **all inclined to assert its** reality in Mr Bradley's
sense of all-inclusive self-sufficience. Obviously, the self
of any individual, **in the** determinations of its character
and the occasions **of** its activity, carries us beyond the
self, just as in the case of things which are not selves.
The self cannot be torn from its environment except by
a process of violent abstraction; and the environment,
if we are to be exact, must be ultimately extended so
as to include all time and all existence. To my mind,
it requires no argument to establish the position that

there can be only one individual as a *res completa*, and consequently, in Mr Bradley's sense, only one reality, namely, the Absolute or the universe as a whole. To fail to realise this is to fail to rise to the light of reason at all ; it is, in Spinoza's phrase, to remain at the stage of " imagination," with its blind substantiation of the individuals of sense just as we find them, or seem to find them.

In this whole line of argument, therefore—including his admirable exposure of the fallacy of a plurality of independent reals—Mr Bradley is certain to meet with hearty acquiescence in most quarters that are worth considering. But this line of argument does not seem sufficient of itself to justify the sweeping condemnation of phenomena as " mere appearance," " illusion," " self-contradictory appearance," " irrational appearance," " essentially made of inconsistencies," and the other terms of excommunication in which Mr Bradley indulges. Because a thing is not the Absolute, and never pretended to be, it seems a little hard to " ruin " its character by a string of bad names like this. And, as a matter of fact, the " ruin " in which Mr Bradley involves the phenomenal is more properly the consequence of a second line of argument, which is on the whole more prominent throughout the First Book. This argu-

ment is neither more nor less than the complete discrepancy of the One and the Many—the impossibility
of realising at all in thought any kind of identity in
diversity. The passages quoted in the earlier part of
this essay illustrate sufficiently the constant recurrence of this idea. At the very outset, in dealing with
substantive and adjective, it is referred to as "the
old dilemma." If you predicate what is different, you
ascribe to the subject what it is *not ;* and if you predicate what is *not* different, you say nothing at all (p. 20).
The dilemma is, in truth, as old as the early Greek
nominalists and sceptics who denied on these grounds
the possibility of predication altogether, except in the
form of an identical proposition. To say that "Socrates
is good," would be to say the thing that is not; for
"Socrates" and "good" are not the same, but different.
"Socrates" is one idea, and "good" is another. "Socrates
is Socrates," and "good is good;" but that the one should
be the other, is quite unintelligible. We are limited,
therefore, to the one kind of proposition which we
never make, A = A. Now, strange as it may seem, Mr
Bradley's First Book is, in essence, neither more nor less
than a restatement and re-enforcement of this sceptical
thesis. He adopts this logic of abstract identity
apparently without reserve, and because it brings him

to a dead-lock, he pronounces the actual world to be
" unintelligible," " inconsistent," " self - contradictory,"
" irrational," " untrue," " illusory."   His multitudinous
repetitions seem designed to leave us in no doubt that
it is everywhere the same touchstone which he applies.
Thus, the conclusion of the third chapter, on " Relation
and Quality," is, as we have seen, that a relational way
of thought is "a mere practical compromise, most
necessary, but in the end most indefensible."

We have to take reality [he continues] as Many, and to
take it as One, and to avoid contradiction. . . . But
when *these inconsistencies* are forced together, as in metaphysics they must be, the result is an open and staring
discrepancy. . . . Our intellect, then, has been condemned to confusion and bankruptcy, and the reality has
been left outside uncomprehended (pp. 33, 34).

In the next chapter, " Space . . . is a peculiar form
of the problem which we discussed in the last chapter,
and is a special attempt to combine the irreconcilable "
(p. 36).   In the fifth chapter (in the passage already
quoted) the problem of change

points back to the dilemma of the One and the Many, the
differences and the identity, the adjectives and the thing,
the qualities and the relations. *How anything can possibly
be anything else* was a question which defied our efforts.
Change is little beyond an instance of this dilemma in

principle. . . . Change, it is obvious, must be a change of something, and it is obvious, further, that it contains diversity. Hence *it asserts two of one*, and so falls at once under the condemnation of our previous chapters (p. 45).

So in the following chapter, on " Causation ":—

If the sequence of the effect is different from the cause, how is the ascription of the difference to be rationally defended? If, on the other hand, it is not different, then causation does not exist, and its assertion is a farce (p. 55). . . . *We assert something of something else.* . . . It is the old puzzle, how to justify the attributing to a subject something other than itself, and which the subject is not (p. 57).

Having found things "go to pieces" when confronted with this test, he finds the same result on applying it to the self.

It is the old puzzle as to the connection of diversity with unity. As the diversity becomes more complex and the unity grows more concrete, we have, so far, found that our difficulties steadily increase, and the expectation of a sudden change and a happy solution, when we arrive at the self, seems hence little warranted. . . You may say that we are each assured of our personal identity in a way in which we are not assured of the sameness of things. But this is unfortunately quite irrelevant to the question. That selves exist, and are identical in some sense, is indubitable. But the doubt is whether their sameness, as we apprehend it, is really intelligible. . . . Does it give an experience by the help of which we can really *understand* the way in which diversity is harmonised [1] (pp. 103, 104).

The self, as feeling, thrusts upon us, " in a still more apparent form, the discrepancy that lies between identity and diversity, immediate oneness and relation" (p. 107). If, again, self-consciousness is proposed as "a special way of intuition or perception," we are forced to ask (supposing such a "self-apprehension of the self as one and many" to exist) how it can "satisfy the claims of understanding." "For the contents of the intuition (this many in one), if you try to reconstruct them relationally, fall asunder forthwith. . . . I am, in short, compelled to this conclusion, even if your intuition is a fact, it is not an *understanding* of the self or of the world. It is a mere experience" (p. 108). In whatever aspect the self is taken, therefore, it does not teach us "how to understand diversity or unity" (p. 112). What we want is "a view . . . combining differences in one so as to turn the edge of criticism" (p. 114), and this we have not met with. The self, as will or volition, leaves us involved in all "the old troubles as to

---

[1] The italics in the passage last quoted are Mr Bradley's own, and I desire specially to call attention to the emphasis, as it corroborates my contention and contains the key to Mr Bradley's position.

diversity in union with sameness" (p. 115). In commenting on the theory of Monads, towards the close of his discussion, he repeats his old question :—

Will it in the least show us *how*[1] the diversity can exist in harmony with the oneness, (p. 118). . . . We have found so far [he says] that diversity and unity cannot be reconciled. Both in the existence of the whole self in relation with its contents, and in the various special forms which that existence takes, we have encountered *everywhere the same trouble*. We have had features which *must* come together, and yet were willing to do so in no way that we could find. In the self there is a variety, and in the self there is an unity; but in attempting to understand how, we fall into inconsistencies which, therefore, cannot be truth (p. 118).

The self, he finally concludes, does not yield us "any defensible thought, *any intellectual principle, by which it is possible to understand how diversity can be comprehended in unity*. It is this, to repeat it once more, on which everything turns. The diversity and the unity must be brought to the light, and the principle must be seen to comprehend these" (pp. 119, 120). The short chapter on "Phenomenalism" adds two further references to "the metaphysical problem of the Many in One" (pp. 124, 125); and, in the last chapter, things-in-themselves are found to "offer pre-

[1] The italics are again Mr Bradley's own.

cisely the old jungle in which no way could be found"
(p. 130).

I have multiplied these references, at the risk of
wearying the reader, in order to convince him, if he
needs convincing, of the uniform and persistent nature
of Mr Bradley's demand. It seems to me, moreover,
that Mr Bradley's position here conditions the whole
nature of the results he arrives at later. For the logic
of abstract identity which he brings into the field
against phenomena is fatal in the end to his Absolute
also, reducing it, in spite of Mr Bradley's disclaimer—
in spite of his sincere endeavour to avoid such a consummation—to the undifferentiated unity of Spinoza's
Substance. According to this logic, each qualityless
point remains identical with itself $(A = A)$, and so
does each unreferred quality, flying loose in the heaven
of abstraction (red is red, a is a, and b is b). But the
living synthesis of fact—the qualified thing, A that is
a, b, c, d, any number of differences, in unity—this, if
not actually denied as in some sense existing, is yet
declared to be unintelligible, hopelessly contradictory.
But surely such an argument marks the very acme of
logical perversity. Such an argument, in truth, imports
into predication a meaning or intention of which predication never dreams. When we say "man is mortal,"

or "the beech has a smooth stem," we do not mean that the concept "man" is identical with the concept "mortal," or that the two concepts "beech" and "smooth - stemmed" are actually one and the same concept. What we mean is that the reality, which we have already qualified as "man" or "beech," is further qualified as "mortal" or "smooth-stemmed." All predication, in short, is about facts, not about concepts — except in the special cases where we happen to be defining a word. Certainly every concept or meaning remains itself, and only itself, to all eternity. That at least is the convention on which logic stands; our terms must bear the same meaning throughout, otherwise all reasoning would be impossible. The law of identity or of non-contradiction means no more than this obviously indispensable con-vention—a convention which, if we are so minded, we may truthfully describe as a fundamental and necessary law of thought, so long as we see clearly its innocent and unobtrusive meaning. The law of identity says that, if we predicate mortality of man, we cannot also predicate non-mortality; it says that, if it is the nature of the beech to be smooth - stemmed, it cannot also be its nature to be rough-stemmed. But, as to the nature of predication, or as to the possibility or impossibility of a thing existing as the unity of diverse qualities, it gives no verdict one way or another. These are questions of fact or of metaphysics which lie beyond its scope. To proceed, therefore, on the strength of the law of identity, to condemn the idea of a thing possessing qualities, or, in general, the idea of unity in diversity, as a contradiction in terms, is logically a complete μετάβασις εἰς ἄλλο γένος.

Now Mr Bradley tells us that "a thing without qualities is clearly unreal" (p. 130), and in his chapter on "Phenomenalism" he proves that the opposite attempt, to rest in qualities without a thing, is equally untrue to reality. But his own doctrine is that the attempt to think a thing *with* qualities, or, in general, the attempt to think a unity in diversity, ends in hopeless contradiction. It looks, therefore, as if thought were brought face to face with an absolute *impasse*. The whole force of his argument appears, however, to rest on this illegitimate extension to reality or experience of a law which holds true only of concepts, as concepts, in the narrow sense just explained. Reality, it may be said boldly, is essentially a many-in-one, and this holds true of any part of reality—*i.e.*, of any existent fact. This, it seems to me, was the insight that lent force and cogency to Hegel's life-long polemic against the abstract understanding and its vaunted law of non-contradiction. Against its abstract identity he held up the concrete facts of experience: there is nothing which is a mere one, an eternal self-sameness. Identity only exists through difference, unity through multiplicity. Such is the constant thesis of the Hegelian philosophy, of which Mr Bradley is one of the profoundest students; and it was, I confess, a surprise to me to find the ancient weapon of the sceptical schools so carefully furbished up and so confidently brandished. All the more so, because Mr Bradley himself, *aliud agendo*—with the atomic sensationalism of the English tradition in view —gives a most impressive statement of the true position, and declares in his own emphatic way that "every movement of our intellect rests wholly upon it," and that the contrary opinion is founded upon "one-sided and uncritical metaphysics," or "in short had no basis but confusion and traditional prejudice" (pp. 349-351). "There will be neither change nor endurance, and still less motion through space of an identical body; there will neither be selves nor things, nor, *in brief, any intelligible fact,* unless on the assumption that sameness in diversity is real. Apart from this main principle of construction, we should be confined to the feeling of a single moment." *Now these "intelligible facts" are the very facts paraded as unintelligible in Book I.*

Hegel no doubt gave a dangerous opening to misconception, when he spoke of the dialectic as exhibiting itself in the conceptions of the "Logic." It is only by a sustained use of metaphor that the appearance of success is obtained; for conceptions, as such, are precisely what do not "pass over" into their opposites. The conception "One" never becomes the conception "Many." What is true is, that every fact can be shown to combine in itself these two aspects. It is in this way that Hegel uses the nature of reality to explode, and (by exploding) to unite, the fixed opposites of conceptual thought. These opposites, it must be remembered, are, and remain, opposites in the abstract world of logic; viewed, that is to say, simply as meanings, the one remains just the opposite of the other. But this opposition of the two as meanings, as concepts, tells us nothing about the possibility or impossibility of a fact to which, in different aspects, both shall be applicable. On that the nature of reality itself must decide: we must appeal to experience.

In making this appeal, we have no need to go further than the fact of our own existence, which is indeed the key of the whole position. The self is very severely handled by Mr Bradley, though **he does admit at the** close that it is "no doubt the highest form of experience which we **have**" **(p. 119).** His argument **consists** largely in enumerating, and setting **against** one another, different senses **in** which the **term "self" has been,** or is currently, **used.** Some of these may **be dismissed** as irrelevant—that is to **say,** we may surrender them at once to Mr **Bradley's criticism as of no particular** interest. The remainder **of** his argument seems to me **to rest** partly **on** the **first line of** thought—viz., that **no** self **of** which **we** have experience **is an absolute,** perfect, or self-sufficient unity, which, **again, may be** fully granted — and partly on the practical difficulty of precisely defining the amount of diversity **which** shall **be included** within the **unity of the** individual self. **Here also** many **a point might be** surrendered to meet **Mr** Bradley's criticism. He reminds us, for example, that **"in the** lifetime **of a** man there are irreparable changes. **Is he literally** *not* the same man if loss, or death, **or love, or** banishment has turned the current of his life ?" **(p. 79.)** **This is** a question of degree. The wrench *may* be so great as actually, in the common phrase, to unhinge the mind; and **in** that case, we admittedly cease to regard the **man as the** same. **His** personality is altogether suspended; he

is insane. So with "the strange selves of hypnotism,"
to which Mr Bradley several times refers. Such abnormalities involve practical difficulties, just like the
"monsters" to which Locke so frequently recurs, or
the cases where it may be difficult to decide whether
an object belongs to the animal or the vegetable
kingdom. But they do not touch the question of
principle with which we are here concerned. It is
not necessary that a self should be an all-inclusive
whole; nor is it necessary that we should be able, in
every case, to say what is a self and what is not a
self. It is enough if there is such a thing as self-
consciousness or personal identity at all. For that
self - consciousness is the living experience of unity
in diversity.

Now Mr Bradley admits that "of course the self,
within limits and up to a certain point, is the same,"
though, as we saw, he strangely treats this consciousness of personal identity as "almost irrelevant." The
key to this utterance is found in the following page,
where he adds, "This, of course, shows that self-
sameness exists as a fact, and that hence somehow
an identical self must be real. But then the question is how?" (p. 113.) To this I see no answer
save Lotze's retort in similar circumstances, that

such a question is as unreasonable, and as perfectly impossible to satisfy, as the demand to know how being is made. **How there** comes to be existence at all, and **how** existence **or** experience **in its** basal characteristics comes to **be what it is** — these **are** questions **which, so far as one can see,** omniscience itself would not enable **us to answer.** The fundamental nature **of experience may enable us** to explain derivatively **any** special feature of experience; **but** that fundamental nature **itself must** be **learned** from experience and simply accepted. **Now** I maintain that unity in multiplicity, identity in diversity, **is just** the ultimate nature of universal **experience.** Such **a** unity or identity is lived or experienced **in** every **instance of** self-conscious existence; **and it** cannot **be** other than a misleading use of language to speak **of our most** intimate experience, the ultimate bed-rock **of** fact, **as** unintelligible or contradictory. The whole procedure **of** thought belies such a supposition; for, instead **of** stumbling over this unity and identity **as** unintelligible, we proceed to make it the measure or standard of the intelligibility of everything **else.** The thing and its qualities is a mere analogue **of** the self as a many in one; all our terms **of** explanation, all the categories of thought, are drawn in like manner from the life of the self. They either reproduce it with more or less fulness, or, if they do not do this, then they express one or other of its aspects. But it is our own fault if we choose to substantiate these aspects, stated thus for the moment in logical or ideal separation ; for they are never given or experienced separately. On the contrary, their concrete unity is the one fact behind which we cannot go. Thought, when it occupies itself in dissecting its own nature, is led into many a bog by the will-o'-the wisp of a false subtlety—by none more so than by this phantasm of abstract identity. But thought, which is directed on its object, and bent only on learning more and more of the nature of things, never seeks thus to overleap itself, and consequently finds none of the unintelligibility of which Mr Bradley complains. In truth, as Berkeley happily puts it, philosophers are often indebted to their own pre-conceptions "for being ignorant of what everybody else knows perfectly well."

And seriously, according to the well-worn brocard, if water chokes us what shall we drink ? If our own existence is unintelligible to us, where are we likely to find intelligibility ? If the one and the many are as absolutely incompatible as they have been represented, how are they to be brought together at all? In other words, if the criticism in the First Book is really valid, it would seem to be equally fatal to the construction of the Absolute attempted in the Second. For the Absolute, we have seen, must "own" or include appearances, and it must do so in such a way as to exclude contradiction. It is to be "a single and all-inclusive experience, which embraces every partial diversity in concord" (p. 147). Doubtless this is our ideal of what an Absolute should be; but surely (to quote Mr Bradley's own words) we have here "at once upon our hands the One and the Many." This Absolute "offers precisely the old jungle in which no way could be found"; and it is irrational to suppose that a sheer contradiction will prove more amenable, when multiplied to infinity, and housed in the Absolute. An unkind critic might say, indeed, with some show of reason, that Mr Bradley has the air of swallowing at a gulp, in Book II., what he had choked over in the successive chapters of Book I. For, if, as was insisted in the case of the self, "the question is how," the Second Book is full of the most ample acknowledgments that the "how" remains as insoluble as ever. "Certainly in the end," we are told, "to know *how* the One and the Many are united is beyond our powers. But in the Absolute, somehow, we are convinced the problem is solved" (p. 281). But this is the language of pious conviction rather than of scientific demonstration ; and though the attentive reader discerns plainly the author's resolve that the Absolute has *got* to include all differences and solve all contradictions, he will be apt to feel that the contradictions forced upon his notice throughout the book have been handed back to him, to digest as best he may.

In the end, this impression would not, I think, be substantially incorrect ; and yet it would certainly not be entirely just to Mr Bradley, for he certainly does attempt in the Second Book to give in outline a theory of the "how." What he would undoubtedly have us regard as his real contribution towards a solution of the difficulty, is to be found in the chapter on "Thought and Reality." He still maintains that the "contradiction" is insoluble on the level of relational thought ; but founding in this chapter on the analogy of feeling, as containing the immediate experience of a whole, he throws out the idea of a supra-relational existence of the Absolute, which shall, so to speak, fuse once more, in an immediate unity, the differences which the process of knowledge has shown were implicit in the primitive undifferentiated unity of feeling. On examination, however, it will be found, I think, that, **in the** end, this theory meets the difficulty by abolishing the differences. Instead, therefore, of being a real solution, it is at bottom a reaffirmation of Mr Bradley's fundamental preconception as to the incompatibility of the **One and the Many.** Notwithstanding **this,** the presentation **of the** theory **is full of** speculative interest.

It is not a new thing in philosophy to attempt to name, and even to conceive, the divine life in this way, as a knowledge that is more than relational, that does not proceed from part to part, but sees the whole in every part, or rather sees all differences in unity, by a species of immediate apprehension or intuition. So much may be said to be a commonplace of philosophical theology. And **in** the Kantian and post-Kantian philosophy of Germany, as is well **known,** the doctrine of a perceptive understanding or an intellectual intuition played **an** important part. But what lends importance to this fresh attempt to put a meaning into the phrase is the independence **of** the treatment—the way in which the idea is seen to grow organically out of the author's whole scheme **of** thought — and also the deliberate endeavour which **is** made really "to form the idea" of such an apprehension, even though only "in vague generality." But, ungracious return as it may seem for the metaphysical feast which Mr Bradley has spread, the objection must still be urged that this supra-relational reconciliation either remains, on the one hand, altogether a name for "we know not what," or, on the other hand, if we press the analogy of feeling, as Mr Bradley frequently does, and endeavour to construct, even in vague generality, the nature of the absolute experience, the conviction is forced upon us that this Absolute excludes contradiction, only because it excludes all variety and difference. In the former case, the diversity is acknowledged, but no light is thrown upon the problem of combining Many in One without contradiction. "In the end," says Mr Bradley, "the whole diversity must be attributed as adjectives to a unity which is not known" (p. 469). Our assertion of a unity becomes then no more than an expression of the faith that with God all things are possible. In the latter case, finite existence is an illusion, which ceases when the standpoint of the Absolute is reached.

Finite existence is said to be harmonised, or, in Mr Bradley's favourite expression, "transmuted" in the Absolute; but for transmuted, we also find such sinister

synonyms as "suppressed," "dissolved," "lost." In
one place, "transmuted and destroyed" are expressly
coupled; while, in another, we are told that the "process of correction" which finite existence undergoes in
the Absolute may "entirely dissipate its nature."

Of course, Mr Bradley protests in numerous passages
against this interpretation of his Absolute as a blank
or undifferentiated unity, like Spinoza's Substance or
Schelling's Neutrum, the night in which all cows are
black. And we may readily believe that he does not
mean simply to "merge" or "fuse" all distinctions into
an indistinguishable mass, but somehow to retain them,
in a richer form, in a single concrete experience. I
will go further, and say that one whole line of Mr
Bradley's thought—the line in which he stands nearest
to Hegel—leads him to emphasise the function of difference and the permanence of distinctions even within
the Absolute. But that line of thought is more than
neutralised by the Spinozistic or Schellingian tendency
which we are at present considering. The best of
intentions cannot avail him, therefore, against the
manifest destiny of this way of thinking.

In the very title of his book, Mr Bradley seems to
me to have started upon the road which leads to this
goal, for "appearance" is certainly, on the whole, a

term of condemnation ; and, as we have seen, it is
frequently qualified throughout the first book, and
also in the second, as " mere appearance," and even
as " illusion." Appearance, therefore, takes on, whether
we will or no, the sense of illusory or unreal.

And it is to be observed that Mr Bradley is consistent, to the end, in his refusal to tolerate difference.
The distinction of subject and predicate remains to
him a contradiction, an imperfection, and consequently
must disappear in the Absolute ; and, with it, the distinction of subject and object from which it is derived.
And that the last vestige of difference may be seen to
disappear from the pure æther of " all-pervasive trans-
fusion," we have the position pushed to its most
quixotic length in the sections of the concluding
chapter which remind us that " not even absolute
truth is quite true." It is not true, for the extraordinary reason that it is only true *of* reality ; it is not
itself reality. The fatal " difference between subject
and predicate" remains, and therefore "even absolute
truth in the end seems thus to turn out erroneous"!
I cannot but think that speculation is here upon an
entirely false track. What Mr Bradley really means,
I suppose, is to renew his famous, and in my view
important, protest against the identification of reality

with "an unearthly ballet of bloodless categories."
He is arguing against the tendency, observable in some
representatives of Hegelian thought, to overstate the
position and function of knowledge. Because knowledge (especially in its highest form as philosophy)
is in its own sphere, as Mr Bradley puts it, "utterly
all-inclusive "—that is, because knowledge, if perfect,
may be said ideally to grasp or include every aspect
of reality—these thinkers speak as if such knowledge
were the reality "bodily," as if the universe were
nothing but an intellectual process, a species of dialectic. Against this tendency Mr Bradley rightly
urges, that "truth" or perfect knowledge is only one
aspect of the universe or of experience. "The universe is not known, and it never, as a whole, can be
known, in such a sense that knowledge would be the
same as experience or reality " (p. 547). "This general
character of reality is not reality itself" (p. 547).
Truth is not *intellectually* defective or limited, for the
idea of an unknowable may easily be shown to be
self-contradictory; it is not, therefore, "intellectually
corrigible"—" it cannot be intellectually transcended."
Still there are other aspects of experience besides the
intellectual, and if we are to have reality "bodily," we
must "take in the remaining aspects of experience."

But this sound and valuable contention is surely presented in a misleading form, when Mr Bradley talks of an " internal discrepancy " which belongs to truth's proper character, and represents truth as achieving its consummation " in passing beyond itself, and in abolishing the difference between the subject and predicate " (p. 547). For " in this passage the proper nature of truth is, of course, transformed and perishes." But this extinction of difference throws us back at once on the distinctionless supra-essential one of mysticism, in which all " details are utterly pervaded and embraced." The collapse of the distinction between subject and predicate (or subject and object) means, however, the extinction of self-consciousness altogether, and throws us back upon the state of dull, diffused feeling, which we suppose to be asymptotically approached in the lowest organisms, and from which (in the same asymptotic fashion) we are accustomed to derive the beginnings of conscious life. Here, therefore, extremes would meet with a vengeance, and the highest become interchangeable with the lowest.

Dissatisfaction with the form of knowledge as such seems to me, I must confess, chimerical ; and I am sure that repudiation of it leads not to any higher unity, but to the pit of undifferentiated substance out of which Hegel dug philosophy. And I venture to add that this is verified in Mr Bradley's own case. On this whole side of his thought, he seems to me to reproduce in essence, and often almost in expression, the Spinozistic doctrine of "imagination," which reduces finite existence to a species of illusion. No doubt there were two tendencies at strife in Spinoza also. But his dominant thought is, "all determination is negation"; and therefore all determinations are devoured, like clouds before the sun, in the white light of the *unica substantia*. But if finite experience is illusory, and its distinctions simply disappear, then, of necessity, the unity which we reach by the denial of these distinctions is quite characterless; we have illusion on the one side, and, as the counter-stroke, nonentity on the other. For does not Erigena tell us at the end of a similar line of thought, "*Deus propter excellentiam non immerito nihil vocatur*"—a phrase the piety of which seems to me with difficulty to conceal its humour?

Mr Bradley displays an extraordinary fertility in metaphors to describe the consummation of finite appearance in the Absolute; but the nature of these metaphors involuntarily confirms the view of his Absolute which we have already arrived at on general

principles.   Appearances are merged, fused, blended,
absorbed, run together, dissolved in a higher unity,
transformed, transmuted; but to transform is found
to mean the same thing as to dissipate, and to trans-
mute is to "destroy" or to "suppress."   To "embrace"
and "harmonise" self-consciousness by transmuting
and suppressing it as such (p. 183) recalls too vividly
the Roman method of pacification: *ubi solitudinem
faciunt, pacem appellant*.   And if Spinoza's Absolute
has been called a lion's den, the description is at least
as applicable to Mr Bradley's.   "All the content, which
the struggle has generated, is brought home and is laid
to rest undiminished in the perfect" (p. 244).   Does
not this suggest the stillness of the grave?   Or when
we are told that "the finites blend and are resolved"
(p. 429); that "every finite diversity is supplemented
and transformed; its private character remains and is
but neutralised by complement and addition"; does it
not seem like saying "yes" and "no" in the same
breath?   How can a private character remain, if it is
neutralised?   *Plus* and *minus* are equivalent to nothing; our result is a blank Schellingian Neutrum.
And Mr Bradley's statement, that "the theoretic object moves towards a consummation in which all distinction and all ideality must be suppressed," is almost

verbally identical with Schelling's account of the ulti-mate goal of the finite Ego.

The ultimate goal of the finite Ego is enlargement of its sphere till the attainment of identity with the infinite Ego. But the infinite Ego knows no object, and possesses, there-fore, no consciousness or unity of consciousness, such as we mean by personality. Consequently, the ultimate goal of all endeavour may also be represented as enlargement of the personality to infinity—that is to say, as its annihil-at'on. The ultimate goal of the finite Ego, and not only of it but also of the Non-Ego—the final goal, therefore, of the world—is its annihilation as a world.[1]

The coincidence seems worth noting, because it in-dicates that both thinkers are haunted by the same ideal, the ideal against which Hegel protests.

So again, when talking of the finite self, Mr Bradley uses a metaphor which, though he excuses its "mise-rable inaccuracy," I cannot help regarding as exceed-ingly significant in this connection. " Because I can-not spread out my window until all is transparent, and *all windows disappear*, this does not justify me in insist-ing on my window-frame's rigidity. For that frame has, as such, no existence in reality, but only in our impotence" (p. 253). This seems to me as exact a re-production as can well be imagined of the Spinozistic

---

[1] Vom Ich als Princip der Philosophie, § 14.

doctrine of *imaginatio*. The window-frames of the self disappear or melt away, because in reality they do not exist at all; it is our impotence which causes us to imagine this severance from others and from the source of all. According to the metaphor by which Erdmann illustrates Spinoza's system, wipe out from any spatial surface the lines which mark it off into distinct figures, and pure or empty space remains. Abolish, in like manner, all window-frames, and "limited transparencies" disappear, as Mr Bradley puts it, in "an all-embracing clearness." But, as we know, the distinction of subject and object has disappeared with the other distinctions of finite appearance; and the clearness, therefore, is not a vision seen by any self. It is the viewless unity of the absolutely infinite Substance.

On whatever line of metaphor or analogy we follow Mr Bradley, the same result is arrived at—the same inherent tendency of his thought is revealed. This is curiously seen in his recurring illustration from Love. Thought, he says, desires "a consummation in which it is lost." And he adds, by way of establishing such a possibility, "does not the river run into the sea and the self lose itself in love?" (p. 173.) The river does run into the sea, but so far is the self from losing it-

self in love, that it may be said therein to attain **to its**
intensest realisation—not realisation in Mr Bradley's
equivocal sense of "disappearing" or "ceasing," but
realisation in the sense of intensest life and enjoyment
in that particular finite centre. So, again, Mr Bradley
tells us (p. **182) that,** in feeling, thought, or volition, the
one reality is present in "a form which does not satisfy."
"In each it longs for that absolute self-fruition which
comes only when the self bursts its limits and blends
with another finite **self."** But **the self never "bursts"**
and "blends" in the way suggested. In all enjoyment,
in all fruition, there is the return of the self upon
itself, without which consciousness would be impossible.
What is meant by a *self*-fruition, in which the self
disappears? **I do** not mean to deny that in extreme
sensual passion, and in the curiously allied mystical
straining **to swoon, as it were,** into Deity, this **self-**
deception is observable **as to** the goal pursued. But I
assert that, in both cases, the desire is self-contradictory; for of love, whether sexual or divine, the poet's
words (in another sense) **are** true, that its dearest
bond is "like in difference." If difference could be
abolished, whether as regards two human beings **or
as regards a** finite individual and its creative source,
"sweet love were slain"—its **very** conditions would be

destroyed. Consciousness itself would be abolished, existence would collapse into nothingness.

We come back, therefore, to our main contention. There is no contradiction in the form of knowledge as such, nor in finite experience merely on the ground that it is in this form. On the contrary, knowledge is rather, as Hegel said, the absolute relation; and all speculation which proceeds by repudiation of this form is found historically to lead straight to the "abyss" of the older mystics. Mr Bradley's speculation simply repeats this lesson. Clearly, the finite is, in Mr Bradley's phrase, essentially self-transcendent. That is as much as to say, more simply, that our experience is *fragmentary;* and however much we enlarge it, it still remains fragmentary. On all sides it seems to stretch infinitely beyond itself. Knowledge, it cannot be denied, is in our experience an infinite progress; and if to have this character is to be contradictory, then the charge must be freely admitted. But it does not seem as if this defect—this contradiction—were inherent in the form of knowledge as such (the form of subject-object, unity in difference); the cause lies rather in our finite position, as that is determined in time and space. We work along infinite radii from an individual locus, but we cannot actually transport ourselves, as it were, to the central hearth of the universe, from which we conceive that all may possibly be seen resumed into unity as a harmonious system. For an intelligence occupying that standpoint, the contradictions of finite experience might possibly disappear, without any abandonment of the form of knowledge. But what is quite plain is, that we cannot by any possibility conceive the nature of that insight. We cannot step out of the infinite progress ourselves. So it is that in Spinoza's system the two sides are never brought together. We may transcend "imagination," and refuse to take facts in isolation; we may trace out endlessly the dependence of any given fact upon the infinite series of its determining causes (nay, upon an infinite number of such converging series), but we never reach the absolute Substance, the immanent cause of the whole. So from the other side there is no process of self-determination by which we can pass from Substance to its infinite attributes, or from any attribute to its particular finite modes. If we could really contemplate existence from the point of view of the Absolute, doubtless the derivation of the finite world might not be so inexplicable; but we never do reach that specular mount. When we attempt to assume such a standpoint, the result is, as with Spinoza, simply emptiness. Abstracting from

the finite, we have nothing left within our grasp. So
it is again with Schelling ; and the side of Mr Bradley's
thought which we have been considering verifies this
experience afresh.

Moreover, an analysis of the arguments by which
Mr Bradley reaches his Absolute throws, I think, an
instructive light upon its nature, and upon the value
which the result can have for us. The Absolute is a
high-sounding title, and rouses proportionate expecta-
tions. Let us inquire whether these are satisfied ; let
us ask ourselves precisely how much Mr Bradley's arguments suffice to establish. "Reality," he says, "must
be a single whole." "The character of the real is to
possess everything phenomenal in a harmonious form."
Absolute Reality, therefore, "embraces all differences in
an inclusive harmony" (pp. 140, 143). "The standard "
is always "the same," and it is applied always under
the double form of inclusiveness and harmony" (p.
371). Now if this were advanced as a definition of
the Absolute, it would obviously be a true, though not
an exhaustive, definition. Taken as implying the existence of the Absolute, it might also be accepted as
the expression of an inextinguishable metaphysical
faith. But when the Absolute in this sense is thrust

upon us as "indubitably real," something which it is
actually impossible to doubt, the very excess of pro-
testation awakens suspicion as to how much the harmony and all-inclusiveness imply. And upon scrutiny,
it seems to me, I must confess, that the assertion resolves itself into something very like an identical
proposition. The mere consideration, it might be
urged, that the universe exists—that Being is—proves
that it is in some sense a harmony. All its aspects
co-exist, and the business of the universe goes on.
Then, as to the systematic unity of the real, I doubt
much, here too, whether what is really proved is not
unduly magnified by the nature of the terms employed.
Mr Bradley successfully disposes of the idea of a
plurality of reals; for each real would in that case be
a universe by itself, or rather a bare unqualified point,
and plurality could never emerge. The mere co-exist-
ence of objects in Knowledge—the fact that we are
able to pass from one object to another—is sufficient
proof that they are not absolutely independent reals,
but exist as parts of one universe—that is, exist, in
some sense, together. To suppose anything else would
be to imagine the continuity of existence to come, as it
were, suddenly to a stop *in mediis rebus*. But does the
postulate that the universe is one, in this sense, carry

us beyond the fact which it explains or names, the
fact that we *are* able to pass indefinitely from one fact
to other facts, reducing them to law as we proceed?
Does it carry us beyond the infinite progress of finite
knowledge, and give us any real idea of an experience
which resumes the life of all the worlds in a central or
focal unity? I do not see that it does. Yet unity,
harmony, system, must mean more than the almost
tautologous result we have just considered, if their
presence or absence is to be of any vital concern to
men.

But it will be said that these formal and abstract
criteria must be supplemented by the further principle that reality, existence of any kind, is one with
" sentience" or " sentient experience." Even if this
be granted, however, I do not see that Mr Bradley's
criteria enable us to pass from an aggregate of experience to " one comprehensive sentience" or " total
experience" (elsewhere spoken of as " an absolute
intuition," " an individual intuition") in the sense of
a living, or, if I may so express myself again, a focal
unity. They do not guarantee unity or harmony, except in the abstract and tautological sense already considered; and the fact that all the varieties of sentient
experience coexist somehow, and are therefore com-

patible—resulting even in a balance of pleasure on **the whole**—is by no means equivalent **to** the assertion **of** a single Being by whom these experiences are felt as a whole, and who enjoys the balance of pleasure which, when " neutralised," " complemented," and " blended," they may **be supposed to yield. The notion of a single** life, in which and for which the experiences are **organically** related and **unified, is** derived **by Mr** Bradley not from his criteria, but from the **nature of** the self; although, strangely enough, in the sections of his book devoted to the **self he does** his **best to disintegrate it** into a mere aggregate. **To** extend the analogy **of** the self to the Absolute is probably inevitable, and **I am far** from objecting to it; although, **in the form in** which Mr Bradley presents the idea, it seems **to come** dangerously near to the crude conception **of** a *Weltseele*, or **soul of** the world—a fused aggregate or mass of sentience. **As a** speculation, however, that might pass, criticism **in detail being reserved. But** what I cannot **see is, how Mr** Bradley can claim the result **as** the immediate consequence **of his** criteria, and **how** he can speak **of it as** absolutely " certain " **and** " indubitably real."

This claim is repeatedly **made by Mr Bradley**, in **a piece of** reasoning which is sufficiently remarkable to challenge examination. The **argument** is introduced a great many times, almost in the same words, as finally closing discussion; and evidently great stress is laid upon it. Curtly stated it is this—"what is *possible* and what a general principle compels us to say *must be*, that certainly *is*" (p. 196); or still more shortly, "what *may* be, if it also *must* be, assuredly *is*" (p. 199).[1] "Here, as before, possibility is all we require to prove reality" (p. 218). The first of these passages is the concluding sentence of the chapter on "Error"; the second occurs in the chapter which follows on "Evil"; and the third in the chapter on "Temporal and Spatial Appearance." In the next chapter (chap. xix.), on "The This and the Mine," the argument is again repeated in exactly the same way, to clinch Mr Bradley's position: "This consummation evidently is real, because on our principle it is necessary, and because again we have no reason to doubt that it is possible" (p. 227). These four chapters deal with recalcitrant facts or aspects of experience, which an opponent might advance as inconsistent with the view of the Absolute just expounded. In them, it must be said that Mr Bradley treats the difficulties in question somewhat lightly. He expressly repudiates the design

---

[1] The italics in these two quotations are Mr Bradley's.

of "showing how" the facts are reconciled in the Absolute, and limits himself to the suggestion of possibilities
—which he seems sometimes not to take very seriously
himself. Having done so, he turns upon us with the
assertion that the abstract possibility is enough, for we
have behind us the general principle of a "must." The
Absolute *must* be all-inclusive and harmonious; there
is nothing about which we cannot say that possibly
it *may* be included in the Absolute; therefore everything *is* included in the Absolute. I cannot see that
there is any real advance in the argument here. Unless we can "show how"—*i.e.*, give some reasonable
theory of the relation of these aspects to the Absolute
—we may as well remain content with the first step:
the Absolute *must* be all-inclusive and harmonious,
though we are quite unable to see how. How far we
are from being able to see how, may be exemplified
from a passage in Mr Bradley's treatment of evil:—

Our old principle may still serve to remove this objection.
The collision and the strife *may* be an element in some
fuller realisation. Just as in a machine the resistance and
pressure of the parts subserves an end beyond any of them,
if regarded by itself—so at a much higher level it *may be*
with the Absolute. Not only the collision but that specific
feeling, by which it is accompanied and aggravated, *can be*
taken up into an all-inclusive perfection. *We do not know*

how this is done, and ingenious metaphors (if we could find them) would not serve to explain it. . . . Such a perfect way of existence *would*, however, reconcile our jarring discords; and I do not see how we can deny that *such a harmony is possible* (p. 203).

This language is surely far more suggestive of pious hope than of philosophic insight; and yet Mr Bradley proceeds in the very next sentence to conclude, " But if possible, then, as before, it is indubitably real." The reference here—and repeatedly—to "our old principle" recalls us, however, to the precise meaning which we found that principle must bear. It is simply the principle that reality must be one. "It must be single, because plurality contradicts itself" (p. 519). "Reality is one system, which contains in itself all experience" (p. 536). "It must include and must harmonise every possible fragment of experience" (p. 548). These statements, taken from the recapitulatory and concluding chapters of the volume, prove afresh that the general principle, on which the whole is founded, is so extremely general as to be of no avail in "harmonising" experience in any vital sense. The "conclusion is certain, and to doubt it logically is impossible" (p. 518); but it is the perfectly abstract conclusion or assumption already discussed, that existence is in some sense one, and does not fundamentally contradict itself, inasmuch as we see that "birth proceeds and things subsist." We are forced, therefore, to conclude that this argument, from necessity through possibility **to reality, is** more specious than **sound,** seeing that it passes from a unity and harmony **which,** as necessary, **are purely abstract, to a unity** and harmony which, as **real,** are understood to imply the **concrete** "perfection" **of** a single Being, and to include the "consummation" **of** "the main tendencies **of** our **nature"** (p. 148). It is, to all intents and purposes, an argument based on our ignorance of **the** possibilities, coupled with the general conviction that things must get along together somehow; since **it is** plain that existent fact contains **all** opposites within itself, and still **exists.** This is certainly **"a faith as vague as** all **unsweet";** but **I** greatly fear that all conclusions about **the universe which it is** logically impossible to doubt **will be found, on** examination, to partake of a similar tautology, **and to be of no** more real value in proving **the universe** a harmonious and perfect **system.**

Lest I should seem to exaggerate the vagueness of **the result, I will** add here **a few** quotations from Mr Bradley's Second Book, **a selection** from a larger anthology. These passages seem to me to bear out the contention that, instead of solving the contradictions of the First Book, the Second Book is mainly devoted to "laying them to rest in the Absolute" with a large draft upon our metaphysical faith. "*Somehow* an identical self must be real," said Mr Bradley in Book I., "but then the question is *how?*" And accordingly the identical self was curtly dismissed, as riddled with contradictions. But "somehow" is the very word which has inscribed itself on page after page of Book II., with an almost pathetic frequency of repetition. Or, if the word itself does not occur, there is the admission that "we do not know how" the reconciliation is effected; but still "we may be sure" that the reconciliation is a fact.

We may say that everything, which appears, is *somehow* real in such a way as to be self-consistent (p. 140).

The bewildering mass of phenomenal diversity must hence *somehow* be at unity and self-consistent (p. 140).

We know what is meant by an experience, which embraces all divisions, and yet *somehow* possesses the direct nature of feeling (p. 160).

If we can realise at all the general features of the Absolute, if we can see that *somehow* they come together in a way known vaguely and in the abstract, our result is certain (p. 160). ·

We cannot understand how in the Absolute a rich

harmony embraces every special discord. But, on the other hand, *we may be sure* that this result is reached (p. 192).

As with error, even our one-sidedness, our insistence and our disappointment, *may somehow* all subserve a harmony and go to perfect it (p. 201).

Then follows the significant passage already quoted as to the possibility of collision and strife being an element in some fuller realisation :—

We do not know how *this is done.* Such a perfect way of existence *would,* however, reconcile our jarring discords (p. 202).

All differences, we have urged repeatedly, come together in the Absolute. In this, *how we do not know,* all distinctions are fused, and all relations disappear (p. 203).

We do *not know how* all these partial unities come together in the Absolute, but *we may be sure* that the content of not one is obliterated (p. 204).

To explain time and space, in the sense of showing how such appearances come to be, and again, how, without contradiction, they can be real in the Absolute, is certainly not my object. Anything of the kind, I am sure, is impossible (p. 205).

Hence we are led to the conclusion that subject and predicate are identical, and that the separation and the change are only appearance. . . . They *somehow* are lost except as elements in a higher identity (p. 220).

The plurality of presentations is a fact, and it, therefore, makes a difference to our Absolute. . . . And the Universe is richer, *we may be sure,* for all dividedness and variety.

Certainly in detail *we do not know how the separation is overcome.* . . . But our ignorance here is no ground for rational opposition. *Our principle assures us* that the Absolute is superior to partition, and *in some way* is perfected by it (p. 226).

The collision is resolved within that harmony where centre and circumference are one (p. 229).

We have no basis on which to doubt that all content comes together harmoniously in the Absolute. . . . All this detail is not made one in any way which we can verify. *That it is all reconciled we know, but how, in particular, is hid from us* (p. 239).

The Reality, therefore, must be One, not as excluding diversity, but as *somehow* including it in such a way as to transform its character (p. 241).

We laid stress [he says in his " Recapitulation " (p. 242)] on the fact that *the how was inexplicable.*

The material world is an incorrect, a one-sided, and self-contradictory appearance of the Real. . . . In other words it is a diversity which, as we regard it, is not real, but which *somehow*, in all its fulness, enters into and perfects the life of the Universe. But, *as to the manner in which it is included*, we are unable to say anything (p. 266).

Certainly, in the end, to know *how* the one and the many are united is beyond our power. *But in the Absolute somehow, we are convinced, the problem is solved* (p. 281).

How these various modes come together into a single unity *must remain unintelligible* (p. 457).

We have seen that the various aspects of experience imply one another, and that all point to a unity which comprehends and perfects them. And I would urge next, that the unity of these aspects is unknown. By this I

certainly do not mean to deny that it essentially is experience, but it is an experience of which, as such, we have
no direct knowledge. . . . *In the end the whole diversity
must be attributed* as adjectives to *a unity which* is not
known (pp. 468, 469).

Mr Bradley's candour in this array of passages is
obviously beyond all praise, but they surely amount
precisely to the assurances of the mystic choir at
the end of 'Faust': "*Das Unzulängliche, hier wird's
Ereigniss; Das Unbeschreibliche, hier ist es gethan.*" Or
in plain prose, so far as the result is metaphysically
certain, it seems too vague to be of use; where it offers
itself as more, it remains the expression of a deep-
seated faith, whose roots are ethico - religious and
æsthetical rather than purely intellectual.

II.

That brings us, however, to an important turning-
point in our investigation. It has been hinted more
than once that Mr Bradley's volume seems the product
of two conflicting tendencies or lines of thought. The
first of these, the Spinozistic or Schellingian tendency,
which is, on the whole, predominant, has been criticised

in the preceding pages. It shapes, perhaps unconsciously, the general view of the Absolute. In his
second line of thought, Mr Bradley stands much more
closely under the influence of Hegel. I propose, in
what follows, to examine this second line of thought,
and to consider the relation of Mr Bradley's theory as
a whole to the Hegelian philosophy, and also to the
limitations of human knowledge.

The Spinozistic tendency, I have said, is, on the
whole, the predominant tendency; but the second line
of thought appears in some important chapters, and
also in the author's statement, towards the close, of
the purpose he had in view in writing the book. The
chapter which seems to me most fully to represent the
second point of view is that on "Degrees of Truth and
Reality." According to the Spinozistic view, appearance is throughout illusion; and the nature of the
Absolute is to be reached by passing beyond appearances to a wholly different mode of being. But this
Being, above or behind appearances, we naturally find
to be entirely predicateless, for in abstracting from
appearance we cut ourselves off from all positive knowledge. According to the second view, which I have
called for convenience the Hegelian, appearances are
not contrasted in a body with the Absolute, and

branded as untrue or illusory; on the contrary, it is recognised that, except in the world of appearances, we have, and can have, no clue to the nature of the Absolute. Attention is concentrated, therefore, in Hegelianism upon the world of appearances, with the result that this world is shown to be a graded or hierarchical system. In this system as a whole, the Absolute is said to be realised or revealed. But appearances only become a safe guide, when regard is had to the systematic or hierarchical character of the revelation.

This doctrine of degrees belongs unquestionably to the abiding essence of the Hegelian philosophy; and, although we have seen that Mr Bradley's speculations often convey another impression, it would appear from his account of the purpose of his volume (given in the concluding paragraphs) that this is the lesson his pages were meant to enforce. The immense importance of the Hegelian position, as against a twofold error, could not in fact be more forcibly put than is done by Mr Bradley in these sentences:—

It is a simple matter to conclude . . . that the Real sits apart, that it keeps state by itself and does not descend into phenomena. Or it is as cheap, again, to take up another side of the same error. The Reality is viewed, perhaps, as immanent in all its appearances, in such a way

that it is, alike and equally, present in all.[1]   Everything
is so worthless on one hand, so divine on the other, that
nothing can be viler or can be more sublime than anything
else.   It is against both sides of this mistake, it is against
this empty transcendence and this shallow Pantheism, that
our pages may be called one sustained polemic.   The positive
relation of every appearance as an adjective to Reality ; and
the presence of Reality among its appearances in different
degrees and with diverse values — this double truth we
have found to be the centre of philosophy (p. 551).

This view is most consistently maintained, as I have
indicated, in the chapter on "Degrees of Truth and
Reality" (chapter xxiv.), and those that follow.   It is
recognised as the ideal of a system of metaphysics " to
show how the world, physical and spiritual, realises by
various stages and degrees the one absolute principle "
(p. 359).   In another place he sketches the task of a
"philosophy of Nature" thus :—

All appearances for metaphysics have degrees of reality.
We have an idea of perfection or of individuality ; and, as
we find that any form of existence more completely realises
this idea, we assign to it its position in the scale of being.
And in this scale (as we have seen) the lower, as its de-
fects are made good, passes beyond itself into the higher.
The end, or the absolute individuality, is also the principle.
Present from the first, it supplies the test of its inferior

---

[1] " As full, as perfect in a hair as heart," according to a line which
Hegelian writers are fond of putting in the pillory.

stages, **and, as** these are included in fuller wholes, the principle grows in reality. Metaphysics, in short, can assign **a** meaning to perfection and progress—

though, as he immediately explains, there would, in setting **out the** various kinds of material phenomena "in an order **of merit,**" be no reference to the scientific **questions of genesis and progress in time.**

In a **complete** philosophy [he proceeds] the whole world **of** appearance would be **set** out as **a** progress. It would **show** a development of principle, though not a succession in time. . . . On **this** scale pure Spirit would mark the **extreme** most removed **from** lifeless Nature. And, at each rising degree of this scale, we should find more of the first character with less of the second. The ideal **of** spirit, we **may say, is** directly opposed to mechanism. Spirit **is a unity of the** manifold in which **the externality of the manifold has utterly** ceased (pp. 497, **498).**

And in the opening of the final chapter he returns to emphasise **this hierarchical aspect of** appearances : " In **the** end no appearance, **as such,** can be real. But appearances fail of reality **in varying** degrees ; and to assert that one **on the whole is** worth **no** more than **another, is** fundamentally vicious " **(p.** 511).

Yet, all through these chapters too, **Mr Bradley is** still **bent upon** reaching an esoteric existence of the **Absolute, *as such*, in** contradistinction to its existence in the system of its appearances. And if this quest does not lead him exactly to an "empty transcendence," it lands him in an abyss of Brahmanic indifference, which threatens to throw us back into the "shallow Pantheism" from which the doctrine of degrees was to deliver us. It prompts him to a series of utterances which, though the qualification of an "as such" may save them from the charge of direct verbal contradiction, are still the expression of two opposite philosophies. Thus, when he tells us (p. 486) with the aid of italics, "The Absolute *is* its appearances," and again, with the same aid (on p. 411), "The Absolute is *not* its appearances," he may perhaps claim with some reason to be enunciating two complementary half-truths. But when he declares emphatically in an eloquent passage (p. 550)—

There is no reality anywhere except in appearance, and in our appearance we can discover the main nature of reality. . . . It is, really and indeed, this general character of the very universe itself which distinguishes for us the relative worth of appearances. . . . Higher, truer, more beautiful, better and more real—these, on the whole, count in the universe as they count for us—

or, again (p. 430), "Whether anything is better or worse does without doubt make a difference to the

absolute; and certainly the better anything is, the **less
totally** in the end is **its being** overruled"; **and** when
he yet says, **at** other times, that "The Absolute is perfect in all its **detail, it** is equally true and **good** throughout" (p. 401); **that,** "viewed in relation to **the Absolute,**
there is **nothing either good or bad, there is not any-**
thing **better or** worse" (p. 411); that "**we may even say**
that **every feature in the universe is absolutely good**"
(p. 412)—the burden **of** the contradiction threatens to
become excessive. We feel that **we are losing** our hold
upon the first view altogether, and drifting **back** into
the gulf of absolute indifference which the poets of
mysticism, Eastern and Western, have hymned. The
passages last quoted all occur, **it is** perhaps **worth
noting, in the** chapter on Goodness, **in which Mr**
Bradley's **zeal** against what **he** calls "the common
prejudice **in favour of the ultimate truth** of morality
or religion" **is** perhaps not untinctured by counter-
prejudice. **His** anxiety **to expose** what he quaintly
calls "the radical **vice of all** goodness" betrays him
into expressions which **seem to** take all vital meaning
out of his first set of phrases, and make the doctrine
of degrees itself an illusion, instead of reflecting, as
he says **elsewhere,** "the essential nature of the world."
The essential **nature** of the world for metaphysics

turns out once more to be the identity in which all distinctions vanish—to which all things, therefore, are the same. This is brought out, with almost startling distinctness, in the description in this chapter of the kind of consummation which the finite attains in the Absolute :—

In the Absolute everything finite attains the perfection which it seeks; but, upon the other hand, it cannot gain perfection precisely as it seeks it. For, as we have seen throughout, the finite is more or less transmuted, and, as such, *disappears in being accomplished*. This common destiny is assuredly the end of the Good. The ends sought by self-assertion and self-sacrifice are, each alike, unattainable. The individual never can in himself become a harmonious system. . . . *In the complete gift and dissipation of his personality*, HE, as such, must vanish; and, with that, the Good is, as such, transcended and submerged. . . . Most emphatically no self-assertion nor any self-sacrifice, nor any goodness or morality, has, as such, any reality in the Absolute (pp. 419, 420).[1]

Comment would but weaken the audacious irony of phrases which make accomplishment tantamount to disappearance, and interpret the "gift" of personality

---

1 In this short passage it will be observed the phrase "as such" occurs no fewer than four times ; it would be interesting to calculate how often it occurs in the course of Mr Bradley's volume. It exactly corresponds to Spinoza's *quatenus*, which has been described as the magic formula which makes all things possible in his system.

as meaning the "dissipation" of the personality in question. But it is plain that, if every aspect of finite existence—if all appearances, even the highest—cease or disappear, "as such," in the Absolute, and we have no knowledge whatever of the Absolute as such, in which it is said to be preserved ("transmuted," "merged and recomposed," p. 306), then surely the Absolute is **for us, in the** Kantian phrase, as **good** as nothing at all. To say we know that it is experience, when it is not like any experience that we know, does not seem greatly helpful. Mr Bradley tells us himself that "an **a**bsolute experience **for us**, emphatically, could be nothing" (p. 550); **and again** he says more explicitly **in a passage** which has been already quoted: **"The unity of these** aspects is unknown. But this **I** certainly **do not** mean to deny, that it essentially is experience, but it is an experience of which, as such, **we can have no** direct knowledge. . . . *In the end the whole diversity must be attributed as adjectives to a unity which is not known*" (pp. 468, 469).

The last passage certainly carries us very near the perilous verge **of** Agnosticism, if indeed it does not take **us** well **over it.** What becomes of the sustained polemic **against** "empty transcendence" (of which

Agnosticism is the most accentuated expression) if
we are forced to admit that, though the Absolute en-
gulfs, and in engulfing harmonises, all we know, it
is itself not known ? We have no reason to suspect
either the good faith or the accuracy of the account
which Mr Bradley gives of the purpose of his book
Much of the polemic of the latter part of the book
is directed against empty transcendence and shallow
Pantheism; and when this polemic is going on, and
Mr Bradley is insisting that the Absolute *is* its appearance ("there is no reality at all anywhere except
in appearance," p. 550), then he is also found teaching
the doctrine of degrees, and insisting that our scale
of worth discovers to us the main nature of reality.
But when he is engaged in his favourite occupation
of dissolving finite experience in contradictions, and
insisting that the Absolute is *not* its appearances, the
other half-truth seems entirely forgotten. In discard-
ing appearance, he falls back himself into an empty
transcendence which, by the very energy with which
it repudiates all the distinctions of finite existence, reduces all the aspects of experience to a dead level
of indifference, and thus strikes round once more into
that shallow Pantheism from which we were promised
a deliverance—the Pantheism to which "nothing can

be viler or can be more sublime than anything else."
For empty transcendence and shallow Pantheism are
two sides of the same mistake, and although Mr Bradley
makes a strenuous effort, in his second or Hegelian line
of thought, to combat and disavow the error, he cannot
cut himself loose from the implications of his Spinozistic logic. The result is, that what I have called the
Hegelian passages have the air of being more or less
inconsequent disclaimers in a book which, as a whole,
expresses an essentially Brahmanic attitude of mind.

Nevertheless, Mr Bradley seems to me to have
rendered a very important service to philosophy in
this book. I will endeavour shortly to indicate what
I consider that service to be. Mr Bradley has attempted to supplement Hegel, or to make an advance
upon Hegel, in one important particular. Hegel's
philosophy is notoriously a philosophy of immanence,
and a vindication of the validity of knowledge. Its
polemical emphasis is directed against the agnostic
relativism of the Kantian "Critique," with its doctrine
of the thing-in-itself, and against the easy mysticism
of the Schellingian *Identitätsphilosophie*, which are
both expressions, in different directions, of an empty
transcendence. By exposing the impossible nature of

the ideals which underlie these doctrines, and vindicating the omnipresence of difference, as woven into the very fibre of existence, Hegel closed one long chapter of philosophical thought—although his results in this respect may doubtless not have been assimilated, even yet, by many of our popular leaders of opinion. But in reaction against this error, Hegel's gift of forcible statement led him into expressions which seem to imply a no less questionable extreme. In preaching the truth that the nature of the Absolute is revealed in the world of its appearances, not craftily concealed behind them, he seems to pass to a sheer identification of the two. Now it is unquestionably true that the two aspects must be everywhere combined: an Absolute which does not appear or reveal itself, and an appearance without something which appears, are correlative abstractions. But that is not tantamount to saying that the appearance of the Absolute *to itself* is identical with the appearance which the world presents to the Hegelian philosopher. Hegel, however, tends to put the philosopher in the place of Deity, and literally to identify the history of humanity with the development of the Absolute. It was this aspect of the Hegelian system which called forth Lotze's sarcastic reference to the

dialectical idyll of an Absolute whose spiritual evolution was confined to the shores of the Mediterranean. I do not think the presence of this tendency in Hegel can fairly be denied. It is an overstatement, as I hold, and as I may **partly be** able to show, of **a great truth**; but, to my mind, the deification of humanity only **requires** to be clearly stated, in order to condemn **itself.** This aspect **of the Hegelian** system found an inadequate counterpoise in the logical dialectic of the categories, from which standpoint the time-process is reduced to **a projection of** thought - distinctions in a series of dissolving views, and the ultimate reality **of** existence seems to be placed in a timeless system **of** abstract conceptions. The **logical** strain in Hegelianism **had** been showing **some signs of** vitality in England, when Mr Bradley, **in his 'Principles of Logic'** (1883), uttered his **memorable** protest against **the** reduction of the universe to **an** " unearthly ballet of bloodless categories." Since then, it may **be** said to have fallen into the background, much as it did in Germany, and the school has mainly devoted itself to the historical development of God. Sometimes this is done, as it is by Hegel himself, with an attempt, either unconscious or deliberate, **to** keep out of **view the** ultimate implications **of** the **position,** as bearing on the doctrine of the being and nature of God. At other times, the identification of man with God is made with an under-current of negative polemic, resulting in a phase of thought which may fairly be described as Hegelian positivism.

If I read Mr Bradley aright, he has clearly realised that neither of these positions can be entertained for a moment, as literal and ultimate truth. Life is more than logic, and God is more than man. The categories —that is to say, the structure of reason—may be said to constitute the essence of God, the ground-plan of the world; we can understand such a statement and recognise the truth it expresses. But "neither gods nor men are in very truth logical categories." And again, God is in history without doubt; but yet we trust He has a richer outlook than He enjoys through any pair of human eyes. Realising, then, these twin defects of the Hegelian position, Mr Bradley, in this volume, has made a strenuous attempt to treat the life of the Absolute as a reality. With the instinct of the true thinker, he recalls us from a too narrow Humanism to an insight into the vastness of the sustaining life that "operates unspent" throughout the universe. This insight is no doubt as simple as it is profound; and it is sufficiently strange that man should forget his position as a finite incident in the plan of things, and measure himself with the immeasurable Spirit of the Universe. Still the fact remains, that the most elementary truths are sometimes most easily forgotten, in the eagerness of a polemic against some particular error. We become so preoccupied with the ideas which we perceive to be true in that particular reference, as against the error we are combating, that we forget the essentially limited nature of the truth we are defending. We forget the limited sphere within which both affirmation and denial have relevancy. Indeed, we become so jealous on behalf of the truth for which we fight, that we cannot brook the least criticism upon it. We confound in a common condemnation the man who denies its legitimate truth, because he lags at the standpoint of exploded error, and the man who, having got beyond these controversial issues, calls attention to the modifications which the principle must submit to, before it can be advanced as the absolute verity.

Elemental, therefore, as the truth is, the stress which Mr Bradley lays, throughout his volume, upon the necessarily superhuman character of the Absolute— its inexpressible and incomprehensible transcendence of human conditions of being and thinking — is a salutary correction to a good deal of current speculation. After all, if it comes to a question of reality, the Absolute is the great and only Reality. *We* have reality only within its all - comprehensive bounds. True, therefore, as it is, in the proper reference, to say that the Absolute realises itself in human self-consciousness, it becomes fundamentally absurd, if the saying is taken to mean that the Absolute exists, so to speak, by the grace of man, and lives only in the breath of his nostrils. Is it not both absurd and blasphemous to suppose that the Power which cradles and encompasses all our lives is not itself a living fact, and that it is reserved for man to bring the Absolute, as it were, to the birth? A moment's reflection convinces us that it is so, and also that it must be essentially impossible for a finite being to realise the manner of that Absolute Life.

But Mr Bradley has not been content simply to restore to us this fundamental insight. He is a metaphysician, and his book, if not presenting a complete system of philosophy, yet contains a pretty definite theory of the Absolute. And the curious thing is that, based as it is upon an important truth, and aiming at correcting an undoubted defect in the Hegelian statement, the theory turns out to be further from the truth —turns out, at all events, to be more misleading— than the theory it attempts to improve. But I perhaps exaggerate the strangeness of the phenomenon, for the result is, in the circumstances, inevitable, as soon as we proceed to a constructive account of absolute experience. As water cannot rise higher than its source, so our speculative grasp cannot transcend the experience which is ours in this seed-plot of Time. The higher may comprehend the lower, but how shall the lower reach out to comprehend the higher? Denying, therefore, that the life of the Absolute can be construed in terms of our actual human experience, even in its highest reaches, Mr Bradley is obliged, as we have seen, to fall back upon the analogy of a lower life, out of which our conscious experience seems to rise—the life of feeling.

It would be trite to dwell here on the ambiguities of the term "feeling" and the varieties of usage in its regard. It will be sufficient if we understand the meaning Mr Bradley intends to convey. Mere feeling, he would probably acknowledge, is a state which we never actually realise, though we seem to approximate to it at times, and conceive it to be approached asymptotically in the lowest forms of organic life. Nevertheless, it is not to be denied that feeling, in Mr Bradley's usage, represents one feature — one fundamental aspect — of our actual experience. All our experience is rooted in the immediacy of perception; and feeling names this perceptual or immediate aspect, as opposed to the conceptual or abstract world, which we rear on the basis of inner or outer perception, and offer as its explanation or interpretation. I foresee the outcry that will be raised, in certain quarters, against this way of stating the fact, and I hasten to add that this in no way implies the separability of these two aspects in actual experience. Our actual perceptions are full of the distinctions of thought; a state of pure perception, entirely without the shaping presence of the conceptions of the understanding, can only be regarded as a πρώτη ὕλη, a vanishing-point or limitative conception, essentially unrealisable within experience. The notion from which empiricism started, that the object of perception is given, as we perceive it, without any activity of thought —the notion that thought simply analytically assorts the objects of which we thus passively become aware, doing them up into classes and discovering their laws of combination—this complete severance of perception from thought we are surely at liberty to treat nowadays as an exploded fiction. But the amplest acknowledgment of the victory of transcendentalism in this controversy leaves the immediacy of perception untouched, and leaves the difference as wide as ever between **the concrete world of** fact, which reveals **itself in perception** (inner and outer), and the abstractions of conception **as** such.

Conception deals wholly **with** *abstracta*, **with isolated** aspects or points **of view. Such are the discrete or** abstract **units which, from** its very nature, it cannot fuse **into** continuity, **and the multiplicities** which **it cannot** resolve **into** unity. It can never, therefore, express the facts of experience as they **exist ; in trying** to do so, it inevitably falls into contradictions **or antinomies.** It then proceeds, on the **basis of** its **own** impotence, to impeach our whole experience **as contradictory,** and no better than an illusion. **But if its** impotence is **perfectly** intelligible—is **seen** indeed **to be inevitable—then** experience **itself can hardly be** called unintelligible. **It may be** unintelligible in a technical use of the word ; **in** the sense that it cannot be reduced to, or exhaustively **expressed** in, the abstractions **which the isolating touch of understanding frames.** But this is merely to say that understanding **is not itself life,** but a useful instrument **in** the service **of life. In the** only reasonable sense **of** intelligibility, **life or experience** is itself the **norm** of intelligibility. **We find united there all the** aspects which, **merely by** detecting

and naming them, understanding tends to fix in isolation and mutual repugnance. Take the typical instance
of unity and multiplicity, which furnished forth Mr
Bradley's whole First Book. The unity of the self and
its states is the sufficient, and the only possible, answer
to the so-called contradiction. True, you cannot *name*
unity and multiplicity, in the same indivisible moment
of time; you must get your breath, as it were, after
articulating the one, before you go on to the other.
And what applies to the articulation of the words
applies to the mental thinking of the thoughts. If you
think of the unity of the Self, you necessarily pause
upon that aspect, before supplementing it by turning
round the eye of the mind to the other aspect, multiplicity. In conception, the mind *takes a step*, as it were,
from the one to the other, and so the two come to appear separate. Then dialectic supervenes, and tells us
that A is A, and, consequently, these two can never
be brought together; whereas we have simply looked
at one fact from two sides. That one fact—our own
inmost experience—exhibits the two sides indissolubly
united, and, accordingly, instead of calling this a contradiction, we adopt it as the norm of all our explanations.

All our experience, then, is rooted in the immediacy

of perception, and experience, from the perceptive side, is a continuum in which we make distinctions. **As we do** not "make" them **in** an arbitrary sense, we may also be said to find them. They were not **there** *for us* till **we made them**; but, in making them, we hold **our-selves** to be analysing **more exactly** what was implicit in the **presentation from** the **first—to** be acquiring, **in** short, **a** fuller and truer knowledge **of** the fact. The whole progress **of knowledge** appears, therefore, as the breaking up of what is given as a vague mass of feeling or undefined consciousness, which can hardly as yet be described even as general awareness. Inasmuch as this state is assumed to occur in the experience **of** some individual **creature, and** to constitute the whole **state** of **the creature in** question, it may be permissible to speak **of it (with** Mr Bradley) **as an** undifferentiated unity, **an** undivided **whole. This** inexhaustible back-ground of "feeling" **constitutes for us the** *being* of the world (including ourselves), **and, in** that sense, it is the ultimate subject of all predication; but, obviously, **it** is only so far as it becomes determined or formed, **that** we can say anything about it. **In** its character of unexhausted remainder, it is not anything we actually realise; **it cannot** itself be properly spoken of as ex-perience, although it is that out of which all experience seems to arise. It is essentially a limitative conception, and, as such, it is the necessary implicate of our experience; but again, as such, it cannot be constructed within experience. We approach it *per viam negativam*, only approximating towards it by throwing out one determination after another; and, if we examine our supposed realisation, we find that we have merely thrown our negatives into a positive form.

But what is itself describable only by negatives, and what, if realisable, would mean a lapse into unconsciousness, cannot be expected to throw any valuable light upon the nature of an absolute experience. That experience, as we have seen, is to be a whole in which the distinctions elicited in the progress of knowledge are again to be merged in such a way that thought returns to the immediacy of feeling; but it is added that, "in that higher unity no fraction of anything is lost" (p. 182). We have already examined this notion, and come to the conclusion that, though Mr Bradley *says*, and is bound to say, that all the "richness," all the distinctions, of the world we know are somehow conserved for the Absolute, the main principle on which his criticism depends points directly to the collapse of all distinction whatever; and he seems himself continually impelled in that direction. Here we need only add that, if the **utter unity** of feeling, out of which our experience seems to take its rise, is an utter unity into which all distinctions collapse, and so a **purely negative conception**, it will be equally negative when transferred to the other end of the scale, and used to illustrate the transcendent unity in which all the differences of finite experience are resolved. In short, in the one case as in the other, we are dealing with a limitative conception, which it is sheerly impossible for us positively to construct, or, in any true sense, to conceive. Our experience has the stamp of incompleteness upon it; it has the appearance of moving from an unknown source to an unknown goal. This incompleteness is expressed in the two limitative conceptions we have had before us, the unity below and the unity above experience, the extreme of mere sense and the extreme of omniscience. Within experience we may approximate to one extreme or the other, but any attempt positively to realise either leaves us baffled, with nothing in our grasp. Beyond experience, in short, all is and must be, for us, absolute emptiness; and whatever "sail-broad vans" we spread for flight, we drop at once plumb down, like Milton's Satan, in a vast vacuity.

It is impossible, therefore, to construct for ourselves, even in outline or vague generality, the nature of an absolute experience. Our general descriptions are seen, on examination, to be either purely formal, and, as I have argued, identical propositions, or they are postulates of faith, realised, we believe, somehow, but always with this for an afterword, that the " how " is hidden from us. And this is so for the simplest of all reasons, because we are men and not God. We are ourselves immersed in the process of the universe. We can only live our own life, and see through our own eyes. If we could do more, that would mean that we ourselves had vanished from the universe; the place which had known us would know us no more, and there would be, as it were, a gap created in the tissue of the world.

Take the crucial case of time. " If time is not unreal," says Mr Bradley, "our Absolute is an illusion " (p. 206). But, however "contradictory" we may find the infinite progress to be, which time involves, can we even adumbrate to ourselves what " a timeless reality " would be? I am quite certain, for my own part, that the utmost we can attain is the idea of something permanent *in* time, lasting unchanged through time; but that leaves us with all the difficulties of the infinite series still on our hands. Mr Bradley's suggestion that there may be many time-series in the Absolute, unrelated to one another, seems to me to throw no light on the subject whatever. The notion of many " times " seems to me one of these empty possibilities— inconceivable verbal combinations—which Mr Bradley elsewhere, I think, discourages. All our notions of reality being drawn necessarily from our own experience, and all our experience being in time, a timeless reality remains for our minds as inconceivable as wooden iron. Besides, the difficulty of passing from the timed to the timeless remains just as great, whether the times be many or one.

Mr Bradley's attempt to determine the Absolute " as such "—i.e., the Absolute as beyond or more than the process of human experience—has the unexpected result, therefore, which I indicated a few pages back. It proves an unexpected vindication of the real strength of the Hegelian position. The cloud of negations in which the attempt involves us, the abstract and empty character of the Absolute supposed to be reached, are a fresh and involuntary confirmation of Hegel's wisdom in refusing to step beyond the circle of knowledge and the process of history. I have said, and I repeat, that Hegel's identification of the Absolute with human experience is indefensible. Nevertheless, his refusal to seek the character of the Absolute elsewhere than in its appearances—*i.e.*, in human experience—was entirely justified. As we have no predicates save those drawn from this experience, the attempt to determine the Absolute, so far as it is something more than this experience, necessarily throws us back upon the purely indeterminate, and we drift easily towards the doctrine of the Unknowable. Professor Royce has already accused Mr Bradley of this tendency.[1] The fruitfulness of Hegel's philosophy lay in his repudiation of this barren search. The real is revealed in its appearances, and is not to be sought behind or beyond them. Extension of experience will bring increased and deepened knowledge of the Absolute :—

> " For all experience is an arch wherethrough
> Gleams that untravelled world whose margin fades
> For ever and for ever when I move."

But as we shift our margin and enter that untravelled world, however far we go, the new is still an extension of the old on the same plane—the plane of finite experience—not a passage to another species of insight. Along with this resolute correlation of the real with its manifestations, there goes in Hegel the organisation of the phenomenal world itself. Relieved from an impossible quest, he devotes himself to the exposition of

[1] Philosophical Review, vol. iii. p. 217.

experience as the only possible revelation of the Absolute for us, and he finds it to be not an indifferent congeries, but a graded system. The significance of this doctrine of degrees I have already dwelt on, in commenting upon what seem to me two conflicting lines of thought in Mr Bradley's book. The result for Hegel of this doctrine, taken together with his fundamental correlation of the real with its manifestation, was, not unnaturally perhaps, a theory which identified, or seemed to identify, the Absolute with the culminating aspects of human experience in art, religion, the State, and philosophical system. The theory is false only so far as it is taken to confine the Spirit of the universe to these earthly tabernacles. So understood, it cabins the spirit of man within a narrow and self-sufficient positivism. It undermines the sentiment of reverence, and dulls our sense of the infinite greatness and the infinite mystery of the world. But it is profoundly true, so far as it asserts that, only by predicates drawn from these spheres, can we determine the Absolute at all, and that, moreover, such determination is substantially, though doubtless not literally, true :—

> " So weit das Ohr, so weit das Auge reicht,
>   Du findest nur Bekanntes, das ihm gleicht,
>   Und deines Geistes höchster Feuerflug
>   Hat schon am Gleichniss, hat am Bild, genug."

The dangers that lurk in any attempt to determine the Absolute as such are well exemplified, I think, in the negations to which Mr Bradley is driven. Thus "morality cannot (as such) be ascribed to the "Absolute" (p. 197). "Goodness as such is but appearance, and is transcended in the Absolute" (p. 429). "Will cannot belong as such to the Absolute" (p. 413). In the Absolute even thought must "lose and transcend its proper self" (p. 182). "If the term 'personal' is to bear anything like its ordinary sense, then assuredly the Absolute is not merely personal" (p. 531). "The Absolute is not personal, nor is it moral, nor is it beautiful or true" (p. 533). What is the inevitable effect upon the mind of this cluster of negations? Surely it will be this: Either the Absolute will be regarded as a mere Unknowable with which we have no concern, or the denial of will, intellect, morality, personality, beauty, and truth will be taken to mean that the Absolute is a unity indifferent to these higher aspects of experience. It will be regarded as non-moral and impersonal in the sense of being below these distinctions; and our Absolute will then remarkably resemble the soulless substance of the materialist. Nothing is more certain than that extremes meet in this fashion, and that the attempt to reach the super-human falls back into the infra-human. Now Mr

Bradley, of course, intends his unity to be a higher, not a lower unity. "The Absolute is not personal, because it is personal and more. It is, in a word, super-personal" (p. 531). But he is not blind to the danger that lurks in his denials. "It is better," he even warns us, if there is a risk of falling back upon the lower unity, "to affirm personality than to call the Absolute impersonal." But there is more than a risk, I maintain; there is a certainty that this will be the result. And therefore the conclusion deducible from Mr Bradley's discussion seems to me to be that the attempt, metaphysically, scientifically, or literally[1] to determine the Absolute as such, is necessarily barren. Where the definition is not tautologous, it is a complex of negations, and if not technically untrue, it has in its suggestions the effect of an untruth. Our statements about the Absolute — *i.e.*, the ultimate nature of things—are actually nearer the truth when they give up the pretence of literal exactitude, and speak in terms (say) of morality and religion, applying to it the characteristics of our own highest experience. Such language recognises itself in general (or, at least, it certainly should recognise itself) as possessing only symbolical truth, — as being, in fact, "thrown out," as Matthew Arnold used to say, at a

[1] I use these for the moment as equivalent terms.

vast reality.   But both religion and the higher poetry
—just because they give up the pretence of an impossible exactitude—carry us, I cannot doubt, nearer
to the meaning of the world than the formulæ of an
abstract metaphysics.

Such a conclusion may be decried as Agnostic, but
names need frighten no one.   The Agnosticism which
rests on the idea of an unknowable thing-in-itself—
the Agnosticism which many of Kant's and Spencer's
arguments would establish—is certainly baseless; but
there are regions of speculation where Agnosticism is
the only healthy attitude.   Such a region I hold to be
that of the Absolute as such.   If it be objected that
the mere mention of such an Absolute is an acknowledgment of the Thing-in-itself, I must allow myself
Mr Bradley's privilege, and simply "doubt if the ob-
jector can understand" (p. 183).   It is, in a word, not
an Absolute-in-itself, but the Absolute-for-itself, of
which we are speaking.   It is the nature of the
existence which the Absolute has or enjoys for
itself.   This is incomprehensible, save by the Absolute itself.   Because it is incomprehensible by the
finite mind, it does not, however, follow that such
an all-embracing experience is not a Reality; and the

denial of such a possibility would seem to be more than presumptuous. So far, therefore, as the Hegelian philosophy disregarded this wider outlook, and implicitly identified the Absolute with the process of finite experience, its scheme of things is out of proportion, and the ineffable transcendence of the Absolute as such required reassertion. But this reassertion must not be construed to mean that our own existence is a vain show which throws no light on the real nature of things. Rightly Agnostic as regards the nature of the Absolute as such, no shadow of doubt need fall on our experience as a true revelation of the Absolute for us. Hegel was right in seeking the Absolute within experience, and finding it too; for certainly we can neither seek it nor find it anywhere else. The truth about the Absolute which we extract from our experience is, doubtless, not the final truth. It may be taken up and superseded in a wider or fuller truth; and in this way we might pass, in successive cycles of finite existence, from sphere to sphere of experience, from orb to orb of truth. But even the highest would still remain a finite truth, and fall infinitely short of the truth of God. Such a doctrine of relativity in no way invalidates the truthfulness of the revelation at any given stage. The fact that the truth I reach is the truth for me, does not make it, on that account, less true. It is true, so far as it goes; and if my experience can carry me no further, I am justified in treating it as ultimate, *until it is superseded*. Should it ever be superseded, I shall then see both how it is modified by being comprehended in a higher truth, and also how it and no other statement of the truth could have been true at my former standpoint. But *before* the higher standpoint is reached, to seek to discredit our present insight by the general reflection that its truth is partial and requires correction—this is a perfectly empty truth which, in its bearing upon human life, may easily come to have the effect of an untruth. We hear much in denunciation of the practice of testing truth by its supposed consequences. And no doubt the argument is often a weapon in the hands of obscurantism and timid conservatism. Yet, in the long-run, truth and life are not dissevered, and there is a line of Goethe's which expresses, with his usual calmness and breadth, the insight of which the popular doctrine is a superficial distortion, *Was fruchtbar ist, allein ist wahr.*

While Mr Bradley's main thought, therefore, undoubtedly possesses a real importance as emancipating us from the too narrow humanism of a dogmatic

Hegelianism, the impression produced by his volume upon an unbiassed mind will be, I fancy, to foster a wise Agnosticism in regard to assertions about the Absolute as such. Human experience, not as itself the Absolute "**bodily**," but as constituting the only accessible and **authentic revelation of its** nature **to us, is the** true subject-matter **of** Philosophy. And here, as **Mr** Bradley says, "the doctrine of degrees in Reality and **Truth is the** fundamental answer to our problem" (p. 487). **Mr Bradley, as** we have seen, acknowledges his special indebtedness to Hegel in this part of his discussion; but, in its general form, **the** doctrine is no exclusive property of any philosophical school. **Rather** it has always been

> "Der Völker löblicher Gebrauch
> **Dass jeglicher** das Beste was er kennt,
> **Er Gott, ja seinen Gott, benennt.**"

We speak most **truly, most in** accordance with the **real** nature **of things, when we thus** characterise the Absolute in terms **of the best** we know.

But that Hegel has given systematic expression **to** this old world-wisdom gives his system **a** place in **history** quite beyond the brilliant but arbitrary speculations **of** individual genius, **and** ensures for it an abiding influence upon modern thought. It must be acknowledged, however, that, in his hands, the doctrine of degrees tends to assume a too purely intellectual and formalistic character. If we look simply at his own methodic statement, the scale seems to resolve itself into a series of repetitions of the fundamental formula of the One and the Many. As we rise in the scale, we get more comprehensive wholes—wholes, too, which include a more intricate complexity of detail, and which embrace their detail in a more intimate union. We have thus a series of types (different powers or *Potenzen*) of the same formula. But the realisation of this abstract scheme possesses in itself no interest or importance. It is the content of any experience which makes it "higher" in any vital sense, and makes it of decisive importance in an inquiry as to the meaning of experience as a whole. Hegel's results in this connection are substantially true, just because they are based not upon the mere application of a formula, but upon an implicit reference to the content of experience and the judgments of value which that legitimates. The formula itself is derived, in fact, from the self-conscious life of man, and to Hegel, in even a wider sense than to Kant, man in his typical activities is an End-in-himself.

The life, that is to say, which is guided by the ideals of Truth, Beauty and Goodness, and which partially realises these, possesses an absolute and indefeasible worth. It is only in such judgments of value that we can be said to possess "an absolute criterion." Mr Bradley says in more than one place that we possess such a criterion, but he also, like Hegel, confines himself too exclusively throughout his book to the intellectual necessities of all-inclusiveness and internal harmony, which, we found, did not carry us so far as he supposed. Our idea of what the Absolute must be is founded on the ideal necessities which our nature compels us to acknowledge. But the ideal necessities in question are not merely intellectual; they are æsthetical, ethical, and religious as well. For "we must believe" (to quote Mr Bradley's own words) "that reality satisfies our whole being; our main wants—for Truth and Life, and for Beauty and Goodness — must all find satisfaction" (p. 159). The necessity of our belief is not due, however, to any esoteric assurance on the point which we possess direct from the Absolute. It is an absolute certainty in the sense simply that it is an ultimate judgment on our part. It represents our deepest conviction as to absolute and relative worth—a conviction which does not admit of being supported, and therefore does not admit of being assailed, by argument.

P

MR BALFOUR AND HIS CRITICS.

THERE is some danger that the philosophical importance of Mr Balfour's 'Foundations of Belief' may
be obscured by the very circumstances which gave
the book for a time such an extraordinary prominence.
The tide of reviews and criticisms, which flowed so
high in the weeks and months immediately following
its appearance, has, for the time at least, completely
ebbed; and the volatile curiosity of the general public
has doubtless been transferred to other themes. But
the book appeals to deeper interests and a more permanent audience. To that audience I venture to
submit the following reconsideration of the subject.
The multifarious and divergent estimates of the book
may themselves serve, I think, by the very misap-
prehensions they reveal, to set its essential argument
in a clearer light. And in the second place, I de-

sire to call attention to an important change, an important advance, as it seems to me, in Mr Balfour's philosophical position, since the publication of his earlier volume. No critic, so far as I know, has commented on this change, although it serves, in great measure, to explain the conflicting judgments of Mr Balfour's argument; and the author himself seems hardly aware that he has in any way shifted his ground. But however insensible the advance may have been, and however closely the two positions may still seem at times to approach one another, the difference between them, from the point of view of philosophical construction, is vital.

Reviews and criticisms always indicate the personal equation of the reviewer. But in Mr Balfour's case the divergence of the critical voices had in it some of the elements of surprise. It was to be expected that naturalists and theologians would judge the book by different standards, and take diametrically opposite views of its value; and it is true that in general the Naturalist denounced it as "a plea for supernaturalism," or as "written in the interest of the powers that be and the established creed." But theologians themselves were found as widely at issue with one another. It would have been natural, again, to find reviewers of a Radical tendency inclined to pick flaws in the book, and those of a Conservative colour inclined to bless it altogether. And no doubt such a stream of tendency may be traced in some of the less important notices of the daily and weekly press. But perhaps the most acrid and unsympathetic notices that were written appeared in the Tory columns of 'Blackwood' and the 'Saturday Review.' The contrast of opinions was fairly typified in the titles given in the same week to their articles by two of our prominent weeklies. "Mr Balfour as a Christian" was the one headline; "Mr Balfour the Sceptic" was the other. Both are written avowedly from an orthodox Christian standpoint; yet the one finds "the last hundred pages of the book," that is to say, the constructive suggestions towards a provisional philosophy, "almost unreadable." "We are supposed," says the critic, "to be taught theories of 'beliefs and realities'; but we find the beliefs qualified out of existence, and the reality attenuated till it is slighter than a shadow." The other reviewer is of opinion that Mr Balfour writes in these sections of his book "with amazing freshness and interest"; and he concludes by saying that "preachers will find much in it to repay their study, and to contribute to their work." If we confine our attention to theologians who write above their own signature, Principal Fairbairn confesses to "deep disappointment." "Pleasure turned to pain, as the underlying philosophy was seen to be shifting sand rather than solid rock; the farther the reading proceeded, the less satisfactory the argument appeared." Professor Marcus Dods, on the contrary, declares that "if Mr Balfour's volume is the result of his enforced absence from the helm of the State, it is a strong argument for the continuance of the Liberal Government." He compares the book to Butler's 'Analogy,' and adds that "there are many who have read the older master with dissatisfaction, who will find in the teacher of to-day the conviction and help they seek."

Looking at another part of the field, we find Mr Alfred Benn, who writes in the main from the Naturalistic standpoint, confidently recommending the book to Roman Catholic believers "as bringing water to their mill." But Dr Barry, who is doubtless more entitled to speak for the Roman Catholic theologians, pronounces, in the 'Dublin Review,' that "the foundation is not true and will never stand." "Universal doubt, rather than religious dogma, will gain by the stroke that smites reason to the ground." "Montaigne had said all these things before, with infinite vivacity and eloquence, but to the praise of a dissolving and pernicious doubt rather than to the gain of Christianity." For Montaigne, the writer in 'Blackwood' substitutes Pilate and Mephistopheles. "God forbid," he ejaculates, "that religion should ever be led to rest its case on pleadings like these!"

In sum, it may be said that while many representatives of the Churches accept the new champion with acclamation, and without too narrow a scrutiny of his weapons or methods of warfare, an important section will have none of such a defender. They are more afraid of what they take to be the sceptical premisses of the book, than grateful for its orthodox conclusions. "*Non tali auxilio*," they seem to say; "we prefer to fight with our own weapons, and take the chances of the war."

Which of these two last-named parties is the better advised, and what is the truth about the scepticism which is said to pervade the book, and to defeat what was avowedly the author's intention in writing it? In general, is there any explanation to be found in the book itself of these contradictory estimates of its con-. tents and result? If, as I am convinced, the volume is much more than the *tour de force* of an eminent statesman, and the wonder **of** a literary season, this is a question which it will well repay us to consider. I do not speak here of the classical graces and felicities of the style, which have been on all hands sufficiently acknowledged. Whether the argument, moreover, is **in** all points **consistent with itself,** whether all the positions advanced are equally tenable, these are questions **on which we may** easily differ; but to fail to recognise the vitality of the discussions, the mastery with which **the** great philosophical debate **is** handled, is to show **a** mind which either cannot rise above long-incrusted prejudice, or cannot detach itself from **the** technical shibboleths **of** its own philosophic sect.

What then, let us ask, does the book itself profess to **be? It is an** inquiry into "the foundations of belief," and **the** sub-title ("**Notes** introductory to the Study of Theology") indicates at **once** the practical, or perhaps one might rather say more broadly the human, interest that underlies and prompts the investigation. Through**out** the book, nothing is more remarkable than the spirit of intellectual detachment which it exhibits, the perfect freedom, at times one might say the airy free**dom,** with which the discussion **is** conducted. Yet **we** are made **to feel that it has not** been undertaken for the mere delight of dialectic fence.   The book is inspired by a keen human interest, which breaks through, from time to time, in passages of deep feeling or indignant irony.   The author conceives the spiritual heritage of mankind to be endangered by certain current assumptions of a would-be philosophic nature. He submits these assumptions, accordingly, to scrutiny (and with them the assumptions that underlie the whole fabric of human knowledge), in order to discover whether we are really under an intellectual obligation to surrender the beliefs in question—beliefs as to the cause of the world and man's place in it, which form the basis of all theological teaching, and which constitute what may be called the spiritual view of the world.

Mr Balfour's attitude, it will be seen from what has been said, is to a large extent the same as when he wrote his ‘Defence of Philosophic Doubt’ in 1879. The fact that the earlier work is described, in a subtitle, as “an Essay on the Foundations of Belief,” indicates the amount of ground which the two volumes occupy in common; and the second part of the present work (“Some Reasons for Belief”) is largely a more popular restatement of some of the criticisms contained in ‘Philosophic Doubt.’   The motive of the two books is also the same; for, in his first publication also, the avowed occasion of Mr Balfour's attack was the aggressive attitude assumed towards religion by "advanced thinkers," who claimed to speak in the name of science. But though the two books have much in common, it would be a mistake to suppose that Mr Balfour has, in the second, simply repeated, with variations, the theme of the first. The many resemblances of the two volumes have fostered the impression that this is the case; and I cannot but think that injustice has been thereby done to the scope of the argument in the 'Foundations of Belief.'

Under this impression, the sceptical criticism of Empiricism and Transcendentalism, and the laudation of Authority, assumed an undue importance, overshadowing what I take to be the substantive thesis of the book and its more enduring contribution to philosophical thought. Some have maintained, indeed, that 'The Foundations of Belief' is a misnomer (like the chapter on snakes in Iceland), inasmuch as the whole purpose of the book is to prove that belief has no foundations. This, as I hope to show, is true of the more recent argument only in a technical sense which robs the assertion of its sting. But it might claim to be a fairly accurate description of the position in

which we are left at the conclusion of the earlier
volume. The 'Defence of Philosophic Doubt' is really
an exposition of the purest scepticism. It is, according to the author's own description, a piece of purely
destructive criticism, directed against the foundations
of scientific knowledge, or what claims to be such. The
argument is conducted, it is true, with an *arrière pensée*
in the shape of "practical results" which it is supposed
to yield in the interests of religious truth. But the
actual conclusion drawn is, that *both* the creed of
religion and the creed of science are equally baseless,
in the sense of being "incapable of any rational defence." Hence Mr Balfour concludes that "religion
is at any rate no worse off than science in the matter
of proof" (pp. 315-319). We have as much right
to believe the one as the other. "I am content to
regard the two great creeds by which we attempt to
regulate our lives as resting in the main *upon separate
bases*. So long, therefore, as neither of them can lay
claim to philosophic probability, discrepancies which
exist, or may hereafter arise, between them cannot be
considered as bearing more heavily against the one
than against the other" (p. 322). Both science and
theology have "claims on our belief," but these
claims are not to be construed as reasons.

Whatever they may be, they are not rational grounds of conviction. . . . It would be more proper **to describe** them as a *kind of inward inclination or impulse*, falling **far** short of—or, I should perhaps **rather say,** altogether differing in **kind** from—philosophic certitude, leaving the reason, **therefore,** unsatisfied, **but amounting, nevertheless, to a practical cause of belief, from the** effects **of which we do not even** desire **to be released (p. 317).**

If **it be** objected that this **" impulse " is not universal, Mr Balfour** rejoins that to build upon **the** universality **of the** impulse would be **to erect** the impulse to believe **into a** reason for believing, and **so entirely to** misread **the** situation. The contention **expressly is that there is no** reason for **belief in either case ; and where** the **impulse is wanting in any number of individuals, we simply** note **its** absence in their case, **as we note its presence in other** individuals. **But** there can **be no** argument **in such a** matter **from** one individual **to** another.

I and an indefinite **number of other** persons, if we contemplate religion and science **as** unproved systems of belief standing side **by** side, feel a practical need for both. . . . But as no legitimate argument can be founded on the mere existence of this need or impulse, so **no** legitimate argument **can be founded** on any differences which psychological **analysis may** detect between different cases of its manifestation. **We are** in this matter, unfortunately, *altogether outside* **the** *sphere* **of** *Reason* **(p. 320).**

Such passages are obviously a formulation of the purest scepticism which can well be conceived.   To find their parallel we must go back to Hume—the Hume of the 'Treatise,'—who also concludes that

after the most accurate and exact of my reasonings, I can give no reason why I should assent to it, and feel nothing but a *strong propensity* to consider objects strongly in that view under which they appear to me. . . . I may, nay, I must yield to the current of nature in submitting to my senses and understanding; and in this *blind submission* I show most perfectly my sceptical disposition and principles. . . . If we believe that fire warms or water refreshes, it is only because it costs us too much pains to think otherwise (part iv. section 7).

Moreover, the earlier volume contains no indication, or next to none, of the precise nature of the theological beliefs by which the author would supplement the creed of science.   Mr Balfour apparently identifies himself with "the ordinary believer" (p. 325).   His language seems to imply an uncriticised acceptance of the traditional creed as a whole.   It can hardly, however, be argued with any plausibility that the impulse to religious belief extends to the details of a dogmatic scheme like that of historical Christianity. Hence, the man who believes on such terms seems to have no course open to him but unquestioning submission to authority and tradition.

The impression, therefore, produced by the earlier volume—and I think not unnaturally produced—was that it was essentially a new version of the often-repeated attempt to aggrandise authority by sapping the foundations of all rational certainty; an attempt, therefore, to found religious faith upon intellectual scepticism. Taken barely thus, and as historically exemplified in writers like Pascal, Newman, and Mansel, such an attitude obviously surrenders all claim to rational criticism of the dogmas offered for acceptance, and offers no safeguard against the re-invasion of the grossest superstition. A more dangerous defence of religious truth cannot, I think, be imagined. And if this is supposed to be the sum of Mr Balfour's contribution in the 'Foundations of Belief,' I can understand Principal Fairbairn's "deep disappointment" with the volume, and his comparison of the author's method to that of "the blind Samson who sacrificed himself, in order that he might the more effectually bury the Philistines under the ruins of their own temple." As Dr Barry puts it, "Universal doubt, rather than religious dogma, will gain by the stroke that smites Reason to the ground." But, in this respect, the two books do not appear to me to stand upon the same level. It is not without

significance that the title of the first has for its leading
word "doubt," while the leading word of that of the
second is "belief." Although the later volume takes
up into itself the distinctive theses of the earlier,
and elaborates them in some cases with far greater
resources of irony and felicitous illustration (for
example, in Part III. on "Some Causes of Belief"),
the second work is undoubtedly to be understood, in
the main, as the constructive complement of the first.
Its principal line of argument, that from needs to their
satisfaction, is implied in a few phrases in the concluding pages of the 'Defence of Philosophical Doubt';
but it is here developed in such a way as to overshadow,
and, indeed, to place in a new light, the sceptical
argumentation with which it is associated. The first
and the last of the four parts into which the book is
divided are, in this respect, completely new, and could
almost be read—perhaps, I might say, they would retain
their substantive value—without the intervention of
the sceptical analysis contained in Parts II. and III.
At all events, when the argument of the volume is
considered as a whole, and in its logical sequence,
Mr Balfour's "scepticism" is seen to be of a strictly
limited and hypothetical character. If its scope has
been exaggerated, that is largely due to the influence

of an unfortunate terminology. But the majority of the critics, coming to the book with the current idea of the author's position derived from the previous volume, were not prepared to catch the true perspective of the argument. Those parts of it with which they seemed to be already familiar bulked more largely in their eyes than the more fundamental, but perhaps more unassuming, line of thought upon which Mr Balfour here depends for his positive conclusions.

Mr Balfour has himself also partly to blame for the misconception. In the chapters on "Philosophy and Rationalism" and on "Reason and Authority," he has devoted himself, with manifest relish, to the task of exposing the ineptitude of much of the language habitually indulged in by the devotees of pure reason. In this part of the book he has given the reins to his powers of epigram and irony, and he displays an almost wilful pleasure in shocking the reader by the audacity with which he tears to pieces the most respectable commonplaces. The outcome of these chapters, taken by themselves, appears to be a depreciation of reason which verges on cynicism, and a corresponding glorification of authority as the principle of coherence and continuity in human life and society. The very choice of the obnoxious term "authority" to designate the group of causes which Mr Balfour here opposes to "reason" may be looked upon as part of the "delight of battle" which so plainly inspires this section of the book. The defence of authority might have been supposed in these days to be limited to those whom Professor James lately described—with more force than politeness—as "the stall-fed officials of an established Church." Yet, meeting it here in Mr Balfour's pages, the exasperated critics, after the first impulse of indignation, determined that it was the natural and becoming attitude of the Tory leader, and communicated this to the British public as the gist of the book. It has to be added, however, in extenuation of this misapprehension, that the chapters in question are so brilliantly written, and, in spite of apparent paradoxes, so full of the wisdom of life, that they cannot but dwell in the memory of most readers, when they come to give an account of the book.

But for my own part, sorry as I should be to miss these brilliant and suggestive dissertations, taken as such on their own merits, I am so far from regarding them as the essence of the book that, looking merely to the coherence of the main argument, I have sometimes been inclined to echo Dr Barry's complaint that Mr Balfour has interposed these sections "almost wantonly, between his criticism of the Naturalist and his apology for the Theologian." Such a drastic "cut" is, of course, not seriously to be thought of. The author in these chapters unquestionably advances positions which are much too important to be treated merely as incidents; and their elimination would greatly alter the character of the book. I refer especially to the limitation of Reason to conscious ratiocination, and the treatment of Rationalism as undeveloped and inconsequent Naturalism. Both these propositions, if understood in the sense which has been commonly put upon them, appear to me philosophically untenable, as well as inconsistent with Mr Balfour's own argument. But a closer examination of the sections in question, in their relation to the rest of the book, has convinced me that the general impression of their meaning is largely a misapprehension, caused by Mr Balfour's terminology, and that, when taken in their true intention, they bear a much more harmless, indeed, a perfectly defensible, sense. Without proposing to defend his terminology, I am prepared, therefore, to do more justice to the logical sequence of Mr Balfour's thought than is implied in Dr Barry's stricture. But I have no hesitation in saying that *if* it were necessary to put upon these chapters the interpretation put by

Dr Barry and many other critics, it would be impossible to reconcile this part of the book with the constructive philosophy suggested in Part IV. This, as I take it, is the explanation of the divergences of critical opinion, to which reference was made at the outset. Failing to detect the coherence between these two parts of the book, the critic is, in a manner, obliged to choose between them; and, according as he chooses the one or the other, he effects a corresponding change in the centre of gravity of the volume.

A short review of the course of the discussion will, I think, substantiate this view of the true perspective of the argument. It will at the same time furnish evidence of the change which has, to some extent unconsciously, effected itself in Mr Balfour's own position.

The book is divided, it will be remembered, into four parts, called respectively, "Some Consequences of Belief," "Some Reasons for Belief," "Some Causes of Belief," and "Suggestions towards a Provisional Philosophy." Mr Balfour begins, that is to say, by drawing out the implications of Naturalism in the domain of ethics and aesthetics, and exhibiting the general aspect which the world presents according to

" this theory of the non-rational **origin of reason.**" The substance of current **morality, he points** out, **is taken for** granted **by the naturalistic evolutionist, as it is,** curiously **enough, by the** most various **schools of** moralists. **But, in this** case, there **is** a fundamental " incongruity **between the sentiments** subservient to morality and **the** naturalistic **account of their** origin." Nature's **sole aim, according to the theory,** is the survival **of the individual or the race in** the struggle for **existence.** There **can be no** ground, therefore,

for drawing **a** distinction **in favour of any of the processes, physiological or** psychological, **by** which **the individual or the race is** benefited. . . . We **can hardly doubt that the august sentiments** which **cling to the ideas of duty and sacrifice are nothing better than a device of nature to** trick **us into the performance of altruistic actions. . . . It is** because, **in the** struggle **for existence,** the altruistic virtues are an advantage to the **family, the tribe, or the** nation, but not always an **advantage to the individual ; it is** because man comes into **the world richly endowed** with the inheritance of **self-regarding instincts and** appetites required by **his animal progenitors, but poor** indeed in **any** inbred **inclination to the** unselfishness necessary to the wellbeing of **the society in which** he lives ; **it is because in no** other **way can the original impulses be displaced by those of** later **growth to the degree required by public utility, that** Nature, **indifferent to our happiness, indifferent to** our morals, but **sedulous of our survival, commends** disinterested virtue to our practice by decking it out in all the splendour which the specifically ethical sentiments alone are capable of supplying (pp. 16, 17).

In a world, indeed, in which we recognise that "our conduct was determined for us by the distribution of unthinking forces in pre-solar æons," the emotions with which we are wont to contemplate virtuous actions become entirely unmeaning. Moreover, there is the same want of harmony "between the demands of the ethical imagination and what naturalism tells us concerning the final goal of all human endeavour " (p. 26). "We desire, and desire most passionately when we are most ourselves, to give our service to that which is universal and to that which is abiding." But man, according to Naturalism, is "no more than a phenomenon among phenomena, a natural object among other natural objects. His very existence is an accident, his story a brief and transitory episode in the life of one of the meanest of the planets;"[1] and as this lesson is driven home, "we may well feel inclined to ask whether so transitory and unimportant an accident

[1] Did space permit I would fain transcribe the whole of the striking passage in which Mr Balfour depicts the ultimate issue of Naturalism—a passage in which speculative imagination and intense human feeling have combined to add a page of rare and moving eloquence to English literature.

in the general scheme of **things as the** fortunes **of** the **human** race can any longer satisfy aspirations and emotions nourished **upon beliefs in** the Everlasting and the Divine." We may expect, **in short, in the case** of those holding the naturalistic **creed,** " that the more thoroughly **the intellect is saturated with** its essential teaching, the **more** certain are **the** sentiments violently and unnaturally **associated with it to** languish **or to die."**

The obvious objection that among **the** professors of **naturalism** are to be found some of the **most shining** examples of unselfish virtue, **is** met **by the parable of the** parasites. " Biologists tell us of parasites which **live, and can only** live, within **the bodies of animals more highly** organised than they." **Similarly, the** spiritual life of **such men is " sheltered by convictions** which belong not to them but to the society **of** which they form a part; it is nourished **by** processes in which they take **no share." The** argument based upon such examples would not hold, therefore, of a society completely impregnated by naturalistic principles.

But the further and apparently more radical objection **has** been raised, that Mr Balfour has presented **the** world with a caricature of Naturalism, even in its purely theoretical aspect. **He is fighting, it** is said,

with a man of straw, with a bogy of his own creation.
There are no Naturalists, in Mr Balfour's sense of the
term; existing Naturalists would disclaim, with one
accord, the creed which he puts in their mouth. The
disclaimer has, as a matter of fact, been made in many
quarters since the appearance of the volume, with considerable display of indignation; and I think we may
readily admit the sincerity of those who make it,
without concluding, on that account, that Mr Balfour
has been terrifying himself and his readers by a fancy
sketch. Few persons take the trouble to connect their
various opinions into a coherent system of belief;
many points have commonly been left vague, others
have been qualified by inconsistent admissions. Hence
they fail to recognise the lineaments of a system which
they have never consciously surveyed as a whole, much
less embraced, and from which, when stated with rigor-
ous consistency and remorseless clearness, they shrink
with unaffected horror. But this constitutes no im-
peachment of Mr Balfour's method. Only by the
development of a system into all its consequences can
the true features of the system be discerned, and judgment passed upon its adequacy. And, for my own
part, I cannot admit that Mr Balfour's picture is too
highly coloured.

The distinction between **Naturalism and** Science has **also** to be kept carefully **in** view at this point. **Many** critics have fallen intó the mistake of supposing that Mr Balfour **has a quarrel** with Science, **and that his** object is **to discredit its methods and results.** They have accused **him of identifying Naturalism and Science,** of treating **the** former creed **as the** inevitable inference **from scientific facts and theories, and of** attributing **it accordingly to all scientific men.** Many honest **protests have been** made, from the side of **Science, against this** supposed identification. On the other hand, the Naturalists, less ingenuously perhaps, **have** sedulously fostered the same impression. As no one can seriously **hope to** prevail **in** a contest with **Science, they have put it about that the** whole attack is **no more than a display of** dialectic fireworks, of which **nobody is a** penny **the worse.** They have pursued in this their accustomed **tactics; it** has been long their practice to seek shelter behind **the ægis** of Science. But, on the present occasion, **it is not Mr Balfour's** fault if the stratagem succeeds; he has denounced it in advance. In concluding his criticism of " The Philosophic Basis **of** Naturalism," he is at special pains to expose

the speculative, but quite illusory, title by which the empiri**cal school have** endeavoured to associate Naturalism and

Science in a kind of joint supremacy over the thoughts and consciences of mankind. . . . . With empirical philosophy [he says in a characteristic passage], considered as a tentative contribution to the theory of Science, I have no desire to pick a quarrel. That it should fail is nothing; other philosophies have failed. Such is, after all, the common lot. . . . . But that it should develop into Naturalism, and then, on the strength of labours which it has not endured, of victories which it has not won, and of scientific triumphs in which it has no right to share, presume, in spite of its speculative insufficiency, to dictate terms of surrender to every other system of belief, is altogether intolerable. Who would pay the slightest attention to Naturalism if it did not force itself into the retinue of science, assume her livery, and claim, as a kind of poor relation, in some sort to represent her authority and to speak with her voice. Of itself it is nothing. It neither ministers to the needs of mankind, nor does it satisfy their reason (p. 135).

It is not with Science, or with scientific results as such, that Mr Balfour has any quarrel. I do not know any modern philosophical book which indicates more unqualified acceptance of these results, or which is more pervaded by the atmosphere of the most recent science. It is *the naturalistic interpretation of science* which he attacks, the attempt to make Science do duty for philosophy, to substitute the history of a process for a theory of its ultimate ground and source. There is not a proposition of science, even the most materialistic in seeming, which may not be unhesitatingly accepted, if combined with Bacon's acknowledgment of "a divine marshal." And this is a question on which Science, dealing only with secondary causes and the sequences of phenomena, is necessarily dumb.

Having thus in Part I. reduced Naturalism to its essentials, and developed it into its consequences, Mr Balfour proceeds (in Part II.) to examine the philosophic basis of the theory, and the rational justification which it has to offer of its first principles. For such a justification he naturally turns first to empirical philosophy. He begins, however, by remarking most truly upon the comparative neglect by all schools (at least before Kant) of a philosophy of science, or, to put it more broadly, of a theory of knowledge, and in particular upon the tendency of the empirical school to substitute psychology for philosophy—to deal "with the origins of what we believe rather than with its justification." "A full and systematic attempt, first to enumerate, and then to justify, the presuppositions on which all science finally rests, has, it seems to me, still to be made." And he lays down the unquestionably sound position that "no general theory of knowledge has the least chance of being successful, which does not explicitly include within the circuit of its

criticism, not only the beliefs which seem to us to be
dubious, but those also which we hold with the most
perfect practical assurance." "Nothing stands more
in need of demonstration than the obvious."

After effectively contrasting the common-sense view
of the world, based upon the immediate judgments of
perception, with the scientific account of material reality,
and contrasting both with the train of psychical sequences from which they are supposed to be deduced,
he proceeds to apply to empirical philosophy his test
of a satisfactory theory, securely grounded and firmly
concatenated. Does it admit of being stated "as a
series of premisses and conclusions, starting from those
which are axiomatic — *i.e.*, for which proof can be
neither given nor required—and running on through a
continuous series of binding inferences until the whole
of knowledge is caught up and ordered in the meshes of
this all-inclusive dialectic network ?"

The argument proper is compressed here within
small compass, partly because Mr Balfour is able to
refer to his more detailed and technical treatment in
' Philosophic Doubt,' partly because it is, in reality, so
easy to show that Hume's is the only legitimate conclusion that can be drawn from any philosophy "which
depends for its premisses in the last resort upon the

particulars revealed to us in perceptive experience alone." As he pointedly says:—

Nothing in the history of speculation is more astonishing, nothing, if I am to speak my whole mind, is more absurd, than the way in which Hume's philosophic progeny, a most distinguished race, have, in spite of all their differences, yet been able to agree, both that experience is essentially as Hume described it, and that from such an experience can be rationally extracted anything even in the remotest degree resembling the existing system of the natural sciences.

The whole fabric of the sciences depends upon the principle of universal causation, but it is impossible to extract from particular experiences anything more than the habit of expecting

among sequences familiar to us in the petty round of daily life the recurrence of something resembling a former consequent, following on the heels of something resembling a former antecedent. . . . When we come to the more complex phenomena with which we have to deal, the plain lesson taught by personal observation is not the regularity, but the irregularity, of Nature. . . . This apparent irregularity of Nature, obvious enough when we turn our attention to it, escapes our habitual notice, of course, because we invariably attribute the want of observed uniformity to the errors of the observer. And without doubt we do well. But what does this imply? It implies that we bring to the interpretation of our sense-perception the

principle of causation ready-made. It implies that we do
not believe the world to be governed by immutable law,
because our experiences appear to be regular ; but that we
believe that our experiences, in spite of their apparent
irregularity, follow some (perhaps) unknown rule, because
we first believe the world to be governed by immutable law.
*But this is as much as to say that the principle is not proved
by experience, but that experience is understood in the light
of the principle* (pp. 132, 133).

With this important conclusion Mr Balfour passes
to the consideration of "Transcendental Idealism."
This chapter is printed by the author in smaller type
than the rest of the book, and the general reader is
recommended to omit it. I propose on this occasion
to claim the privilege of the general reader for a variety
of reasons. In the first place, the position which Mr
Balfour has himself assigned to it indicates that it
stands to some extent apart from the main argument
of the book, which is intelligible and sufficiently complete without it. Moreover, it is limited, for the most
part, to a criticism of the idealistic theory as it appears
in the works of the late Professor Green. As a matter
of fact, I am in agreement with most of the criticisms
which Mr Balfour here makes upon Green's formulæ.
But the weaknesses of Green's version of idealism
have (thanks largely to Mr Balfour's criticisms of

earlier date) come to be pretty widely acknowledged, even by Idealists themselves, and his specific doctrines do not occupy, therefore, the position of authority in the school which they held when Mr Balfour began to write. It may be said also, that in pressing his critical advantage over Green, Mr Balfour, in this chapter, is disposed to put out of sight the larger aspects of idealism, and to forget the real affinities of the idealistic theory to his own constructive doctrines. I will try to show, before I close, that these affinities have been underestimated, both by Mr Balfour himself and by his idealist critics.

In what follows, we enter upon the most questionable part of Mr Balfour's speculations, a part in which his use of terms has proved, and could hardly fail to prove, misleading. The sections to which I refer, the last two chapters of Part II. and the whole of Part III., begin by drawing from the foregoing investigations the ill-omened, and purely Humian, conclusion that "Certitude is found to be the child, not of reason, but of custom." "If this be true," continues Mr Balfour, "it is plainly a fact of capital importance. It must revolutionise our whole attitude towards the problems presented to us by science, ethics, and theology." Obviously, we must refuse "arbitrarily to erect one department of belief (the scientific) into a lawgiver for all the others."

Here Mr Balfour, for the moment, does not advance beyond the attitude which he inculcated as the " Practical Result" of 'Philosophic Doubt.' Both creeds, he there argued, the creed of Science and the creed of Religion, being equally without rational foundation, it is quite indefensible to make one the norm of the other. Later on in the present volume, Mr Balfour expressly discards the remedy which "consists in simply setting up, side by side with the creed of natural science, another and supplementary set of beliefs which may minister to needs and aspirations which Science cannot meet" (p. 186). He recognises how impossible it is " to acquiesce in this unconsidered division of the 'whole' of knowledge into two or more unconnected fragments" (p. 187), and accepts as a necessary ideal, and one which, at least in part, he attempts himself to realise, "the unification of all belief into an ordered whole, compacted into one coherent structure under the stress of reason " (p. 233). But, in the sections we are considering, he continues to work the earlier sceptical vein. This is exemplified in the account of reason and rationalism which follows, certain passages of which are among the most unguarded in the book, and have given offence in quarters where, it is certain, they were never intended **to do so.** Mr Balfour, it will be remembered, repeatedly connects rationalism and naturalism, treating the latter **as the** logical outcome of the former, the former as merely a half-way house to **the latter,** occupied by thinkers too **timid or too inconsequent to** realise their proper destination. "**Naturalism,"** he says, "**is** the completed **product** of Rationalism" **(p. 173)**; again he speaks of "rationalising **methods and** naturalistic **results" (p. 174);** "Rationalism," **he repeats, "is the high road to** naturalism" (p. 175); "Rationalism **is** Naturalism in **embryo"** (p. 185).

Now if Reason **is used here in** the **large, philosophic** sense **of the word,** and if by Rationalism is understood any system **of** thought which builds unreservedly upon Reason, and involves **no other** organ for the apprehension of truth, **then it must** be admitted that these propositions are **among the most** insidious and subversive which it is possible to conceive. It must have been such statements that Mr Benn had in view when **he** recommended the volume **to** Roman Catholics as bringing water **to** their mill. So interpreted, they would compel us to class the systems of Plato and Aristotle, **Kant and** Hegel, **as** Naturalism in embryo, because they build throughout upon the rational nature of man, without feeling it necessary to invoke, without, indeed, leaving any place for, the supernatural in the ecclesiastical sense of the term. Mr Balfour explains, however, at the outset that he proposes to "employ the word in a much more restricted sense." He will use it, he says, to indicate

a special form of that reaction against dogmatic theology which may be said with sufficient accuracy to have taken its rise in the Renaissance, to have increased in volume during the seventeenth and eighteenth centuries, and to have reached its most complete expression in the Naturalism which has occupied our attention through the first portion of these Notes (p. 168).

Even this definition, as it stands, is too wide, if we are to acquiesce in the censures heaped upon Rationalism, and in the account which Mr Balfour gives of its necessary goal. For the definition would naturally include the whole movement of modern thought— Descartes and Leibniz, as well as Hobbes and Hume, Kant, Fichte, and Hegel, as well as Comte, Mill, and Spencer. And, in that case, it cannot easily be distinguished from similar dicta of Newman and other Catholic theologians. But, in point of fact, Mr Balfour uses the term in a still more special and restricted sense than his own definition might lead us to expect. He understands by it, he says, "a view of the universe based exclusively upon the prevalent mode of interpreting sense-perception" (p. 170); it involves "the assumption that the kind of 'experience' which gave us natural science was the sole basis of knowledge" (p. 171). His definition would therefore apply, at most, to the empirical or sensationalist philosophies; and the course of the discussion makes it plain that he has in view, not so much the systems of philosophers,[1] as the body of thought occupied largely with theological and social discussion, which arrogated to itself, in the second half of the eighteenth century, the prerogatives of reason and common-sense. To this widespread movement in England and Germany — a movement characteristic of the eighteenth century, though doubtless having its origin in an earlier period, and continuing its influence into the present century —the name Rationalism, in a specific sense, is very frequently applied in philosophical and theological writing. It is the period which Hegelian writers commonly designate as that of the *Aufklärung* or Enlightenment. That these are the discussions and

---

[1] "Rationalists," he says, "as such, are not philosophers. . . They judge as men of the world" (p. 171).

this the temper of mind which Mr Balfour intends
to condemn, is proved, to my mind, beyond doubt,
by the chapter on "Rationalist Orthodoxy," which
concludes this part of the book. It has often been
remarked that the orthodox defenders of Christianity
were as completely under the influence of the dominant spirit as its assailants. The presuppositions and
methods of both parties were the same. The attack
was delivered and the defence conducted with the
same weapons. Mr Balfour accordingly turns, in this
chapter, to the defenders of the faith, and condemns
unsparingly the inadequacy both of the systems of
" Natural Religion" and of the "Christian evidences"
which were then so much in vogue. By this method
of treatment, he declares, theology becomes

a mere annex or appendix to Science, a mere footnote to
history. . . . We are no longer dealing with a creed whose
real premisses lie deep in the nature of things. . . . We are
asked to believe the Universe to have been designed by a
Deity for the same sort of reason that we believe Canter-
bury Cathedral to have been designed by an architect; and
to believe in the events narrated in the Gospels for the
same sort of reason that we believe in the murder of Thomas
à Becket (p. 178).

Professor Wallace is one of the critics who censures
most severely Mr Balfour's dealings with Reason and

Rationalism; but in a chapter **of his recent Pro-
legomena** to Hegel's 'Logic,' entitled **"Two Ages of
Reason,"** he comments in a similar strain upon the
period and spirit in question, **and even** while **emphasising the larger** use of Reason, his language **acknowledges** the frequent appropriation of Reason and
Rationalism **(but especially of the latter) in** a narrower
or lower sense:—

The eighteenth century, it has been often said, was **a**
rationalising, unhistorical age. . . . To simplify, to level,
to render intelligible and self-consistent, was the task **of**
enlightenment in dealing with all institutions. **It was**
assumed that the standard of adjudication **was** to **be found**
in the averagely educated and generally cultured **individual**
among the class of more or less "advanced thinkers" **who
asked the** questions and set up the aims. . . . They took
themselves **as the types** of humanity and what *their* under-
standings **found** acceptable they dubbed rational: all else
was **a survival from the** ages of darkness.

But, **in course of time, he proceeds,**

it was made apparent that intelligence, with its hard-and-fast
formulæ, its logical principles, its keen analysis, was not deep
enough or wide enough to justify its claim to the august title
of reason. . . . There are more things in heaven and earth
than are heard of in the philosophy of the logical intellect.

This phrase, "the logical intellect," or, as he elsewhere
varies **it, the** "merely intellectual and abstract in-

telligence," exactly covers the old Rationalism which Mr Balfour attacks. Professor Wallace contrasts it with " the Reason of German Idealism," which he describes as "intelligence charged with emotion, full of reverence, reverent above all to the majesty of that divinity which, much disguised and weather-beaten, like Glaucus of the sea, resides in common and natural humanity." But these words might have been written as a description of the provisional philosophy which Mr Balfour sketches in his concluding chapters, and proposes to substitute for Naturalism and abstract Rationalism. They dwell, at any rate, with felicitous emphasis on its leading characteristics; and, on this showing, Mr Balfour's 'Suggestions,' no less than German Idealism, might fairly be styled a doctrine of the larger Reason.

In the substance of his contention, therefore, Mr Balfour may claim to have powerful philosophical support from a quarter sufficiently free from the suspicion of clericalism or supernaturalism; and even his terminology, when examined, is found not to stray so far from common usage. Rationalism is, I think, most commonly used in the hard and narrow sense he attributes to it. At the same time, the usage is undeniably open to misconception; and it was a thousand pities that it was not more carefully fenced about with explanation. Moreover, what a **man** may safely do often depends on **his own past record.** Mr Balfour's antecedent reputation for scepticism (**not** undeserved, as we saw) **made it almost certain that, in** his **case,** an attack on Rationalism **would be** interpreted **in the** worst **sense.** And when to this was added the glorification of **authority at the** expense **of** reason, in **the** chapters which immediately follow, this interpretation became inevitable.

The dissertation on Authority **and Reason may be** best understood as a supplement **to the criticism of** Rationalism which precedes **it.** After denying the competency **of the logical** intellect **to solve the philosophical**· **problem,** Mr Balfour proceeds **to show, by reference to everyday** experience, how few human beliefs **have been** reached by a conscious process of ratiocination **in the minds of the** individuals who hold them. He amplifies, that **is to say,** the Humian dictum **quoted** above, that certitude **is the** child not of reason **but** of custom. The vast majority **of** our beliefs, of our ethical, social, and religious beliefs in particular, are **in this sense** without a logical substructure; they **have been** generated in the individual by "custom, **education, public opinion,** the contagious convictions

of countrymen, family, party, or Church." Immense
tracts of human life thus lie apparently altogether outside the purview of the abstract reason; indeed, so
far from the mass of our fundamental beliefs de-
pending on the reasoned assent of the individuals
who entertain them, we know from history that
when men do begin to analyse their beliefs and
usages, their abstract theorising is apt to be purely
disintegrative in its tendency. Stated in this form,
Mr Balfour's contention is so obviously true that it
is difficult to imagine any one dissenting from it. But
he has chosen to express his meaning by opposing
Authority to Reason, and contrasting its beneficent
and all - pervading influence with "the comparative
pettiness of the *rôle* played by reasoning in human
affairs."

To Reason we are in some measure beholden, though
not, perhaps, so much as we suppose, for hourly aid in
managing so much of the trifling portion of our personal
affairs intrusted to ourselves by nature as we do not happen
to have already surrendered to the control of habit. By
reason also is directed, or misdirected, the public policy of
communities within the narrow limits of deviation permitted by accepted custom and tradition. . . . (But) if
we are to judge with equity between these rival claimants,
we must not forget that it is Authority rather than Reason
to which, in the main, we owe, not religion only, but ethics

and politics; that it is Authority which supplies us with
essential elements in the premisses of science; that it is
Authority rather than Reason which lays deep the foundations of social life; that it is Authority rather than
Reason which cements its superstructure (pp. 227-229).

Mr Balfour must have foreseen that round phrases
like these there would gather at once a hubbub of
excited and ill-informed controversy; and the love of
mischief would seem to have had some share in prompting their use. Both the terms are, in this respect,
unfortunate. In the case of "Reason," Mr Balfour
remarks, in a note, that the term is used "in its
ordinary and popular, not in its transcendental sense;
there is no question here of the Logos, or Absolute
Reason"; and the course of the discussion makes it
plain that he uses it as strictly equivalent to "reasoning," or conscious logical ratiocination. The two terms,
"reason" and "reasoning," sometimes cross and recross
one another several times in the course of the same page,
with no distinction between them. Now, this usage is
no doubt common among the older English thinkers;
but it is certainly not the ordinary sense of the term
in recent philosophic writing. Reason, if it does not
always explicitly convey a larger meaning, at least
constantly tends to assume that sense, and by no

means only with thinkers of a transcendental cast. Mr Balfour himself speaks of Naturalism as deposing "Reason from its ancient position as the ground of all existence" (p. 75); he speaks of Reason as "the roof and crown of things"—of the universe as "the creation of Reason" (p. 72), and of all things as working together "towards a reasonable end" (p. 83). Clearly, when he uses these expressions, he has something more in view than the "intellect," or "discursive reason," which is only "permitted to have a hand in the simplest jobs" (p. 72). It is the limited range of the latter which he intends to contrast with the omnipresent action of authority; but by insisting, as he does repeatedly, on the "non-rational" character of the causes which he groups under that name, he conveys the impression that they have no relation to Reason in the larger sense—that they are really what he calls in one place "utterances of unreason."

Then, again, the use of the term Authority in this connection has even less excuse. It has no justification in ordinary usage; on the contrary, owing to the fixed associations of the word, it is a use which *invites* misconception. What are the causes which Mr Balfour groups under this head? He enumerates them variously, but they include "custom, education, public opinion" (p. 213), "the contagious convictions of countrymen, family, party, or Church," and, not least, "the spirit of the age," producing a certain "psychological 'atmosphere,' or 'climate,' favourable to the life of certain modes of belief, unfavourable, and even fatal, to the life of others" (p. 206). Habit, in the management of our personal affairs, is also contrasted with Reason, as we have seen, in the same way as "accepted custom and tradition," in the direction of the public policy of communities; and both are apparently included under the head of authority. "Authority," he says in the passage which most nearly approaches to a definition—"Authority, as I have been using the term, is in all cases contrasted with Reason, and stands for that group of non-rational causes, moral, social, and educational, which produces its results by psychic processes other than reasoning" (p. 219). This appears to me to involve a complete departure from ordinary usage. Newman, it is true, gives a similar extension to the term in a note to his 'Apologia,' but he acknowledges that he is using the word "in a broad sense"; and even there the reference seems to be, not to *the unconscious action* of the forces referred to, but to the conscious use of them as sanctions. Certainly in ordinary usage the term is limited — conveniently

and intelligibly limited—to the conscious adoption by
the individual of the beliefs of some other person, or
of some historical organisation, without personal examination of the beliefs in question. Mr Balfour refers
to this usage, which he distinguishes from his own.
He rightly points out that in this sense Authority
"becomes a species of Reason," but a reason which
can in no case furnish us with the *foundation* for a
system of belief, seeing that there is always involved
a prior reason for submitting individual belief and
conduct to the particular authority in question. But
however inconsistent it may be to appeal to Authority
as a logical foundation for a system of beliefs, the fact
remains that the term Authority has been appropriated,
by almost universal usage, to designate this attitude of
conscious submission on the part of the individual
reasoner; and Mr Balfour can hardly fail, therefore,
to be misunderstood when he uses it in a sense so
widely different. He uses it to cover the manifold
forces that unconsciously mould the belief and conduct of the individual,—his own training in the past,
his social environment, the historic life of the community and the race to which he belongs—above all,
the influence of history. As it is put by a German
reviewer, otherwise sympathetic, who objects to the

misleading implications of the term Authority : " What Mr Balfour says may all be covered by the proposition that we men, in our higher spiritual life, are the **products** of history before we are **its** producers, and that in this double relation of ours to history the weight is permanently **to be placed upon the** first member, upon our dependence **on the** historical factors which surround and determine us." [1]

But if this **is** so, **it** disposes at once of the absolute opposition supposed to exist between **these two groups** of causes. Habits are, as it were, **the deposits of** reason. An action is first performed **consciously,** with minute supervision of every step or detail; but, according to the beneficent provision of nature, **the** action goes more smoothly the oftener it is repeated, and the active supervision of consciousness is no longer required. **The action** has become habitual, and the higher energies of the living creature are set at liberty for the performance **of** new tasks, the acquirement of other dexterities. This applies to the humblest bodily exercises; but we have only to recall Aristotle's definition of virtue as a habit, to recognise that **it** holds equally **in the** highest reaches **of** the ethical life. Habit, being thus the creation of reason, cannot be

---

[1] Professor Kaftan in the ' Preussische Jahrbücher,' vol. lxxxii.

opposed to it as an alien force. And the same is true of custom, tradition, public opinion, the spirit of the age. They are non-rational, certainly, in the sense that their determining influence over the individual does not depend on a conscious process of ratiocination on his part—a progress from premisses to conclusion. But customs and institutions are themselves originally the product of the conscious activities of human beings. They constitute, in their first intention, the objective realisation of a rational system; and so long as they continue to hold society together at all, they still are this in their degree. Doubtless, no customs or institutions are the adequate or final embodiment of Reason; and hence they are subject to progressive modification, or, if you like, rationalisation. In this way, the old comes to be opposed to the new, and to be regarded as a mere obstruction on the path of Reason. But tradition and custom are opposed to Reason, only as the good is opposed to the better. They have their birth from Reason originally, and they continue throughout accessible to its transforming influence.

In fact, it does not seem too much to say that Mr Balfour, continuing in these chapters his attack upon the abstract, or, as he afterwards calls it, the "un-assisted Reason" of the rationalists, is really vindicating, in his own way, that larger sense of Reason, characteristic of the present century, which recognises that thought becomes formal and empty, just in proportion as it cuts itself adrift from the historical development of mankind. To take only the case of ethics, the advance of historical study has long lifted us above the notion of an abstract conscience, promulgating to all men the same perfect moral law. The content of the moral law grows every way from age to age. The progress of man upwards, from "the ape and tiger" to the civilisation of the present day with its altruistic and humanitarian ideals—this whole ethical process with the customs and institutions in which it embodies itself, its laws, its public opinion, its shifting but ever deepening and widening ideals of honour and chivalry, of heroism or saintly life, of justice and self-control— all this development can only be rightly understood when regarded as the progressive revelation from within of an ideal of goodness, which in itself is the most real of realities. From this development we derive the substance of the ethical code. If, like Kant, we neglect to root the individual in the corporate life of humanity, the categorical imperative remains a form void of specific content—a command which refuses to translate itself into any concrete duty.

In ethics, as in other spheres, the advance of speculative thought since Kant has mainly consisted in surmounting the abstract and unhistoric individualism of preceding philosophy. Hence, as Professor Wallace eloquently puts it, in its modern conception, "Philosophy is not the work of abstract or 'unassisted' Reason. The pure reason of philosophers is a reason which has been purified of dross, corruption, and sluggishness by the discipline of the sciences, by the heroism and conscientiousness of religion, by the fair and noble intuitions of art; otherwise it is little worth."[1]

To this view of Reason, to this interpretation of the historical process, Mr Balfour seems to be working his way, even in those sections which appear at first sight, owing to their unfortunate terminology, most uncompromisingly opposed to it. The sheer distinction between Reason and Authority, or, as we may agree to put it, between Reason and History, is not in the end adopted as true. It is employed as a weapon with which to destroy Naturalism and the barren Rationalism whose offspring Naturalism is represented as being. It is in this sense an *argumentum ad hominem*. If we limit reason to the discursive intellect in its conscious

---

[1] 'Fortnightly Review,' April 1895.

exercise, *and if we refuse to take a theistic* **view** *of man and the world,* then undoubtedly the beliefs **and prac-** tices which fill out **our** life must appear as the **products of** non-rational causes, just as our existence as living and conscious **beings is itself, on these terms, the** outcome **of unreasoning material** forces. But the whole **aim of the demonstration is to** impress upon the **reader the necessity of the** theistic postulate. **That this is the real significance of Mr** Balfour's argument, **and the** true place **of this** discussion **in** the sequence of his thought, is proved **by the** account he gives of it himself, in retrospect, in **his concluding** chapter. The fundamental difficulty **of Naturalism,** he says, the difficulty the book **is designed to press** home, is

the ineffaceable **incongruity between the origin of** our beliefs, so far **as these can be revealed to us by** Science, and the beliefs themselves. **This it was that, as** I showed in the first part of this Essay, touched **with** the frost of scepticism **our** ideals of conduct and our **ideals of** beauty. This it was that, as I showed in **the** Second Part, cut down scientific philosophy **to the root.** And all the later discussions with **which I have** occupied the attention of the reader, serve but **to** emphasise afresh the inextricable confusion which the naturalistic hypothesis introduces **into** every department of **speculation and** practice, *by refusing to allow us to penetrate beyond the phenomenal causes,* **by** *which, in the order of*

Nature, our beliefs are produced. . . . When once we have
realised the scientific truth that at the root of every rational
process lies an irrational one; that reason, from a scientific
point of view, is itself a natural product; and that the
whole material on which it works is due to causes, physical,
physiological, and social, which it neither creates nor con-
trols, we shall be driven in mere self-defence to hold that,
behind these non-rational forces, and above them, guiding
them by slow degrees, and, as it were, with difficulty, to a
rational issue, stands that Supreme Reason in whom we
must thus believe, if we are to believe in anything (pp.
321-323).

The last sentences carry us already far into the
heart of **Part IV.**, in which the author passes from
criticism to the more difficult task of construction. If
the preconception of Mr Balfour's misology and scepticism still lingers in any reader's mind, it should be
effectually dispelled by his language here. He expressly denies "that the object aimed at in preceding
discussions is to discredit reason" (p. 246), and declares
that "the unification of all belief into an ordered whole
compacted into one coherent structure under the stress
of reason is an ideal which we can never abandon"
(p. 233). But, as he truly adds, "Reason is not
honoured by pretending that she has done what, as
a matter of fact, is still undone"; "the best system
we can hope to construct will suffer from gaps and

rents, from loose ends and ragged edges. It does not, however, follow from this that it will be without a high degree of value."

If we have to submit, as I think we must, to *an incomplete rationalisation of belief*, this ought not to be because, in a fit of intellectual despair, we are driven to treat Reason as an illusion; nor yet because we have deliberately resolved to transfer our allegiance to irrational or non-rational inclination; but because Reason itself assures us that such a course is, at the lowest, the least irrational one open to us (p. 234).

What is this but an acknowledgment in fitting terms of the incompleteness and imperfection of any finite synthesis? I do not understand, and I do not envy, the state of mind of the thinker who is not prepared to make a similar confession.

Proceeding, then, to "rationalise," to "unify," or "co-ordinate," as far as may be, our various beliefs, Mr Balfour begins by setting the Naturalistic theory aside as inherently irrational. Naturalism had been condemned, in the first part of the volume, because it did not satisfy the demands of our ethical nature. He here pronounces more generally that, inasmuch as the Whole of which we desire a reasoned knowledge includes human consciousness as an element, we must refuse to "regard any system which, like Naturalism, leaves large tracts and aspects of that consciousness unaccounted for and derelict as other than, to that extent at least, irrational" (p. 250). Moreover, it was shown in Part II. that the body of beliefs about the material world which we take for granted in ordinary experience, and which science presents us with in an elaborated form, cannot themselves be exhibited as a series of logical conclusions for which the particulars of sense furnish the premisses. It had to be regarded rather as an assumption which we found it necessary to make in practical life; as Mr Balfour here expresses himself, it is essentially the satisfaction of a need. Doubtless the belief in question possesses an "inevitable" and "coercive" character not shared by other beliefs; but that constitutes no logical justification for erecting the judgments of sense-perception into a norm or standard, by which all other beliefs must be judged. To do so would be to substitute "psychological compulsion for rational necessity." Universality and necessity, as here exemplified, may be "marks of the elementary and primitive character of the beliefs," but hardly "badges of pre-eminence." It is the plain dictate of reason that our scheme, "though it be founded on the last resort upon our needs, shall at least take account of other needs than those we share **with our brute progenitors."** And on this point Mr Balfour **appeals to** the example of the great masters **of** speculation.

Though they have **not, it may be,** succeeded in supplying us with a satisfactory **explanation of the** Universe, at least the Universe **which they have sought to explain** has been something more **than a mere collection of** hypostatised sense-perceptions, **packed side by side in** space, and following **each other with blind uniformity** in time (p. 243).

The argument from needs **to their satisfaction, here** generalised, is the constructive principle **on which Mr** Balfour depends, and **furnishes,** I think, the **key to a** true understanding of **the** book. The **author** himself **recognises that the** argument **is one which** requires **to be applied with** great caution, if the **wish is not to be** father **to the thought; and** he apparently **lays no stress on this particular way of** formulating it.

Whether this **correspondence is best** described as that which obtains between **a "need" and its** "satisfaction," **may** be open **to** question. **But, at all** events, let it be understood that if the relation described is, on the one **side,** something different from that between a premiss **and** its conclusion, **so, on** the other, it is intended **to be** equally remote from that between a desire and its fulfilment. **That** it has not the logical validity of **the** first, I have already admitted, or rather asserted. That **it** has not **the** casual, wavering, and purely "subjective" character of the second,

is not less true. For the correspondence postulated is not
between the fleeting fancies of the individual and the
immutable verities of an unseen world, but between these
characteristics of our nature which we recognise as that in
us which, though not necessarily the strongest, is the highest;
which, though not always the most universal, is nevertheless the best (pp. 247, 248).

Instead of further abstract debate as to the scope and
legitimacy of the argument, let us see how Mr Balfour
applies it. Its true nature will be best shown by the
concrete examples of its use, and we shall then be
better able to form a judgment as to its legitimacy.
It is first applied, in the intellectual sphere, to demon-
strate the implications or presuppositions of the scientific
view itself, or of the mere fact that we know. Mr
Balfour had already pointed out, in dealing with our
belief in the uniformity of nature, that this belief cannot be *proved* by the facts, seeing that it is a postulate
implied in the very idea of investigating facts. In
these constructive chapters, he amplifies this thought
in a remarkably fresh and striking way. After
dealing instructively with some of the usual arguments
for Theism, he proceeds to push the question a stage
further back. But "something may also be inferred
from the mere fact that we know, a fact which, like
every other, has to be accounted for." And after some

luminous pages, in which he presses home the fundamental inconsequence of Naturalism, in requiring us "to accept a system as rational, one of whose doctrines is that the system itself is the product of causes which have no tendency to truth rather than falsehood, or to falsehood rather than truth,"[1] he concludes: "I do not believe that any escape from these perplexities is possible, unless we are prepared to bring to the study of the world the presupposition that it was the work of a rational Being, who made it intelligible, and at the same time made us, in however feeble a fashion, able to understand it" (p. 301). Theism is thus a "presupposition," "not only tolerated but actually required by Science" (p. 321). It is "forced upon us by the single assumption that Science is not an illusion." As he put it before, we are "driven in mere self-defence" to the belief in a Supreme Reason directing the apparently non-rational forces of nature; we "must" believe in Supreme Reason, "if we are to believe in anything." But this admission, if once made, cannot stand alone. If we "postulate a rational God in the interests of Science, we can scarcely de-

---

[1] One might say, indeed, that the very notion of truth is an inexplicable excrescence or inconsequence in a world where everything simply is or happens.

cline to postulate a moral God in the interests of Morality." And, in the light of this presupposition, the whole process by which the ethical code and the moral sentiments have been slowly developed appears in a different setting, as "an instrument for carrying out a divine purpose," as a divine education of the human race.

Such, without following them into details, are the important conclusions which Mr Balfour reaches by the method of argument he follows. When they are thus stated summarily, and detached from some of the discussions which accompany them, the philosophical student can hardly fail to remark the striking resemblance of Mr Balfour's mode of argument to the transcendental method of Kant, and the affinity of his conclusions to those of Kant's idealistic successors. In saying this, it is far from my intention to depreciate the freshness and independence of Mr Balfour's treatment; on the contrary, he has, I think, accomplished a remarkable feat in working his way from a different starting-point, and to a large extent by a different route, to this fundamental argument. And he has made it doubly his own by clothing it in pellucid English, which he who runs may read. It is the transcendental argument stated with a luminous simplicity, **as it** might have been stated by Hume, had **he** returned in maturer life to the metaphysical meditations of his youth. But the argument itself **is in** substance identical with that which Kant patiently dug from the *débris* of rationalism, and built into **a** system, **so** palpably artificial **in** its details and so cumbrously **pedantic in** its terminology, that the philosophical world has been engaged ever since in quarrelling over its interpretation. When we penetrate beneath the portentous phrases to the comparatively humble truth which they labour **to** express, Kant's "objective unity of apperception," **as** the supreme condition of the possibility of experience, is simply the assertion that the idea of "a nature" **or a rational system is not** a conclusion from particular facts, but is **involved, as** a postulate or presupposition, **in** there being **any** experience of facts at all. And when, at the close **of his** investigation, he emphasises the adaptation of phenomena to our faculty of cognition, as proof of a harmony between sense and understanding, that is to say, ultimately, a harmony between the world and the mind; when he argues that this adaptation justifies us in treating reality as everywhere rationalisable, and therefore *as if* it were the product of a supreme reason; this, in more scholastic form, and with Kant's well-known reservation as to the merely regulative character of the Ideas of Reason, is neither more nor less than the argument *from the mere fact that we know*. But to colligate Kant's different statements, and to disengage what is central and vital in his argument from its perplexing and useless integuments, is a task which demands both philosophical and exegetical skill. The English world has as yet failed, for the most part, to grasp Kant's way of putting this argument; we shall be curious to see whether it proves more accessible to Mr Balfour's presentation of it.

Mr Balfour himself does not seem to be aware how closely the general attitude of mind he recommends in Part IV. corresponds to the transcendental proof from the possibility of experience. In the earlier part of his work, he emphasises the impossibility of reaching a satisfactory foundation by means of "inferences of the ordinary pattern" (p. 186). He recognises that, in his own argument, the relation between needs and their satisfaction is "something different from that between a premiss and a conclusion" (p. 248); and at the close of the theistic argument which we have just examined (from the mere fact that we know), he seems to hesitate whether the term *proof* can be properly applied to it. "Theism," he says, "whether or not it can in the strict meaning of the word be described as proved by Science, is a principle which Science . . . requires for its own completion. . . . Our knowledge of that system is inexplicable unless we assume for it a rational Author" (p. 302). In such passages, it seems almost as if the writer were feeling his way to a new point of view, and were hardly aware of the strength of his own method. It is unduly to disparage the nature of his argument to contrast it with logical procedure, or to hesitate to call it a proof. It implies, certainly, the abandonment of the old ideal of a philosophical system, "as a series of premisses and conclusions, starting from those which are axiomatic—*i.e.*, for which proof can neither be given nor required, and running on through a continuous series of binding inferences, until the whole of knowledge is caught up and ordered in the meshes of this all-inclusive dialectic network" (p. 105). If by premisses, in other words, we understand either isolated intuitions or the particulars of sense, then it may be said that the transcendental argument neither starts from premisses nor arrives at a conclusion. Yet, in a more vital sense, experience itself, as a concrete fact demanding explanation, constitutes the premiss from which we advance (or rather regress) to its implied condition or explaining cause. The postulate or presupposition thus reached is, from one point of view, a conclusion; from another, it is the ultimate premiss on which all our conclusions in a certain department— or, in this case, all conclusions whatever—depend. If we can speak, as Mr Balfour himself does, of the presupposition as "actually required by science," as "forced upon us by the mere assumption that Science is not an illusion"—as a necessary assumption, "if we are to believe in anything"—then it seems to me a merely technical question, whether we agree to call the process of reaching it an inference or not. We have, at all events, the element of logical necessity in its most unequivocal form.

The Kantian terms, postulates, presuppositions (implications also, I think) are used from time to time by Mr Balfour, either as nouns or verbs. As a general term, postulate seems to me much the best. Need and satisfaction are probably words of too everyday a character to express a fundamental speculative position; they are too coloured by the associations of life to express a philosophical meaning with precision. No doubt the word "need" often appeals to us, just by its breadth and simplicity, and in some connections no word would seem so appropriate. But to many it seems little more than a glorified wish; and although this is **unjust,** it cannot be denied that the associations of **the** word are too predominantly emotional. Now when we speak even of ethical or religious needs, it is not only the emotional disappointment, the collapse **of** hope and joy, **that** is referred to, but **the fact that** the denial of the postulated reality inverts the whole proportions **of** our life, irrationalises the whole scheme of things presupposed **by** our ordinary experience. **The** word postulate seems to express admirably both **this** element of intellectual necessity in the argument, and, at the same time, the subjective element, which is undoubtedly also present. For universal scepticism admits of no refutation; a man must admit certain aspects **of** experience before any argument **can be** founded upon **them.**

But no **nice question** of terminology need affect our sense of the **importance** and fundamental truth of the argument itself. **The** acknowledgment of rational necessity which **it** involves — rather, I should say, the insistence on rational **necessity** — constitutes the advance **in Mr** Balfour's thought **on** which **I** have desired to lay stress. Although at times his phraseology may waver, and we may catch the echo of passages in 'Philosophic Doubt' **which** identify **"needs" with** "non-rational impulses," yet, on the

whole, the difference of tone is marked. The needs
are here presented as the needs of reason itself. In
the case of the intellectual argument, this may perhaps
be allowed to be obvious. But it is no less so in
the case of the ethical. Whereas he had formerly
said—"I and an indefinite number of other persons
feel a practical need for [ethical and religious beliefs],
but no legitimate argument can be founded on the
mere existence of this need or impulse. We are on
this matter, unfortunately, altogether outside the sphere
of Reason,"—he now condemns the Naturalistic theory
as " irrational," and claims that his own is founded on
" the plain dictates of reason." From the former
standpoint, argument is impossible, and is admitted
to be so; but in the present volume we are no longer
"outside the sphere of Reason." The whole scheme
of construction implies that we have passed from
" psychological compulsion" to " rational necessity."
Mr Balfour may be said to be trying, throughout the
volume, to establish a definition of truth or of Reason
which shall be at once more comprehensive and more
self-consistent than that which limits it to the facts
and laws of physical Science. The truth, if fully
known, must include, he argues, a satisfactory explanation of our ethical, æsthetical, and religious ideas

and sentiments. The self-styled truth that fails to do this is a fragment which men have mistaken for the whole—a fragment, moreover, which cannot even supply its own foundation. Such a system arrogates to itself unjustly the august name of truth, for truth cannot land us in an open contradiction between equally fundamental constituents of our nature. But if this is so, the appeal of the volume is not from truth to authority but from a partial to a fuller truth, from man conceived as mere abstract intellect to human nature as a whole.

In his method, as I have said, Mr Balfour resembles Kant, and, like Kant, he passes from the intellectual to the ethical domain. But, in his conclusions, he approaches more nearly the general position of Hegel. In the metaphysical application of his thought, he enforces the dependence of the subjective reason of the individual on the objective reason of the historic process, and recognises a cosmic or Absolute Reason as the ground of the whole development. What distinguishes all three alike is (in one way of putting it) the unwavering humanism of their point of view, as opposed to the naturalism of those who would crush the spirit of man by thrusting upon it the immensities of physical nature, of infinite space and endless time.

Mr Balfour, in some searching pages, has exposed the fallacy of such a mode of argument: material grandeur and moral excellences, as he well says, are incommensurable quantities. And in the age-long debate which has divided thinkers since the time of Democritus and Plato, this has been the essential import of all the great idealistic systems — πάντων χρημάτων μέτρον ἄνθρωπος. This thesis, first formulated by scepticism, is in point of fact, when properly interpreted, profoundly true. Our own nature is, from the very circumstances of the case, the only measuring-rod which we can apply to the universe. "A harmony of some sort between our inner selves and the universe of which we form a part is a tacit postulate," as Mr Balfour says, "of every belief we entertain about phenomena." Our intellect is, after all, as much *ours* as any other part of our being, and in accepting the account of science as true, the Naturalist is involuntarily postulating harmony, to that extent, between himself and the universe. But why should this harmony be limited to the intellectual activities of sense-perception? It is impossible to show that this limitation is other than arbitrary, and that we have not as good a right to use as our touchstone of reality those inspirations of goodness which are the spur of all our endeavour, and those visions of beauty and of harmonious truth which are a master-light of all our seeing. Man must be anthropomorphic. What we ask is simply that his anthropomorphism shall be deliberate, consistent, and critical, instead of being unconscious, partial, and arbitrary.

But if, in these latter remarks, I have emphasised the affinity of Mr Balfour's thought to these systems of the larger Reason of which Hegel's is the most convenient example, the affinity is obviously not to be understood in any narrow or rigid sense. His whole intellectual temper is different; some might say it is more sceptical, others might say it is more human, by which I mean more cognisant of the limitations of humanity. There is one important Hegelian doctrine at least with which Mr Balfour is strenuously at one—the doctrine of "degrees of truth,"—the insight that all truth is a matter of approximation, that no error is wholly false and no finite truth is wholly true. This doctrine, recently re-expounded by Mr Bradley with so much force, is an integral part of Hegelian thought, but a part strangely forgotten in the claim of the system to represent absolute truth, to be indeed the insight of the Absolute Being into his own essence and history. The temper of Mr Balfour's book is

well exhibited by contrast in a characteristic passage,
with which this long review may fitly close :—

I like to think of the human race, from whatever stock
its members may have sprung, in whatever age they may be
born, whatever creed they may profess, together in the
presence of the One Reality, engaged not wholly in vain, in
spelling out some fragments of its message.   All share its
being; to none are its oracles wholly dumb.   And if, both
in the natural world and in the spiritual, the advancement
we have made on our forefathers be so great that our interpretation seems indefinitely removed from that which
primitive man could alone apprehend, and wherewith he
had to be content, it may be, indeed I think it is, the case
that our approximate guesses are closer to his than they
are to their common Object, and that, far as we seem to
have travelled, yet, measured on the celestial scale, our
intellectual progress is scarcely to be discerned, so minute is
the parallax of Infinite Truth.

NOTE A.

THE USE OF THE TERM "NATURALISM."

ONE of the results of Mr Balfour's 'Foundations of Belief' has been to bring to light some serious, and even remarkable, divergences of view as to the meaning and precise application of current philosophical terms. This was particularly the case in regard to the term Naturalism, which is so prominent in Mr Balfour's argument. Much of the criticism of the book took, in fact, the form of an indignant repudiation of the author's use of names. It may perhaps, therefore, contribute to the fixing of philosophical usage in this case, and in the case of some other terms frequently conjoined with it, if, starting from Mr Balfour's definitions, we examine his usage in the light of some of the chief objections taken to it.

In his introductory chapter, Mr Balfour thus indi-

T

cates the system of thought against which his book is directed :—

Whatever the name selected, the thing itself is sufficiently easy to describe. For its leading doctrines are that
we may know phenomena and the laws by which they
are connected but nothing more. "More" there may or
may not be, but if it exists we can never apprehend it;
and whatever the World may be "in its reality" (supposing such an expression to be otherwise than meaningless),
the World for us, the World with which alone we are concerned, or of which we alone can have any cognisance, is that
World which is revealed to us through perception, and which
is the subject-matter of the Natural Sciences. Here, and
here only, are we on firm ground. Here, and here only,
can we discover anything which deserves to be described
as Knowledge. Here, and here only, may we profitably
exercise our reason or gather the fruits of Wisdom (p. 7).

In another passage he speaks of "the two elements
composing the naturalistic creed: the one *positive*, consisting, broadly speaking, of the teaching contained in
the general body of the natural sciences; the other
negative, expressed in the doctrine that beyond these
limits, wherever they may happen to lie, nothing is,
and nothing can be, known" (p. 92); and again of "the
assumption that the kind of 'experience' which gave
us natural science was the sole basis of knowledge,"
and "the further inference that nothing deserved to be

called Knowledge which did not come within the circle of the natural sciences" (p. 171). "After all," he says in another place, "Naturalism is nothing more than the assertion that empirical methods are valid and that no others are so" (p. 134). In these passages the theory is defined by reference to its presuppositions or method; when we look at the resulting body of doctrine, we find that the theory attempts "the impossible task of extracting reason from unreason" (p. 301). It involves the

deposition of Reason from its ancient position as the ground of all existence to that of an expedient among other expedients for the maintenance of organic life; an expedient, moreover, which is temporary in its character and insignificant in its effects. An irrational Universe which accidentally turns out a few reasoning animals at one corner of it, as a rich man may experiment at one end of his park with some curious "sport" accidentally produced among his flocks and herds, is a Universe which we might well despise, if we did not ourselves share its degradation (p. 75).

And, finally, the naturalistic catechism which he elaborates at the conclusion of the first part of the volume clearly identifies Naturalism with consistent Materialism (pp. 83-85).

To the system whose substantive doctrines he thus

indicates, Mr Balfour applies throughout his volume
the term Naturalism. "Agnosticism, Positivism, Empiricism," he says, "have all been used more or less
correctly to describe this scheme of thought, though
in the following pages, for reasons with which it is
not necessary to trouble the reader, the term which
I shall commonly employ is Naturalism." This passage and the usage it indicates have called forth emphatic disclaimers from the patrons or representatives
of the views which are here practically identified.
Each objects to be identified with any of the others,
and they all disclaim responsibility for the system of
doctrines attributed to them in common. Professor
Huxley, not unnaturally jealous for the honour of the
term which he invented, objected "to making Agnosticism the scapegoat, on whose head the philosophic
sins of the companions with whom it is improperly
associated may be conveniently piled up"; while Mr
Frederic Harrison, as a Positivist, is still more wroth
to find himself identified with the Agnostics, against
whom he has so often gone forth to war in the Reviews. "The passage just quoted," he says, "is a
coagulated clot of confusion and misstatement"—from
which it is easy to see that Mr Harrison is very
angry indeed. Professor Wallace, on the other hand,

though himself accepting in the main an **Idealism of the** Hegelian type, puts a **lance in rest for Naturalism, which he seems to** think has been hardly treated in being identified with **its own extreme consequences.** " Its faults," he **says, "spring from a creditable motive. It** is the **desire to be honest, to** say only **what you** can **prove, to require thorough** continuity and **consistency in the** whole realm **of accepted truths.**[1] **Naturalism was a reaction from the** follies of **Super-naturalism."**

Naturalism [he says again] **was at the outset and in essence** a negation, not of **the supernatural in general,** but of a supernatural conceived as incoherent, arbitrary, and chaotic ; a protest **against a conception** which separated **God from** the **world, as a** potter from his clay, against **the** *ignava ratio* **which took** customary sequences of events as needing

---

[1] **I cannot help remarking** the striking similarity between this account of **Naturalism and Professor** Huxley's truly extraordinary definition of Agnosticism as consisting essentially " in the application of a single principle, which is **the** fundamental axiom of modern science. Positively, this principle **may be** thus expressed : in matters of the intellect, follow your reason **as far** as it will take you, without **regard** to **any other** consideration. And negatively : in matters of **the** intellect, **do not** pretend that conclusions are certain which are not demonstrated **or** demonstrable." On this showing, **we** should all **desire** with **one accord** to take service under the Agnostic flag, for Agnosticism, so defined, is another name for intellectual honesty. Similarly, on **Professor** Wallace's **showing,** no self-respecting person **would permit himself to be called** anything but a Naturalist.

no explanation, and looked for special revelation from por-
tents and wonders.[1]

Understanding Supernaturalism in this sense, Professor
Wallace regrets "that some recognition of the inner
aims of Rationalism and Naturalism is not vouchsafed,"
and he would evidently prefer to rehabilitate the term
Naturalism and follow that banner, rather than be
suspected of any complicity with a discredited Supernaturalism. To this Mr Balfour might easily retort
that his purpose was not an historical review of the
progress of opinion, but an attempt to deal directly
with current ways of looking at the universe, using
terms as nearly as possible in the sense which is most
general in philosophic usage, and which they tend to
bear in the vocabulary of educated people. And although Naturalism, as a matter of etymology and history, may take its rise as merely the denial of an
external and arbitrary Supernaturalism, I think there
can be no reasonable doubt that the name has acquired
within the present century the signification which Mr
Balfour gives it, and that it has, indeed, of late been
gradually supplanting other terms as the most fitting
designation for the system of beliefs in question.

[1] These quotations are from an article by Professor Wallace in the
'Fortnightly Review' for April 1895.

Naturalism, in accepted phraseology, is a name applicable to any system which, as Mr Balfour expresses it, finds the metaphysical or permanent reality of the universe in "the world which is revealed to us through perception and which is the subject-matter of the Natural Sciences." Naturalism is, therefore, practically identical with Materialism, though it may not pretend to explain the origin of the phenomena of consciousness from matter in motion, but may content itself, in that regard, with a doctrine of concomitance. In any case, the fundamental explanation—the central fact—of the universe is to be found, according to the theory, not in the phenomena of consciousness with their rational and ethical implications, but in the mechanical system of causes and effects of which consciousness seems to be the outcome or accompaniment. If that is so, any attempt to re-define Naturalism in such a way that absolute Idealism might reasonably be included under it, could only result in still further confusing the issues. The "New Naturalism," of which Professor Wallace constitutes himself the champion, would have, as he says, "to repair the defects of the Old." But when repairs are so extensive as to alter the whole structure and outlook of the building, the question as to the identity of the edifice becomes a point

of casuistry. Naturalism, in ordinary usage, is the antithesis not merely of the Supernaturalism which finds
its support in supposed divine "interference," but also
of every spiritual or idealistic theory of the universe.
The wide influence of Mr Balfour's book must have
largely contributed to stereotype this use of the term ;
and, from the point of view of philosophical terminology,
I cannot regard this as other than a fortunate result. ·

As a standing designation, it is distinctly preferable
in point of accuracy to any of the terms which Mr
Balfour mentions as currently, but somewhat loosely,
in use as synonyms. The absence of God and im-
mortality from the Positivist scheme may well seem
to the ordinary man to leave no practical difference
between that doctrine and the theory of Naturalism.
Yet, from a philosophical point of view, the difference
is not unimportant. Though, in its denials, Positivism
makes common cause with Naturalism, its constructive
doctrine is borrowed from Idealism, or, if you like,
from Christianity. In the stress which Positivism lays
upon man, even to the extent of calling itself the
religion of Humanity, Positivism echoes the thought
of Pascal, that man—the dying reed—is greater than
the universe by which he dies, that there is no common measure for the immensities of the physical uni-

verse and the spring of love, of thought, of reverence
that wells in a human heart. To this Positivism owes
its vitality, for the germ of the higher religions is this
sense of the truly infinite, the truly adorable, as revealed in man alone. " Comtianism," Dr Hutchison
Stirling has aptly said, " bears to Hegelianism a relation very similar to that of Mahometanism to Christianity" (Schwegler, p. 464). If we generalise the
statement, we may, I think, recognise in Positivism
an idealism *manqué*—an idealism with strange defects
and inconsistencies—but still a doctrine in spirit and
intention widely removed from mere Materialism. It
is well, therefore, not to ignore this difference, but to
continue to use the term in a narrower and specific
sense, as applicable to the different sects which appeal
to Comte as their founder and claim to represent the
Religion of Humanity.

Naturalism seems also more accurately descriptive
than Agnosticism ; for the theory in question is essentially a negative dogmatism, whereas Agnosticism, according to its etymology and according to the intention
of the inventor of the term, is meant to convey only
an expression of ignorance, a balance of the intellect,
a refusal to pronounce upon ultimate problems either
in one sense or in another. " A plague o' both your

houses" is, in effect, the language held by Professor
Huxley to the partisans of Idealism and Materialism
alike, in his well-known essay "On the Physical Basis
of Life," in the essay "On Descartes," and in many
other places.

The materialistic position that there is nothing in the
world but matter, force, and necessity is as utterly devoid
of justification as the most baseless of theological dogmas.
The fundamental doctrines of Materialism, like those of
Spiritualism and most other "isms," lie outside the limits
of philosophical inquiry, and David Hume's great service
to humanity is his irrefragable demonstration of what these
limits are.—(Collected Essays, vol. i. p. 162.)

No doubt it is difficult constantly to keep oneself correctly balanced upon the razor-edge of agnostic orthodoxy.   Professor Huxley tells us that, "the further
Science advances, the more extensively and consistently
will all the phenomena of Nature be represented by
materialistic formulæ and symbols"; and though he
enters his protest against the error of mistaking the
symbols for real entities, he admits, in doing so, that
it is a mistake only too easy to fall into.   The Agnostic,
like David Hume, who is here invoked as patron of
the creed, is apt to reserve his denials for "divinity or
school metaphysics," while he views with something

like equanimity the materialistic conclusions drawn from the advance of science. He is certain that he knows nothing of spiritual realities or agents; theoretically, he should be equally certain of his ignorance of reality or agency in the case of natural phenomena. But, as he is constantly occupied with the latter, his hand becomes subdued to what it works in. As man, moreover, is not a creature of pure reason alone, the senses assert their imperious sway over his practical beliefs, and his position becomes indistinguishable from Materialism pure and simple. Still, in spite of the fatal facility with which the one may glide into the other, we have in strictness no more right to identify the two, than a naturalist would have to deny the difference between two species because of the existence of intermediate forms in which they continuously approach one another. Definition in such cases must be by type. The typical Agnostic, like Huxley, is clearly distinguished from the typical Materialist. It would be an unjustifiable and quite unnecessary removal of landmarks, therefore, to use the two terms indiscriminately. No one in these days will allow that he is a Materialist; but Naturalism supplies exactly the term needed to enable us to surmount this verbal difficulty, while Agnosticism may be conveniently retained to

designate the quasi-sceptical position which it etymo-
logically suggests.[1]

The only legitimate objection to this use of the
term Naturalism is that urged by Professor Wallace.
Naturalism, in a certain context, appears as the antithesis of Supernaturalism; and he who attacks Naturalism may accordingly be supposed to do so in the
interest of "miracles" and other "supernatural" adjuncts
of theology. Some parts of the discussion in Mr
Balfour's concluding chapters certainly seem to favour
this view of his argument. But there are others which
suggest a larger interpretation, as where he expressly
discards what he calls "the common division between
'natural' and 'supernatural.'"

We cannot consent [he proceeds], to see the "preferential
working of Divine Power" only in those religious manifestations which refuse to accommodate themselves to our conception (whatever that may be) of the strictly "natural"
order of the world; nor can we deny a Divine origin to
those aspects of religious development which natural laws
seem competent to explain. The familiar distinction, indeed, between "natural" and "supernatural" coincides
neither with that between natural and spiritual, nor with

---

[1] Empiricism may be disregarded in this connection, as a term which
is no longer much in popular use. It tends to become restricted to
the bloodless controversies of the schools, and even there it suggests,
perhaps, a more or less obsolete formulation of the issues.

that between "preferential action" and "non-preferential,"
nor with that between phenomenal and noumenal. It is
perhaps less important than is sometimes supposed."

Quite in keeping with this is the fine passage which
follows on Inspiration, as "limited to no age, to no
country, no people" (pp. 330, 331).

But whatever Mr Balfour's personal attitude may be
towards the supernatural in the ordinary theological
sense of that word (and that is a matter which does
not concern us here), it is sufficiently plain that this
is not the kernel of the argument. Even when he
comes to deal with the central article of the Christian
faith, it is not on the extra-naturalness of certain
facts that the emphasis is laid, but upon the adaptation of the doctrine to the needs of man—upon what
might be called, therefore, in the highest sense, its
"naturalness." The antithesis which runs through
the volume, and which must impress itself upon any
candid reader, is not that between the natural and
a so-called supernatural, but between the natural and
the spiritual, — between nature, as "revealed to us
through perception," and that higher nature in nature
which makes us men and gives us an earnest of the
Divine. This antithesis also has the sanction of usage
on its side. Both in theological and in philosophical

writing, the natural and the spiritual are as currently
and intelligibly opposed to one another as the natural
and the supernatural. The moral world of persons
is constantly contrasted with the natural world of
things. What other interpretation is to be put upon
Leibniz's " Kingdom of Nature and Kingdom of Grace,"
upon Kant's opposition of the Sensible and the Intelligible World? "Nature," says Jacobi, "conceals
God. Man reveals God." "Man Supernatural" is
the title chosen by Professor Campbell Fraser for one
of his recent Gifford Lectures. "As a merely sentient
being man is wholly, or almost wholly, an event in
the orderly natural system. In his moral acts man
appears to exemplify that final principle on which
natural order ultimately depends." "Nature," says
Green, concluding his long argument for a spiritual
principle, "implies a principle which is non-natural"
(Proleg., p. 56). I quote these prominent expressions
of widely different thinkers, not because I regard
them all as equally sound, or any of them perhaps
as beyond criticism, but simply to prove how widely
current is the narrower sense of "Nature" which is
embodied in Mr Balfour's use of Naturalism. In not
one of the passages quoted is there the least suggestion of the supernatural in the mechanical and external

sense of popular theology. The contrast is substantially between the material and the ideal, the natural and the spiritual. If we turn to the histories of philosophy and their classifications of philosophical doctrine, we find also that the usage is no innovation. When Schwegler applies the term Naturalism to the doctrine of Democritus, when Ueberweg uses it as an equivalent to Materialism in his account of the French Encyclopædists, and describes in the same way the transformation which the Hegelian system underwent at the hands of Feuerbach, both apparently appeal to accepted usage. No apology is offered for the introduction of the term, nor does the reader feel that any explanation is required of a terminology so appropriate. The conjecture is permissible that Mr Balfour's usage would also have been accepted without cavil but for the sub-title of the volume, which seems to make the whole discussion ancillary to the study of theology. The air of England is charged with ecclesiasticism, and this was sufficient to create an inveterate prejudice in many minds, and to rouse in many more the suspicion of an *arrière pensée*. For there are many, unfortunately, who are more jealous of the encroachments of the supernatural than alive to the conservation of the spiritual truths of which it has been the vehicle.

NOTE B.

THE LEGITIMACY OF THE ARGUMENT FROM CONSEQUENCES.

Mr Balfour's general mode of procedure has been unsparingly condemned in many quarters, on the ground that his inquiry is avowedly undertaken in the interest of certain beliefs as to the course of the world and man's place in it. The motive of the investigation, it is said, discredits its results in advance. It is not a disinterested quest of truth, but a piece of special pleading in support of beliefs whose truth is assumed without investigation, on the strength of certain supposed "needs" of the individual and the race. But the needs of the race, still more of the individual, have no relevance, when the question is one of the facts of existence. Proud man has long enough indulged himself in this comforting but fatuous course of reasoning, and imposed his own image upon the world. Man's needs must **bend before** nature's necessities. It is time for **him to accept his** true **place in** the cosmic scheme. **If science teaches us** our insignificance **and** evanescence, we have **no** option but to accept that **teaching, however** wounding to **our** pride or lacerating **to our** emotions it may be.

Thus, **in familiar accents,** with a measure of right **on their side, and a still** greater measure of plausibility, we can hear the devotees of "truth" exclaim. **And** their indignation is naturally redoubled **when Mr** Balfour, **in** the first part **of his book, deliberately proceeds** to test the doctrines of "Naturalism" **by** their consequences—that is to say, **by the consequences, or** supposed consequences, to morality **and life** of their general **adoption as a working creed. Here** at least, we **can hear them say, is a method of** polemic, which it might **have been supposed** was obsolete. Mr Balfour himself **admits that his** procedure **is** not the **most** logical, **but** he blandly **adds that he** has adopted **it in order to** arrest **the** attention of "the **general reader." Could** there be **a more** unblushing admission **or a** more demoralising mode **of** argument?

This line **of** objection, which rests upon the same notion of **truth,** has even more show of reason than **the first; and it may be freely** admitted that the

argument *in terrorem*, from the supposed consequences
of a doctrine, is peculiarly liable to abuse, and also
that it has frequently been idly invoked in the past.
Beliefs which were held to be essential to the religious
life or the stability of the social fabric have been
abandoned without any signs of injury to either, and
doctrines which were declared to strike at the roots
of both religion and society have become part of our
common teaching; and yet the heavens have not
fallen, as it was confidently prophesied they would.
Nothing, in short, is more wonderful than the power
of adaptation which experience shows man to possess
in the matter of belief. Yet while this is both true
and reassuring, we must remember that experience
only proves its truth within certain limits. Profound
as the changes of belief have been in the past, the
doctrines that have been from time to time abandoned
or embraced must still be pronounced to be concerned
with details, as compared with the fundamental issue
between Materialism or Naturalism and a spiritual or
idealistic view of man's place in the universe. This,
it may be fairly argued, is not an issue between
different forms of an ethical or social creed, but between belief and no-belief; inasmuch as the materialistic scheme affords no legitimate basis for ethical

endeavour or ethical precept. No human society has ever been based upon the conclusions of materialism, and wherever this negative creed has become widely spread among individuals (in cultivated society under the Roman empire, for example, or in the same circles in France before the Revolution) the result has been visible in moral deterioration and social disintegration. The teaching of experience, therefore, does not discourage the application of the argument from consequences in an ultimate resort, however much it may cast ridicule upon misguided attempts to invoke this *ultima ratio* for any of the changing forms in which mankind have embodied their spiritual experience. For the *ultima ratio* of every creed, the *ultima ratio* of truth itself, is that it *works;* and no greater condemnation can be passed upon a doctrine or system than that, if it were true, human life, as it has been lived by the best of the race, would cease to be reasonable, or rather, would become a phenomenon whose emergence it was impossible to explain.

This consideration tends also to rob the previous objection of a good deal of its plausibility. "Truth" has become in these days a kind of Juggernaut, whose car is periodically dragged abroad in triumph by its self-immolating worshippers. There is much question-begging done under cover of devotion to " truth." The ethical life has also its certainties and its postulates; and a man is not necessarily evading truth, when he rejects a creed, because it has no place within it for those postulates of the ethical or spiritual life which to him are the most fundamental certainties of all. Nor is he convicted of prejudice, because he avows that the defence of these postulates is the motive of his speculative inquiry. Mr Balfour, as has been argued in the preceding essay, may be said to be trying throughout his volume to establish a definition of truth or of Reason, which shall be at once more comprehensive and more self-consistent than that which limits it to the facts and laws of physical science. But if this is so, then the appeal of the volume is not from truth to authority, or from truth to subjective cravings, but from a partial and fragmentary truth to a fuller truth; and the argument may fairly claim to be judged on its merits, without any importation of the *odium antitheologicum*.

PRINTED BY WILLIAM BLACKWOOD AND SONS.

A STUDY OF ETHICAL PRINCIPLES.

By JAMES SETH, M.A.,

Professor of Moral Philosophy in Cornell University, U.S.A.

Second Edition, Revised.   Post 8vo, 10s. 6d. *net*.

"One of the finest products of scholarship which America has given us for some time.......He does not write merely to convince us of the truth of his own theory, he gives us an orderly and tolerant account of other theories that have been held and still are held by other men. Thus it at once serves the purpose both of the student and of the general reader."—*Expository Times*.

"This is an excellent book, well written and well reasoned, not over subtle, yet with real philosophical grasp and insight, distinguished by competent knowledge, careful analysis, candid yet discriminative criticism, and a moral purpose and conviction, all too rare in ethical treatises, which makes the reader feel that he has to do with an author to whom the ideal is the real, and the obligatory an imperative that will not be denied."—*Speaker*.

"Professor Seth travels over a wide field, and indeed touches upon all the important questions which in recent years have been opened by ethical inquiry.......Sounder and more enlightening criticism it would be impossible to find. There is no emergence at any point of the slightest degree of partisanship, prejudice, or heat.......His style is remarkably lucid and agreeable, so that distinct literary flavour accompanies the severest thinking."—Professor MARCUS DODS in the *British Weekly*.

"One of the most important books which have been published in philosophy in recent years.......Marked not less by keen moral insight than by conspicuous dialectical skill."—*Standard*.

WILLIAM BLACKWOOD & SONS, EDINBURGH AND LONDON.

Catalógue

of

Messrs Blackwood & Sons'

Publications

PHILOSOPHICAL CLASSICS FOR ENGLISH READERS.

EDITED BY WILLIAM KNIGHT, LL.D.,

Professor of Moral Philosophy in the University of St Andrews.

In crown 8vo Volumes, with Portraits, price 3s. 6d.

Contents of the Series.

DESCARTES, by Professor Mahaffy, Dublin.—BUTLER, by Rev. W. Lucas Collins, M.A.—BERKELEY, by Professor Campbell Fraser.—FICHTE, by Professor Adamson, Glasgow. — KANT, by Professor Wallace, Oxford.—HAMILTON, by Professor Veitch, Glasgow.—HEGEL, by the Master of Balliol. —LEIBNIZ, by J. Theodore Merz.—VICO, by Professor Flint, Edinburgh.—HOBBES, by Professor Croom Robertson. — HUME, by the Editor. — SPINOZA, by the Very Rev. Principal Caird, Glasgow.—BACON: Part I. The Life, by Professor Nichol.— BACON: Part II. Philosophy, by the same Author.—LOCKE, by Professor Campbell Fraser.

FOREIGN CLASSICS FOR ENGLISH READERS.

EDITED BY MRS OLIPHANT.

In crown 8vo, 2s. 6d.

Contents of the Series.

DANTE, by the Editor. — VOLTAIRE, by General Sir E. B. Hamley, K.C.B. —PASCAL, by Principal Tulloch. — PETRARCH, by Henry Reeve, C.B.—GOETHE, by A. Hayward, Q.C.—MOLIÈRE, by the Editor and F. Tarver, M.A.—MONTAIGNE, by Rev. W. L. Collins, M.A.—RABELAIS, by Sir Walter Besant. — CALDERON, by E. J. Hasell.—SAINT SIMON, by Clifton W. Collins, M.A.—CERVANTES, by the Editor. — CORNEILLE AND RACINE, by Henry M. Trollope. — MADAME DE SÉVIGNÉ, by Miss Thackeray.—LA FONTAINE, AND OTHER FRENCH FABULISTS, by Rev. W. Lucas Collins, M.A.—SCHILLER, by James Sime, M.A., Author of 'Lessing, his Life and Writings.'—TASSO, by E. J. Hasell. — ROUSSEAU, by Henry Grey Graham.—ALFRED DE MUSSET, by C. F Oliphant.

ANCIENT CLASSICS FOR ENGLISH READERS.

EDITED BY THE REV. W. LUCAS COLLINS, M.A.

CHEAP RE-ISSUE. In limp cloth, fcap. 8vo, price 1s. each.

Two Volumes will be issued Monthly in the following order :—

HOMER: ILIAD, . . The Editor. } *Ready.*	HESIOD AND THEOGNIS, J. Davies. } *Sept.*	
HOMER: ODYSSEY, . The Editor. } *Ready.*	PLAUTUS AND TERENCE, The Editor. } *Sept.*	
HERODOTUS, . . G. C. Swayne. } *Ready.*	TACITUS, ... W. B. Donne. } *Oct.*	
CÆSAR, . . Anthony Trollope. } *Ready.*	LUCIAN, ... The Editor. } *Oct.*	
VIRGIL, ... The Editor. } *Ready.*	PLATO, ... C. W. Collins. } *Nov.*	
HORACE, . Sir Theodore Martin. } *Ready.*	GREEK ANTHOLOGY, Lord Neaves. } *Nov.*	
ÆSCHYLUS, . Bishop Copleston. } *May.*	LIVY, ... The Editor. } *Dec.*	
XENOPHON, . . Sir Alex. Grant. } *May.*	OVID, ... Rev. A. Church. } *Dec.*	
CICERO, ... The Editor. } *June.*	CATULLUS, TIBULLUS, AND PROPERTIUS, ... J. Davies. } 1898. *Jan.*	
SOPHOCLES, . . . C. W. Collins. } *June.*	DEMOSTHENES, . W. J. Brodribb. } 1898. *Jan.*	
PLINY, . Church and Brodribb. } *July.*	ARISTOTLE, . . Sir Alex. Grant. } *Feb.*	
EURIPIDES, . . . W. B. Donne. } *July.*	THUCYDIDES, . . . The Editor. } *Feb.*	
JUVENAL, ... E. Walford. } *Aug.*	LUCRETIUS, . . W. H. Mallock. } *March.*	
ARISTOPHANES, . . The Editor. } *Aug.*	PINDAR, . . Rev. F. D. Morice. } *March.*	

CATALOGUE

OF

MESSRS BLACKWOOD & SONS'

PUBLICATIONS.

ALISON.
  History of Europe. **By Sir Archibald** Alison, Bart., D.C.L.
  1. From the Commencement of the French Revolution to
     the Battle of Waterloo.
       Library Edition, 14 vols., with Portraits. Demy 8vo, £10, 10s.
       Another Edition, in 20 vols. crown 8vo, £6.
       People's Edition, 13 vols. crown 8vo, £2, 11s.
  2. Continuation to the Accession of Louis Napoleon.
       Library Edition, 8 vols. 8vo, £6, 7s. 6d.
       People's Edition, 8 vols. crown 8vo, 34s.
  Epitome of Alison's History of Europe. Thirtieth **Thou-**
     sand, 7s. 6d.
  Atlas to Alison's History of Europe. By A. Keith Johnston.
       Library Edition, demy 4to, £3, 3s.
       People's Edition, 31s. 6d.
  Life of John Duke of Marlborough. **With** some Account of
     his Contemporaries, and of the War of the Succession. **Third** Edition. 2 vols.
     8vo. Portraits and Maps, 30s.
  Essays : Historical, Political, and Miscellaneous. 3 vols.
     demy 8vo, **45s.**

ACROSS FRANCE IN A CARAVAN : Being some Account
     of a Journey from Bordeaux to Genoa in the "Escargot," taken in the Winter
     1889-90. By the Author of 'A Day of my Life at Eton.' With fifty Illustrations
     by John Wallace, after Sketches by the Author, and a Map. Cheap Edition,
     demy 8vo, 7s. 6d.

ACTA SANCTORUM HIBERNIÆ ; Ex Codice Salmanticensi.
     Nunc primum integre edita opera Caroli de Smedt et Josephi de Backer, e
     Soc. Jesu, Hagiographorum Bollandianorum ; Auctore et Sumptus Largiente
     Joanne Patricio Marchione Bothae. In One handsome 4to Volume, bound in
     half roxburghe, £2, 2s.; in paper cover, 31s. 6d.

ADOLPHUS. Some Memories of Paris. **By** F. Adolphus
     Crown 8vo, 6s.

AIKMAN.
  Manures and the Principles of Manuring. By C. M. Aikman,
     D.Sc., F.R.S.E., &c., Professor of Chemistry, Glasgow Veterinary College ;
     Examiner in Chemistry, University of Glasgow, &c. Crown 8vo, 6s. 6d.
  Farmyard Manure : Its Nature, Composition, and Treatment.
     Crown 8vo, 1s. 6d.

AIRD. Poetical Works of Thomas Aird. Fifth Edition, with
     Memoir of the Author by the Rev. Jardine Wallace, and Portrait. Crown 8vo,
     7s. 6d.

ALLARDYCE.
The City of Sunshine. By **ALEXANDER ALLARDYCE**, Author of
'Earlscourt,' &c. New Edition. **Crown 8vo, 6s.**
Balmoral : A Romance of the **Queen's Country.** New Edition.
Crown 8vo, 6s.

ALMOND. Sermons by a Lay Head-master. By **HELY HUTCH**-
INSON ALMOND, M.A. Oxon., Head-Master of Loretto School. **Crown 8vo, 5s.**

ANCIENT CLASSICS FOR ENGLISH READERS. Edited
by Rev. W. LUCAS COLLINS, M.A. Price 1s. each. *For List of Vols. see p.* 2.

ANDERSON. Daniel in the Critics' Den. A Reply to Dean
Farrar's 'Book of Daniel.' By ROBERT ANDERSON, LL.D., Barrister-at-Law,
Assistant Commissioner of Police of the Metropolis; Author of 'The Coming
Prince,' 'Human Destiny,' &c. Post 8vo, 4s. 6d.

AYTOUN.
Lays of the Scottish Cavaliers, and other Poems. By W.
EDMONDSTOUNE AYTOUN, D.C.L., Professor of Rhetoric and Belles-Lettres in the
University of Edinburgh. New Edition. Fcap. 8vo, 3s. 6d.
ANOTHER EDITION. Fcap. 8vo, 7s. 6d.
CHEAP EDITION. 1s. Cloth, 1s. 3d.

An Illustrated Edition of the Lays of the Scottish Cavaliers.
From designs by Sir NOEL PATON. Cheaper Edition. Small 4to, 10s. 6d.

Bothwell : a Poem. **Third Edition. Fcap., 7s. 6d.**

Poems and Ballads of Goethe. **Translated** by Professor
AYTOUN and Sir THEODORE MARTIN, K.C.B. **Third Edition.** Fcap., 6s.

The Ballads of Scotland. **Edited by Professor** AYTOUN.
Fourth Edition. 2 vols. fcap. 8vo, 12s.

Memoir of William E. Aytoun, **D.C.L.** By Sir THEODORE
MARTIN, K.C.B. With Portrait. Post 8vo, **12s.**

BEDFORD & COLLINS. Annals of the Free Foresters, from
1856 to the Present Day By W. K. R. BEDFORD, W. E. W. COLLINS, and other
Contributors. With 55 Portraits and 59 other Illustrations. Demy 8vo, 21s. *net.*

BELLAIRS. Gossips with Girls and Maidens, **Betrothed and**
Free. By LADY BELLAIRS. New Edition. Crown 8vo, 3s. 6d. Cloth, extra
gilt edges, 5s.

BELLESHEIM. History of the Catholic Church of Scotland.
From the Introduction of Christianity to the Present Day. By ALPHONS BEL-
LESHEIM, D.D., Canon of Aix-la-Chapelle. Translated, with Notes and Additions,
by D. OSWALD HUNTER BLAIR, O.S.B., Monk of Fort Augustus. Cheap Edition.
Complete in 4 vols. demy 8vo, with Maps. Price 21s. net.

BENTINCK. Racing Life of Lord George Cavendish Bentinck,
M.P., and other Reminiscences. By JOHN KENT, Private Trainer to the Good-
wood Stable. Edited by the Hon. FRANCIS LAWLEY. With Twenty-three full-
page Plates, and Facsimile Letter. Third Edition. Demy 8vo, 25s.

BEVERIDGE.
Culross and Tulliallan ; or, Perthshire on Forth. Its History
and Antiquities. With Elucidations of Scottish Life and Character from the
Burgh and Kirk-Session Records of that District. By DAVID BEVERIDGE. 2 vols.
8vo, with Illustrations, 42s.

Between the Ochils and the Forth ; **or, From Stirling** Bridge
to Aberdour. Crown 8vo, 6s.

BICKERDYKE. A Banished Beauty. By JOHN BICKERDYKE, Author of ' Days in Thule, with Rod, Gun, and Camera,' ' The Book of the All-Round Angler,' ' Curiosities of Ale and Beer,' &c. With Illustrations. Crown 8vo, 6s.

BIRCH.

Examples of Stables, Hunting-Boxes, Kennels, Racing Establishments, &c. By JOHN BIRCH, Architect, Author of ' Country Architecture,' &c. With 30 Plates. Royal 8vo, 7s.

Examples of Labourers' Cottages, &c. With **Plans for Improving** the Dwellings of the Poor in Large Towns. With 34 Plates. **Royal 8vo, 7s.**

Picturesque Lodges. A Series of Designs for Gate Lodges, Park Entrances, Keepers', Gardeners', Bailiffs', Grooms', Upper and Under Servants' Lodges, and other Rural Residences. With 16 Plates. 4to, 12s. 6d.

BLACK. **Heligoland and the Islands of** the North Sea. **By** WILLIAM GEORGE BLACK. Crown 8vo, 4s.

BLACKIE.

Lays and Legends of Ancient Greece. By JOHN STUART BLACKIE, Emeritus Professor of Greek in the University of Edinburgh. Second Edition. Fcap. 8vo, 5s.

The Wisdom of Goethe. **Fcap. 8vo. Cloth, extra gilt, 6s.**

Scottish Song : Its Wealth, Wisdom, and **Social Significance.** Crown 8vo. With Music. 7s. 6d.

A Song of Heroes. Crown 8vo, 6s.

John Stuart Blackie : A Biography. By ANNA M. STODDART. With 3 Plates. Third Edition. 2 vols. demy 8vo, 21s.
POPULAR EDITION. With Portrait. Crown 8vo, **6s.**

BLACKMORE. The Maid of Sker. By R. D. **BLACKMORE,** Author of ' Lorna Doone,' &c. New Edition. Crown 8vo, **6s. Cheaper Edition.** Crown 8vo, 3s. 6d.

BLACKWOOD.

Annals of a Publishing House. William Blackwood and **his** Sons ; including a History of their Magazine and Friends. By Mrs OLIPHANT. With Four Portraits, demy 8vo. *{Vols. I. and II. in the press.*

Blackwood's Magazine, from Commencement in 1817 to May 1897. Nos. 1 to 979, forming 160 Volumes.

Index to Blackwood's Magazine. Vols. 1 to 50. 8vo, 15s.

Tales from Blackwood. First Series. Price One Shilling **each,** in Paper Cover. Sold separately at all Railway Bookstalls.
They may also be had bound in 12 vols., cloth, 18s. Half calf, richly gilt, 30s. Or the 12 vols. in 6, roxburghe, 21s. Half red morocco, 28s.

Tales from Blackwood. Second Series. Complete in Twenty-four Shilling Parts. Handsomely bound in 12 vols., cloth, 30s. In leather back, roxburghe style, 37s. 6d. Half calf, gilt, 52s. 6d. Half morocco, 55s.

Tales from Blackwood. Third Series. Complete in Twelve Shilling Parts. Handsomely bound in 6 vols., cloth, 15s.; and in 12 vols., cloth, 18s. The 6 vols. in roxburghe, 21s. Half calf, 25s. Half morocco, 28s.

Travel, Adventure, and Sport. From ' Blackwood's Magazine. Uniform with ' Tales from Blackwood.' In Twelve Parts, each price 1s. Handsomely bound in 6 vols., cloth, 15s. And in half calf, 25s.

BLACKWOOD.

New Educational Series. *See separate* **Catalogue.**
New Uniform Series of Novels (Copyright).
Crown 8vo, cloth. Price 3s. 6d. each. Now ready:—

THE MAID OF SKER. By R. D. Blackmore.
WENDERHOLME. By P. G. Hamerton.
THE STORY OF MARGRÉDEL. By D. Storrar Meldrum.
MISS MARJORIBANKS. By Mrs Oliphant.
THE PERPETUAL CURATE, and THE RECTOR. By the Same.
SALEM CHAPEL, and THE DOCTOR'S FAMILY. By the Same.
A SENSITIVE PLANT. By E. D. Gerard.
LADY LEE'S WIDOWHOOD. By General Sir E. B. Hamley.
KATIE STEWART, and other Stories. By Mrs Oliphant.
VALENTINE AND HIS BROTHER. By the Same.
SONS AND DAUGHTERS. By the Same.
MARMORNE. By P. G. Hamerton.

REATA. By E. D. Gerard.
BEGGAR MY NEIGHBOUR. By the Same.
THE WATERS OF HERCULES. By the Same.
FAIR TO SEE. By L. W. M. Lockhart.
MINE IS THINE. By the Same.
DOUBLES AND QUITS. By the Same.
ALTIORA PETO. By Laurence Oliphant.
PICCADILLY. By the Same. With Illustrations.
LADY BABY. By D. Gerard.
THE BLACKSMITH OF VOE. By Paul Cushing.
THE DILEMMA. By the Author of 'The Battle of Dorking.'
MY TRIVIAL LIFE AND MISFORTUNE. By A Plain Woman.
POOR NELLIE. By the Same.

Standard **Novels.** Uniform in size and binding. Each complete in one Volume.

FLORIN SERIES, Illustrated Boards. Bound in Cloth, 2s. 6d.

TOM CRINGLE'S LOG. By Michael Scott.
THE CRUISE OF THE MIDGE. By the Same.
CYRIL THORNTON. By Captain Hamilton.
ANNALS OF THE PARISH. By John Galt.
THE PROVOST, &c. By the Same.
SIR ANDREW WYLIE. By the Same.
THE ENTAIL. By the Same.
MISS MOLLY. By Beatrice May Butt.
REGINALD DALTON. By J. G. Lockhart.

PEN OWEN. By Dean Hook.
ADAM BLAIR. By J. G. Lockhart.
LADY LEE'S WIDOWHOOD. By General Sir E. B. Hamley.
SALEM CHAPEL. By Mrs Oliphant.
THE PERPETUAL CURATE. By the Same.
MISS MARJORIBANKS. By the Same.
JOHN: A Love Story. By the Same.

SHILLING SERIES, Illustrated Cover. Bound in Cloth, 1s. 6d.

THE RECTOR, and THE DOCTOR'S FAMILY. By Mrs Oliphant.
THE LIFE OF MANSIE WAUCH. By D. M. Moir.
PENINSULAR SCENES AND SKETCHES. By F. Hardman.

SIR FRIZZLE PUMPKIN, NIGHTS AT MESS, &c.
THE SUBALTERN.
LIFE IN THE FAR WEST. By G. F. Ruxton.
VALERIUS: A Roman Story. By J. G. Lockhart.

BON GAULTIER'S BOOK OF BALLADS. Fifteenth Edition. With Illustrations by Doyle, Leech, and Crowquill. Fcap. 8vo, 5s.

BRADDON. Thirty Years of Shikar. By Sir EDWARD BRADDON, K.C.M.G. With Illustrations by G. D. Giles, and Map of Oudh Forest Tracts and Nepal Terai. Demy 8vo, 18s.

BROUGHAM. **Memoirs of the** Life and **Times of Henry Lord** Brougham. Written by HIMSELF. 3 vols. 8vo, £2, 8s. The Volumes are sold separately, price 16s. each.

BROWN. The Forester: **A Practical Treatise on** the Planting and Tending of Forest-trees and the General Management of Woodlands. By JAMES BROWN, LL.D. Sixth Edition, Enlarged. Edited by JOHN NISBET, D.Œc., Author of 'British Forest Trees,' &c. In 2 vols. royal 8vo, with 350 Illustrations, 42s. net.
Also being issued in 15 Monthly parts, price 2s. 6d. net each.
[Parts 1 to 4 ready.

BROWN. Stray Sport. By J. MORAY BROWN, Author of 'Shikar Sketches,' 'Powder, Spur, and Spear,' 'The Days when we went Hog-Hunting.' 2 vols. post 8vo, with Fifty Illustrations, 21s.

BROWN. A Manual of Botany, Anatomical and Physiological. For the Use of Students. By ROBERT BROWN, M.A., Ph.D. Crown 8vo, with numerous Illustrations, 12s. 6d.

BRUCE.

In Clover and Heather. Poems by **WALLACE** BRUCE. New and Enlarged Edition. Crown 8vo, 3s. 6d.
A limited number of Copies of the First Edition, on large hand-made paper, 12s. 6d.

Here's a Hand. Addresses and Poems. Crown 8vo, 5s. Large Paper Edition, limited to 100 copies, price 21s.

BUCHAN. Introductory Text-Book of Meteorology. By ALEX-ANDER BUCHAN, LL.D., F.R.S.E., Secretary of the Scottish Meteorological Society, &c. New Edition. Crown 8vo, with Coloured Charts and Engravings.
[In preparation.

BURBIDGE.

Domestic Floriculture, **Window** Gardening, and Floral **Decora-**tions. Being Practical Directions for the Propagation, Culture, and Arrangement of Plants and Flowers as Domestic Ornaments. By F. W. BURBIDGE. Second Edition. Crown 8vo, with numerous Illustrations, 7s. 6d.

Cultivated Plants: Their Propagation and Improvement. Including Natural and Artificial Hybridisation, Raising from Seed, Cuttings, and Layers, Grafting **and** Budding, as applied to the Families and Genera in Cultivation. Crown 8vo, with numerous Illustrations, 12s. 6d.

BURGESS. **The** Viking Path: A Tale of the White Christ. By J. J. HALDANE BURGESS, Author of 'Rasmie's Büddie,' 'Shetland Sketches,' &c. Crown 8vo, 6s.

BURKE. The Flowering of the Almond **Tree, and other** Poems. By CHRISTIAN BURKE. Pott 4to, 5s.

BURROWS.

Commentaries on the History **of** England, from the Earliest Times to 1865. By MONTAGU BURROWS, Chichele Professor of Modern History in the University of Oxford; Captain R.N.; F.S.A., &c.; "Officier de l'Instruction Publique," France. Crown 8vo, 7s. 6d.

The History of the Foreign Policy of Great **Britain.** Demy 8vo, 12s.

BURTON.

The History of Scotland: From Agricola's Invasion to the Extinction of the last Jacobite Insurrection. By JOHN HILL BURTON, D.C.L., Historiographer - Royal for Scotland. Cheaper Edition. In 8 monthly vols. Crown 8vo, 3s. 6d. each. *[Vols. I. to III. ready.*

History of the British Empire **during the** Reign of Queen Anne. In 3 vols. 8vo. 36s.

The Scot Abroad. **Third** Edition. Crown 8vo, 10s. 6d.

The Book-Hunter. **New** Edition. With Portrait. **Crown** 8vo, 7s. 6d.

BUTCHER. Armenosa **of** Egypt. **A** Romance of the Arab Conquest. By the Very Rev. Dean BUTCHER, D.D., F.S.A., Chaplain at Cairo. Crown 8vo, 6s.

BUTE. The Altus of **St** Columba. With a Prose **Paraphrase** and Notes. In paper cover, 2s. 6d.

BUTT.

Theatricals: An Interlude. **By BEATRICE MAY BUTT.** Crown 8vo, 6s.

Miss Molly. Cheap Edition, **2s.**

Eugenie. Crown 8vo, 6s. 6d.

Elizabeth, and other Sketches. Crown **8vo, 6s.**

Delicia. New Edition. Crown 8vo, 2s. 6d.

CAIRD. Sermons. By JOHN CAIRD, D.D., Principal of **the** University of Glasgow. Seventeenth Thousand. Fcap. 8vo, 5s.

CALDWELL. Schopenhauer's System in its Philosophical Significance (the Shaw Fellowship Lectures, 1893). By WILLIAM CALDWELL, M.A., D.Sc., Professor of Moral and Social Philosophy, Northwestern University, U.S.A. ; formerly Assistant to the Professor of Logic and Metaphysics, Edin., and Examiner in Philosophy in the University of St Andrews. Demy 8vo, 10s. 6d. net.

CALLWELL. The Effect of Maritime Command on Land Campaigns since Waterloo. By Major C. E. CALLWELL, R.A. With Plans. Post 8vo, 6s. net.

CAMPBELL. Sermons Preached before the Queen at Balmoral. By the Rev. A. A. CAMPBELL, Minister of Crathie. Published by Command of Her Majesty. Crown 8vo, 4s. 6d.

CAMPBELL. Records of Argyll. Legends, Traditions, and Recollections of Argyllshire Highlanders, collected chiefly from the Gaelic. With Notes on the Antiquity of the Dress, Clan Colours, or Tartans of the Highlanders. By Lord ARCHIBALD CAMPBELL. Illustrated with Nineteen full-page Etchings. 4to, printed on hand-made paper, £3, 3s.

CANTON. A Lost Epic, and other Poems. By WILLIAM CANTON. Crown 8vo, 5s.

CARSTAIRS.
Human Nature in Rural India. By R. CARSTAIRS. Crown 8vo, 6s.
British Work in India. Crown 8vo, 6s.

CAUVIN. A Treasury of the English and German Languages. Compiled from the best Authors and Lexicographers in both Languages. By JOSEPH CAUVIN, LL.D. and Ph.D., of the University of Göttingen, &c. Crown 8vo, 7s. 6d.

CHARTERIS. Canonicity ; or, Early Testimonies to the Existence and Use of the Books of the New Testament. Based on Kirchhoffer's 'Quellensammlung.' Edited by A. H. CHARTERIS, D.D., Professor of Biblical Criticism in the University of Edinburgh. 8vo, 18s.

CHENNELLS. Recollections of an Egyptian Princess. By her English Governess (Miss E. CHENNELLS). Being a Record of Five Years' Residence at the Court of Ismael Pasha Khédive. Second Edition. With Three Portraits. Post 8vo, 7s. 6d.

CHESNEY. The Dilemma. By General Sir GEORGE CHESNEY, K.C.B., M.P., Author of 'The Battle of Dorking,' &c. New Edition. Crown 8vo, 3s. 6d.

CHRISTISON. Life of Sir Robert Christison, Bart., M.D., D.C.L. Oxon., Professor of Medical Jurisprudence in the University of Edinburgh. Edited by his Sons. In 2 vols. 8vo. Vol. I.—Autobiography. 16s. Vol. II.—Memoirs. 16s.

CHURCH. Chapters in an Adventurous Life. Sir Richard Church in Italy and Greece. By E. M. CHURCH. With Photogravure Portrait. Demy 8vo, 10s. 6d.

CHURCH SERVICE SOCIETY.
A Book of Common Order : being Forms of Worship issued by the Church Service Society. Seventh Edition, carefully revised. In 1 vol. crown 8vo, cloth, 3s. 6d. ; French morocco, 5s. Also in 2 vols. crown 8vo, cloth, 4s. ; French morocco, 6s. 6d.
Daily Offices for Morning and Evening Prayer throughout the Week. Crown 8vo, 3s. 6d.
Order of Divine Service for Children. Issued by the Church Service Society. With Scottish Hymnal. Cloth, 3d.

CLOUSTON. Popular Tales and Fictions: their Migrations and Transformations. By W. A. CLOUSTON, Editor of 'Arabian Poetry for English Readers,' &c. 2 vols. post 8vo, roxburghe binding, 25s.

COCHRAN. A Handy Text-Book of Military **Law.** Compiled chiefly to assist Officers preparing for Examination; also for all Officers of the Regular and Auxiliary Forces. Comprising also a Synopsis of part of the Army Act. By Major F. COCHRAN, Hampshire Regiment Garrison Instructor, North British District. Crown 8vo, 7s. 6d.

COLQUHOUN. The Moor and the Loch. Containing Minute Instructions in all Highland Sports, with Wanderings over Crag and Corrie, Flood and Fell. By JOHN COLQUHOUN. Cheap Edition. With Illustrations. Demy 8vo, 10s. 6d.

COLVILE. Round **the Black Man's** Garden. By Lady Z. COLVILE, F.R.G.S. **With 2 Maps** and 50 Illustrations from Drawings **by the** Author and from **Photographs.** Demy 8vo, 16s.

CONDER. **The Bible and the East.** By Lieut.-Col. C. R. CONDER, R.E., LL.D., **D.C.L.**, M.R.A.S., Author of 'Tent Work in Palestine,' &c. With Illustrations and a Map. Crown 8vo, 5s.

CONSTITUTION AND LAW OF THE CHURCH OF SCOTLAND. With an Introductory Note by the late Principal Tulloch. New Edition, Revised and Enlarged. Crown 8vo, 3s. 6d.

COTTERILL. Suggested Reforms in **Public Schools.** By C. C. COTTERILL, M.A. Crown 8vo, 3s. 6d.

COUNTY HISTORIES OF SCOTLAND. **In demy 8vo vol-** umes of about 350 pp. each. With Maps. Price 7s. 6d. **net.**

> Fife and Kinross. **By** ÆNEAS J. **G.** MACKAY, **LL.D.**, Sheriff of these Counties.

> Dumfries and Galloway. By Sir **HERBERT** MAXWELL, Bart., M.P.

> Moray and **Nairn.** By CHARLES RAMPINI, LL.D., Sheriff-Substitute **of these** Counties.

> **Inverness. By** J. CAMERON LEES, D.D. *[Others in preparation.*

CRAWFORD. Saracinesca. By F. MARION CRAWFORD, Author of 'Mr Isaacs,' &c., &c. Eighth Edition. Crown 8vo, 6s.

CRAWFORD.

> The Doctrine of Holy Scripture respecting the Atonement. By the late THOMAS J. CRAWFORD, D.D., Professor of Divinity in the University of Edinburgh. Fifth Edition. 8vo, 12s.

> The Fatherhood of God, Considered in its General and **Special** Aspects. Third Edition, Revised and Enlarged. 8vo, 9s.

> The Preaching of the Cross, and other Sermons. **8vo, 7s. 6d.**

> The Mysteries of Christianity. Crown 8vo, **7s. 6d.**

CROSS. Impressions of Dante, and of the New World; with a Few Words on Bimetallism. By J. W. CROSS, Editor of 'George Eliot's Life, as related in her Letters and Journals.' Post 8vo, 6s.

CUMBERLAND. Sport on the Pamirs and Turkistan Steppes. By Major C. S. CUMBERLAND. With Map and Frontispiece. Demy 8vo, 10s. 6d.

CURSE OF INTELLECT. Third Edition. Fcap. 8vo, 2s. 6d. net.

CUSHING. The Blacksmith of Voe. By PAUL CUSHING, Author of 'The Bull i' th' Thorn,' 'Cut with his own Diamond.' Cheap Edition. Crown 8vo, 3s. 6d.

DAVIES.
  Norfolk Broads and Rivers; or, **The Waterways, Lagoons,** and Decoys of East Anglia. By G. CHRISTOPHER DAVIES. Illustrated with **Seven** full-page Plates. New and Cheaper Edition. **Crown** 8vo, 6s.
  Our Home in Aveyron. Sketches of Peasant Life in **Aveyron** and the Lot. By G. CHRISTOPHER DAVIES and Mrs BROUGHALL. Illustrated with full-page Illustrations. 8vo, 15s. **Cheap Edition, 7s. 6d.**

DE LA WARR. An Eastern Cruise in the ' **Edeline.' By the** Countess DE LA WARR. In Illustrated Cover. 2s.

DESCARTES. The Method, Meditations, and Principles **of Philo-**sophy of Descartes. Translated from the Original French and Latin. With a New Introductory Essay, Historical and Critical, on the Cartesian **Philosophy.** By **Professor** VEITCH, LL.D., Glasgow University. Eleventh Edition. **6s. 6d.**

DOGS, OUR DOMESTICATED: Their Treatment in reference to **Food,** Diseases, Habits, Punishment, Accomplishments. By 'MAGENTA.' Crown **8vo, 2s. 6d.**

DOUGLAS.
  The Ethics of John Stuart **Mill.** By CHARLES DOUGLAS, M.A., D.Sc., Lecturer in Moral **Philosophy, and** Assistant to the Professor of **Moral** Philosophy in the University **of Edinburgh. Post** 8vo, 6s. net.
  John Stuart Mill: A Study **of his Philosophy. Crown 8vo,** 4s. 6d. net.

DOUGLAS. Chinese Stories. **By ROBERT K. DOUGLAS. With** numerous Illustrations by Parkinson, **Forestier, and** others. **New and Cheaper** Edition. Small demy 8vo, 5s.

DOUGLAS. Iras: A Mystery. **By THEO. DOUGLAS, Author of** ' **A** Bride Elect.' Cheaper Edition, in **Paper Cover** specially designed by Womrath. Crown 8vo, 1s. 6d.

DU CANE. The Odyssey of Homer, Books I.-XII. Translated into **English Verse.** By Sir CHARLES DU CANE, K.C.M.G. 8vo, 10s. 6d.

DUDGEON. History **of** the Edinburgh or Queen's Regiment **Light** Infantry Militia, now 3rd Battalion The Royal Scots; with an Account of **the** Origin and Progress of the Militia, and a Brief Sketch of the Old Royal **Scots.** By Major R. C. DUDGEON, Adjutant 3rd Battalion the Royal Scots. **Post 8vo,** with Illustrations, 10s. 6d.

DUNSMORE. Manual of the Law of Scotland as to the Rela-**tions** between Agricultural Tenants and the Landlords, Servants, Merchants, and **Bowers.** By W. DUNSMORE. 8vo, 7s. 6d.

DZIEWICKI. **Entombed in Flesh. By** M. H. DZIEWICKI. In 1 vol. crown 8vo.   [*In the press.*

ELIOT.
  George Eliot's Life, Related in Her **Letters and Journals.** Arranged and Edited by her husband, J. W. CROSS. **With Portrait and other** Illustrations. Third Edition. 3 vols. post 8vo, 42s.
  George Eliot's Life. With Portrait **and** other Illustrations. New Edition, in one **volume.** Crown 8vo, 7s. 6d.
  Works of George **Eliot** (Standard Edition). **21** volumes, crown 8vo. In buckram **cloth,** gilt top, 2s. 6d. per vol.; or in roxburghe binding, 3s. 6d. per vol.
      ADAM BEDE. 2 vols.—THE MILL ON **THE** FLOSS. 2 vols.—FELIX HOLT, THE RADICAL. 2 vols.—ROMOLA. 2 vols.—SCENES OF CLERICAL LIFE. 2 vols.—MIDDLEMARCH. 3 vols.—DANIEL DERONDA. 3 vols.—SILAS MARNER. 1 vol. —JUBAL. 1 vol.—THE SPANISH GIPSY. 1 vol.—ESSAYS. 1 vol.—THEOPHRAS-TUS SUCH. 1 vol.
  Life and Works of George Eliot (Cabinet Edition). 24 volumes, **crown** 8vo, price £6. Also to be had handsomely bound in half and full calf. The Volumes are sold separately, bound in cloth, price 5s. each.

ELIOT.
  Novels by George Eliot. Cheap Edition.
   Adam Bede. Illustrated. 3s. 6d., cloth.—The Mill on the Floss. Illus-
   trated. 3s. 6d., cloth.—Scenes of Clerical Life. Illustrated. 3s., cloth.—
   Silas Marner: the Weaver of Raveloe. Illustrated. **2s.** 6d., cloth.—Felix
   Holt, the Radical. Illustrated. 3s. **6d.**, cloth.—Romola. With Vignette.
   3s. 6d., cloth.
  Middlemarch. Crown 8vo, 7s. **6d.**
  Daniel Deronda. Crown 8vo, 7s. **6d.**
  Essays. New Edition. Crown 8vo, 5s.
  Impressions **of** Theophrastus Such. New Edition. **Crown**
   8vo, 5s.
  The Spanish **Gypsy.** New Edition. Crown 8vo, 5s.
  The Legend **of** Jubal, **and other** Poems, Old and New.
   New Edition. **Crown** 8vo, 5s.
  Wise, Witty, **and** Tender Sayings, in Prose and Verse. Selected
   from the Works of GEORGE ELIOT. New Edition. Fcap. 8vo, 3s. 6d.
ESSAYS ON SOCIAL SUBJECTS. Originally published in
   the 'Saturday Review.' New Edition. First and Second Series. 2 vols. crown
   8vo, 6s. **each.**

FAITHS OF THE WORLD, **The.** **A Concise** History of the
   Great Religious Systems of the World. **By various Authors.** Crown 8vo, 5s.
FALKNER. The Lost Stradivarius. **By J. MEADE FALKNER.**
   Second Edition. Crown 8vo, 6s.
FENNELL AND O'CALLAGHAN. A Prince of Tyrone. By
   CHARLOTTE FENNELL and J. P. O'CALLAGHAN. Crown 8vo, 6s.
FERGUSON. Sir Samuel Ferguson in the Ireland of his Day.
   By LADY FERGUSON, Author of 'The Irish before **the** Conquest,' ' Life of William
   Reeves, D.D., Lord Bishop of Down, Connor, **and** Drumore,' &c., &c. With
   Two Portraits. 2 vols. post 8vo, 21s.
FERRIER.
  Philosophical Works of the late James F. Ferrier, B.A.
   Oxon., Professor of Moral Philosophy and Political Economy, St Andrews.
   New Edition. Edited by Sir ALEXANDER GRANT, Bart., D.C.L., and Professor
   LUSHINGTON. 3 vols. crown 8vo, 34s. 6d.
  Institutes of Metaphysic. Third Edition. 10s. 6d.
  Lectures on the Early Greek Philosophy. 4th Edition. **10s. 6d.**
  Philosophical Remains, including the Lectures on **Early**
   Greek Philosophy. New Edition. **2** vols. 24s.
FLINT.
  Historical Philosophy in France and French Belgium and
   Switzerland. By ROBERT FLINT, Corresponding Member of the Institute of
   France, Hon. Member of the Royal Society of Palermo, Professor in the Univer-
   sity of Edinburgh, &c. 8vo, 21s.
  Agnosticism. Being the Croall Lecture for **1887-88.**
                                                      [*In the press.*
  Theism. Being the Baird **Lecture** for 1876. Ninth Edition,
   Revised. Crown 8vo, 7s. 6d.
  Anti-Theistic Theories. Being **the Baird Lecture** for 1877.
   Fifth Edition. Crown 8vo, 10s. 6d.
FOREIGN CLASSICS FOR ENGLISH READERS. Edited
   by Mrs OLIPHANT. Price 2s. 6d. *For List of Volumes, see page 2.*
FOSTER. The Fallen City, and other Poems. By WILL FOSTER.
   Crown 8vo, 6s.

FRANCILLON. Gods and Heroes; or, The Kingdom of Jupiter.
By R. E. FRANCILLON. With 8 Illustrations. Crown 8vo, 5s.

FRANCIS. Among the Untrodden Ways. By M. E. FRANCIS
(Mrs Francis Blundell), Author of 'In a North Country Village,' 'A Daughter of
the Soil,' 'Frieze and Fustian,' &c. Crown 8vo, 3s. 6d.

FRASER.
Philosophy of Theism. Being the Gifford Lectures delivered
before the University of Edinburgh in 1894-95. First Series. By ALEXANDER
CAMPBELL FRASER, D.C.L. Oxford; Emeritus Professor of Logic and Metaphysics in the University of Edinburgh. Post 8vo, 7s. 6d. net.

Philosophy of Theism. Being the Gifford Lectures delivered
before the University of Edinburgh in 1895-96. Second Series. Post 8vo,
7s. 6d. net.

FRASER. St Mary's of Old Montrose: A History of the Parish
of Maryton. By the Rev. WILLIAM RUXTON FRASER, M.A., F.S.A. Scot.,
Emeritus Minister of Maryton; Author of 'History of the Parish and Burgh of
Laurencekirk.' Crown 8vo, 3s. 6d.

FULLARTON.
Merlin: A Dramatic Poem. By RALPH MACLEOD FULLAR-
TON. Crown 8vo, 5s.

Tanhäuser. Crown 8vo, 6s.

Lallan Sangs and German Lyrics. Crown 8vo, 5s.

GALT.
Novels by JOHN GALT. With General Introduction and
Prefatory Notes by S. R. CROCKETT. The Text Revised and Edited by D.
STORRAR MELDRUM, Author of 'The Story of Margrédel.' With Photogravure
Illustrations from Drawings by John Wallace. Fcap. 8vo, 3s. net each vol.

ANNALS OF THE PARISH, and THE AYRSHIRE LEGATEES. 2 vols.—SIR ANDREW
WYLIE. 2 vols.—THE ENTAIL; or, The Lairds of Grippy. 2 vols.—THE PRO-
VOST, and THE LAST OF THE LAIRDS. 2 vols.

See also STANDARD NOVELS, *p.* 6.

GENERAL ASSEMBLY OF THE CHURCH OF SCOTLAND.
Scottish Hymnal, With Appendix Incorporated. Published
for use in Churches by Authority of the General Assembly. 1. Large type,
cloth, red edges, 2s. 6d.; French morocco, 4s. 2. Bourgeois type, limp cloth, 1s.;
French morocco, 2s. 3. Nonpareil type, cloth, red edges, 6d.; French morocco,
1s. 4d. 4. Paper covers, 3d. 5. Sunday-School Edition, paper covers, 1d.,
cloth, 2d. No. 1, bound with the Psalms and Paraphrases, French morocco, 8s.
No. 2, bound with the Psalms and Paraphrases, cloth, 2s.; French morocco, 3s.

Prayers for Social and Family Worship. Prepared by a
Special Committee of the General Assembly of the Church of Scotland. Entirely
New Edition, Revised and Enlarged. Fcap. 8vo, red edges, 2s.

Prayers for Family Worship. A Selection of Four Weeks'
Prayers. New Edition. Authorised by the General Assembly of the Church of
Scotland. Fcap. 8vo, red edges, 1s. 6d.

One Hundred Prayers. Prepared by the Committee on Aids
to Devotion. 16mo, cloth limp, 6d.

Morning and Evening Prayers for Affixing to Bibles. Prepared
by the Committee on Aids to Devotion. 1d. for 6, or 1s. per 100.

GERARD.
Reata: What's in a Name. By E. D. GERARD. Cheap
Edition. Crown 8vo, 3s. 6d.

Beggar my Neighbour. Cheap Edition. Crown 8vo, 3s. 6d.

The Waters of Hercules. Cheap Edition. Crown 8vo, 3s. 6d.

A Sensitive Plant. Crown 8vo, 3s. 6d.

GERARD.

A Foreigner. An Anglo-German Study. **By E. GERARD.**
Crown 8vo, 6s.

The Land beyond the Forest. Facts, Figures, and Fancies
from Transylvania. With Maps and Illustrations. 2 vols. post 8vo, 25s.

Bis : Some Tales Retold. Crown 8vo, 6s.

A Secret Mission. 2 vols. crown 8vo, 17s.

An Electric Shock, and other Stories. Crown **8vo, 6s.**

GERARD.

A Spotless **Reputation. By DOROTHEA** GERARD. **Third**
Edition. Crown **8vo,** 6s.

The Wrong Man. Second Edition. Crown 8vo, 6s.

Lady Baby. Cheap Edition. Crown 8vo, 3s. 6d.

Recha. Second Edition. Crown 8vo, 6s.

The Rich Miss Riddell. Second Edition. Crown 8vo, 6s.

GERARD. **Stonyhurst Latin Grammar. By Rev.** JOHN GERARD.
Second **Edition. Fcap. 8vo, 3s.**

GILL.

Free Trade : an Inquiry into the **Nature of its Operation.**
By RICHARD GILL. Crown 8vo, 7s. 6d.

Free Trade under Protection. Crown 8vo, 7s. 6d.

GORDON CUMMING.

At Home in Fiji. By C. **F.** GORDON **CUMMING. Fourth**
Edition, post 8vo. With Illustrations and Map. 7s. 6d.

A Lady's Cruise in a French Man-of-War. **New and Cheaper**
Edition. 8vo. With Illustrations and Map. 12s. 6d.

Fire-Fountains. The Kingdom of Hawaii : **Its Volcanoes,**
and **the** History of its Missions. With Map and Illustrations. 2 vols. 8vo, 25s.

Wanderings in China. New and Cheaper Edition. **8vo, with**
Illustrations, 10s.

Granite Crags : **The** Yŏ-semité Region **of** California. Illustrated with 8 Engravings. New and Cheaper Edition. 8vo, 8s. 6d.

GRAHAM. Manual of the Elections (Scot.) (Corrupt and Illegal
Practices) Act, 1890. With Analysis, Relative Act of Sederunt, Appendix con-
taining the Corrupt Practices Acts of 1883 and 1885, and Copious Index. By J.
EDWARD GRAHAM, Advocate. 8vo, 4s. 6d.

GRAND.

A Domestic Experiment. **By** SARAH **GRAND, Author of**
'The Heavenly Twins,' 'Ideala : **A Study** from Life.' Crown **8vo, 6s.**

Singularly Deluded. Crown **8vo, 6s.**

GRANT. Bush-Life in **Queensland.** By A. C. **GRANT. New**
Edition. Crown 8vo, 6s.

GRIER.

In Furthest Ind. The Narrative of Mr EDWARD CARLYON of
Ellswether, in the County of Northampton, and late of the Honourable East India
Company's Service, Gentleman. Wrote by his own hand in the year of grace 1697.
Edited, with a few Explanatory Notes, by SYDNEY C. **GRIER.** Post 8vo, 6s.

His Excellency's English Governess. Crown 8vo, 6s.

An Uncrowned King : A Romance of High Politics. Second
Edition. Crown 8vo, 6s.

GUTHRIE-SMITH. Crispus : **A Drama. By H.** GUTHRIE-
SMITH. Fcap. 4to, 5s.

HAGGARD. Under Crescent and **Star.** By Lieut.-Col. ANDREW HAGGARD, D.S.O., Author of 'Dodo **and I,' '**Tempest Torn,' &c. With a Portrait. Second Edition. Crown 8vo, 6s.

HALDANE. Subtropical Cultivations and **Climates.** A Handy Book for Planters, Colonists, and Settlers. By R. C. **HALDANE.** Post 8vo, 9s.

HAMERTON.

Wenderholme: **A Story** of Lancashire and Yorkshire Life. By P. G. HAMERTON, Author of '**A** Painter's **Camp.' New Edition.** Crown 8vo, 3s. 6d.

Marmorne. **New Edition. Crown** 8vo, 3s. 6d.

HAMILTON.

Lectures **on** Metaphysics. **By Sir** WILLIAM HAMILTON, Bart., Professor of Logic and Metaphysics in the University of Edinburgh. **Edited** by the Rev. H. L. MANSEL, B.D., LL.D., Dean of St Paul's; and JOHN VEITCH, M.A., LL.D., Professor of Logic and Rhetoric, Glasgow. Seventh Edition. 2 vols. 8vo, 24s.

Lectures on Logic. **Edited by the** SAME. Third Edition, Revised. 2 vols., 24s.

Discussions on Philosophy **and Literature,** Education and University Reform. Third Edition. 8vo, 21s.

Memoir **of** Sir William Hamilton, **Bart., Professor of** Logic and Metaphysics in **the** University of Edinburgh. **By Professor** VEITCH, of the University of Glasgow. 8vo, with Portrait, 18s.

Sir William Hamilton: The Man **and his Philosophy. Two** Lectures delivered before the Edinburgh Philosophical Institution, January and February 1883. By **Professor** VEITCH. Crown 8vo, 2s.

HAMLEY.

The Operations of War Explained **and** Illustrated. By General Sir EDWARD BRUCE HAMLEY, K.C.B., **K.C.M.G.** Fifth Edition, Revised throughout. 4to, with numerous Illustrations, 30s.

National Defence; Articles and Speeches. Post 8vo, 6s.

Shakespeare's Funeral, and **other** Papers. Post 8vo, 7s. 6d.

Thomas **Carlyle**: An Essay. Second Edition. Crown **8vo,** 2s. 6d.

On Outposts. Second Edition. 8vo, 2s.

Wellington's Career; A Military and Political Summary. Crown 8vo, 2s.

Lady **Lee's** Widowhood. New Edition. Crown **8vo, 3s. 6d.** Cheaper Edition, 2s. 6d.

Our Poor **Relations.** A Philozoic Essay. **With Illustrations,** chiefly by Ernest Griset. Crown 8vo, cloth gilt, 3s. 6d.

The Life **of General** Sir Edward Bruce Hamley, K.C.B., K.C.M.G. By ALEXANDER INNES SHAND. With two Photogravure Portraits and other Illustrations. Cheaper Edition. With a Statement by Mr EDWARD HAMLEY. 2 vols. demy 8vo, 10s. 6d.

HARE. Down **the Village** Street: **Scenes in a** West Country Hamlet. By CHRISTOPHER HARE. Second Edition. Crown 8vo, 6s.

HARRADEN.

In Varying Moods: Short Stories. By BEATRICE HARRADEN, Author of 'Ships that Pass in the Night.' Twelfth Edition. Crown 8vo, 3s. 6d.

Hilda Strafford, and The Remittance Man. Two Californian Stories. Tenth Edition. Crown 8vo, 3s. 6d.

HARRIS.

From **Batum** to Baghdad, *via* Tiflis, Tabriz, and Persian Kurdistan. By WALTER B. HARRIS, F.R.G.S., Author of 'The Land of an African Sultan; Travels in Morocco,' &c. With numerous Illustrations and 2 Maps. Demy 8vo, 12s.

HARRIS.
Tafilet. The Narrative of a Journey of Exploration to the Atlas Mountains and the Oases of the North-West Sahara. With Illustrations by Maurice Romberg from Sketches and Photographs by the Author, and Two Maps. Demy 8vo, 12s.

A Journey through the Yemen, and some General Remarks upon that Country. With 3 Maps and numerous Illustrations by Forestier and Wallace from Sketches and Photographs taken by the Author. Demy 8vo, 16s.

Danovitch, and other Stories. Crown 8vo, 6s.

HAWKER. The Prose Works of Rev. R. S. Hawker, Vicar of Morwenstow. Including 'Footprints of Former Men in Far Cornwall.' Re-edited, with Sketches never before published. With a Frontispiece. Crown 8vo, 3s. 6d.

HAY. The Works of the Right Rev. Dr George Hay, Bishop of Edinburgh. Edited under the Supervision of the Right Rev. Bishop Strain. With Memoir and Portrait of the Author. 5 vols. crown 8vo, bound in extra cloth, £1, 1s. The following Volumes may be had separately—viz.:
The Devout Christian Instructed in the Law of Christ from the Written Word. 2 vols., 8s.—The Pious Christian Instructed in the Nature and Practice of the Principal Exercises of Piety. 1 vol., 3s.

HEATLEY.
The Horse-Owner's Safeguard. A Handy Medical Guide for every Man who owns a Horse. By G. S. Heatley, M.R.C.V.S. Crown 8vo, 5s.

The Stock-Owner's Guide. A Handy Medical Treatise for every Man who owns an Ox or a Cow. Crown 8vo, 4s. 6d.

HEDDERWICK. Lays of Middle Age; and other Poems. By James Hedderwick, LL.D., Author of 'Backward Glances.' Price 3s. 6d.

HEMANS.
The Poetical Works of Mrs Hemans. Copyright Editions. Royal 8vo, 5s. The Same with Engravings, cloth, gilt edges, 7s. 6d.

Select Poems of Mrs Hemans. Fcap., cloth, gilt edges, 3s.

HERKLESS. Cardinal Beaton: Priest and Politician. By John Herkless, Professor of Church History, St Andrews. With a Portrait. Post 8vo, 7s. 6d.

HEWISON. The Isle of Bute in the Olden Time. With Illustrations, Maps, and Plans. By James King Hewison, M.A., F.S.A. (Scot.), Minister of Rothesay. Vol. I., Celtic Saints and Heroes. Crown 4to, 15s. net. Vol. II., The Royal Stewards and the Brandanes. Crown 4to, 15s. net.

HIBBEN. Inductive Logic. By John Grier Hibben, Ph.D., Assistant Professor of Logic in Princeton University, U.S.A. Crown 8vo, 3s. 6d. net.

HILDEBRAND. The Early Relations between Britain and Scandinavia. Being the Rhind Lectures in Archæology for 1896. By Dr Hans Hildebrand, Royal Antiquary of Sweden. With Illustrations. In 1 vol. post 8vo. [In the press.

HOME PRAYERS. By Ministers of the Church of Scotland and Members of the Church Service Society. Second Edition. Fcap. 8vo, 3s.

HORNBY. Admiral of the Fleet Sir Geoffrey Phipps Hornby, G.C.B. A Biography. By Mrs Fred. Egerton. With Three Portraits. Demy 8vo, 16s.

HUTCHINSON. Hints on the Game of Golf. By Horace G. Hutchinson. Ninth Edition, Enlarged. Fcap. 8vo, cloth, 1s.

HYSLOP. The Elements of Ethics. By James H. Hyslop, Ph.D., Instructor in Ethics, Columbia College, New York, Author of 'The Elements of Logic.' Post 8vo, 7s. 6d. net.

IDDESLEIGH. Life, Letters, and Diaries of Sir Stafford Northcote, First Earl of Iddesleigh. By Andrew Lang. With Three Portraits and a View of Pynes. Third Edition. 2 vols. post 8vo, 31s. 6d.
Popular Edition. With Portrait and View of Pynes. Post 8vo, 7s. 6d.

INDEX GEOGRAPHICUS: Being a List, alphabetically arranged, of the Principal Places on the Globe, with the Countries and Subdivisions of the Countries in which they are situated, and their Latitudes and Longitudes. Imperial 8vo, pp. 676, **21s.**

JEAN JAMBON. Our Trip to Blunderland; or, Grand Excursion to Blundertown and Back. By JEAN JAMBON. With **Sixty Illustrations** designed by CHARLES DOYLE, engraved by DALZIEL. Fourth **Thousand.** Cloth, gilt edges, 6s. 6d. Cheap Edition, cloth, 3s. 6d. Boards, 2s. 6d.

JEBB. A Strange Career. The Life and Adventures of JOHN GLADWYN JEBB. By his Widow. With an Introduction by H. RIDER HAGGARD, and an Electrogravure Portrait of Mr Jebb. Third Edition. Demy 8vo, 10s. 6d. CHEAP EDITION. With Illustrations by John Wallace. Crown 8vo, 3s. 6d.

Some Unconventional People. By Mrs GLADWYN JEBB, Author of 'Life and Adventures of J. G. Jebb.' With Illustrations. Crown 8vo, 3s. 6d.

JENNINGS. Mr Gladstone: A Study. By LOUIS J. JENNINGS, M.P., Author of 'Republican Government in the United States,' 'The Croker Memoirs,' &c. Popular Edition. Crown 8vo, 1s.

JERNINGHAM.
Reminiscences of an Attaché. By HUBERT E. H. JERNINGHAM. Second Edition. Crown 8vo, 5s.

Diane de Breteuille. A Love Story. Crown 8vo, 2s. 6d.

JOHNSTON.
The Chemistry of Common Life. By Professor J. F. W. JOHNSTON. New Edition, Revised. By ARTHUR HERBERT CHURCH, M.A. Oxon.; Author of 'Food: its Sources, Constituents, and Uses,' &c. With Maps and 102 Engravings. Crown 8vo, 7s. 6d.

Elements of Agricultural Chemistry. An entirely New Edition from the Edition by Sir CHARLES A. CAMERON, M.D., F.R.C.S.I., &c. Revised and brought down to date by C. M. AIKMAN, M.A., B.Sc., F.R.S.E., Professor of Chemistry, Glasgow Veterinary College. 17th Edition. Crown 8vo, 6s. 6d.

Catechism of Agricultural Chemistry. An entirely New Edition from the Edition by Sir CHARLES A. CAMERON. Revised and Enlarged by C. M. AIKMAN, M.A., &c. 95th Thousand. With numerous Illustrations. Crown 8vo, 1s.

JOHNSTON. Agricultural Holdings (Scotland) Acts, 1883 and 1889; and the Ground Game Act, 1880. With Notes, and Summary of Procedure, &c. By CHRISTOPHER N. JOHNSTON, M.A., Advocate. Demy 8vo, 5s.

JOKAI. Timar's Two Worlds. By MAURUS JOKAI. Authorised Translation by Mrs HEGAN KENNARD. Cheap Edition. Crown 8vo, 6s.

KEBBEL. The Old and the New: English Country Life. By T. E. KEBBEL, M.A., Author of 'The Agricultural Labourers,' 'Essays in History and Politics,' 'Life of Lord Beaconsfield.' Crown 8vo, 5s.

KERR. St Andrews in 1645-46. By D. R. KERR. Crown 8vo, 2s. 6d.

KINGLAKE.
History of the Invasion of the Crimea. By A. W. KINGLAKE. Cabinet Edition, Revised. With an Index to the Complete Work. Illustrated with Maps and Plans. Complete in 9 vols., crown 8vo, at 6s. each.

—— Abridged Edition for Military Students. Revised by Lieut.-Col. Sir GEORGE SYDENHAM CLARKE, K.C.M.G., R.E. In 1 vol. demy 8vo. [In the press.

History of the Invasion of the Crimea. Demy 8vo. Vol. VI. Winter Troubles. With a Map, 16s. Vols. VII. and VIII. From the Morrow of Inkerman to the Death of Lord Raglan. With an Index to the Whole Work. With Maps and Plans. 28s.

KINGLAKE.
   Eothen. A New Edition, uniform with the Cabinet Edition
   of the 'History of the Invasion of the Crimea.' 6s.
      CHEAPER EDITION. With Portrait and Biographical Sketch of the Author.
      Crown 8vo, 3s. 6d. Popular Edition, in paper cover, 1s. net.

KIRBY. In Haunts of Wild Game: A Hunter-Naturalist's
   Wanderings from Kahlamba to Libombo. By FREDERICK VAUGHAN KIRBY,
   F.Z.S. (Maqaqamba). With numerous Illustrations by Charles Whymper, and a
   Map. Large demy 8vo, 25s.

KLEIN. Among the Gods. Scenes of India, with Legends by
   the Way. By AUGUSTA KLEIN. With 22 Full-page Illustrations. Demy 8vo, 15s.

KNEIPP. My Water-Cure. As Tested through more than
   Thirty Years, and Described for the Healing of Diseases and the Preservation of
   Health. By SEBASTIAN KNEIPP, Parish Priest of Wörishofen (Bavaria). With a
   Portrait and other Illustrations. Authorised English Translation from the
   Thirtieth German Edition, by A. de F. Cheap Edition. With an Appendix, con-
   taining the Latest Developments of Pfarrer Kneipp's System, and a Preface by
   E. Gerard. Crown 8vo, 3s. 6d.

KNOLLYS. The Elements of Field-Artillery. Designed for
   the Use of Infantry and Cavalry Officers. By HENRY KNOLLYS, Colonel Royal
   Artillery; Author of 'From Sedan to Saarbrück,' Editor of 'Incidents in the
   Sepoy War,' &c. With Engravings. Crown 8vo, 7s. 6d.

LANG. Life, Letters, and Diaries of Sir Stafford Northcote,
   First Earl of Iddesleigh. By ANDREW LANG. With Three Portraits and a View
   of Pynes. Third Edition. 2 vols. post 8vo, 31s. 6d.
      POPULAR EDITION. With Portrait and View of Pynes. Post 8vo, 7s. 6d.

LEES. A Handbook of the Sheriff and Justice of Peace Small
   Debt Courts. With Notes, References, and Forms. By J. M. LEES, Advocate,
   Sheriff of Stirling, Dumbarton, and Clackmannan. 8vo, 7s. 6d.

LINDSAY.
   Recent Advances in Theistic Philosophy of Religion. By Rev.
   JAMES LINDSAY, M.A., B.D., B.Sc., F.R.S.E., F.G.S., Minister of the Parish of
   St Andrew's, Kilmarnock. Demy 8vo, 12s. 6d. net.
   The Progressiveness of Modern Christian Thought. Crown
   8vo, 6s.
   Essays, Literary and Philosophical. Crown 8vo, 3s. 6d.
   The Significance of the Old Testament for Modern Theology.
   Crown 8vo, 1s. net.
   The Teaching Function of the Modern Pulpit. Crown 8vo,
   1s. net.

LOCKHART.
   Doubles and Quits. By LAURENCE W. M. LOCKHART. New
   Edition. Crown 8vo, 3s. 6d.
   Fair to See. New Edition. Crown 8vo, 3s. 6d.
   Mine is Thine. New Edition. Crown 8vo, 3s. 6d.

LOCKHART.
   The Church of Scotland in the Thirteenth Century. The
   Life and Times of David de Bernham of St Andrews (Bishop), A.D. 1239 to 1253.
   With List of Churches dedicated by him, and Dates. By WILLIAM LOCKHART,
   A.M., D.D., F.S.A. Scot., Minister of Colinton Parish. 2d Edition. 8vo, 6s.
   Dies Tristes: Sermons for Seasons of Sorrow. Crown 8vo, 6s.

LORIMER.
   The Institutes of Law : A Treatise of the Principles of Jurisprudence as determined by Nature. By the late JAMES LORIMER, Professor of
   Public Law and of the Law of Nature and Nations in the University of Edinburgh. New Edition, Revised and much Enlarged. 8vo, 18s.

LORIMER.

The Institutes of the Law of Nations. A Treatise of the
Jural Relation of Separate Political Communities. In 2 vols. 8vo. Volume I.,
price 16s. Volume II., price 20s.

LUGARD. The Rise of our East African Empire: Early Efforts
in Uganda and Nyasaland. By F. D. LUGARD, Captain Norfolk Regiment.
With 130 Illustrations from Drawings and Photographs under the personal
superintendence of the Author, and 14 specially prepared Maps. In 2 vols. large
demy 8vo, 42s.

M'CHESNEY.

Miriam Cromwell, Royalist: A Romance of the Great Rebel-
lion. By DORA GREENWELL M'CHESNEY. Crown 8vo, 6s.

Kathleen Clare: Her Book, 1637-41. With Frontispiece, and
five full-page Illustrations by James A. Shearman. Crown 8vo, 6s.

M'COMBIE. Cattle and Cattle-Breeders. By WILLIAM M'COMBIE,
Tillyfour. New Edition, Enlarged, with Memoir of the Author by JAMES
MACDONALD, F.R.S.E., Secretary Highland and Agricultural Society of Scotland.
Crown 8vo, 3s. 6d.

M'CRIE.

Works of the Rev. Thomas M'Crie, D.D. Uniform Edition.
4 vols. crown 8vo, 24s.

Life of John Knox. Crown 8vo, 6s. Another Edition, 3s. 6d.

Life of Andrew Melville. Crown 8vo, 6s.

History of the Progress and Suppression of the Reformation
in Italy in the Sixteenth Century. Crown 8vo, 4s.

History of the Progress and Suppression of the Reformation
in Spain in the Sixteenth Century. Crown 8vo, 3s. 6d.

M'CRIE. The Public Worship of Presbyterian Scotland. Histori-
cally treated. With copious Notes, Appendices, and Index. The Fourteenth
Series of the Cunningham Lectures. By the Rev. CHARLES G. M'CRIE, D.D.
Demy 8vo, 10s. 6d.

MACDONALD. A Manual of the Criminal Law (Scotland) Procedure Act, 1887. By NORMAN DORAN MACDONALD. Revised by the LORD
JUSTICE-CLERK. 8vo, 10s. 6d.

MACDONALD AND SINCLAIR. History of Polled Aberdeen
and Angus Cattle. Giving an Account of the Origin, Improvement, and Characteristics of the Breed. By JAMES MACDONALD and JAMES SINCLAIR. Illustrated
with numerous Animal Portraits. Post 8vo, 12s. 6d.

MACDOUGALL AND DODDS. A Manual of the Local Govern-
ment (Scotland) Act, 1894. With Introduction, Explanatory Notes, and Copious
Index. By J. PATTEN MACDOUGALL, Legal Secretary to the Lord Advocate, and
J. M. DODDS. Tenth Thousand, Revised. Crown 8vo, 2s. 6d. net.

MACINTYRE. Hindu-Koh: Wanderings and Wild Sports on
and beyond the Himalayas. By Major-General DONALD MACINTYRE, V.C., late
Prince of Wales' Own Goorkhas, F.R.G.S. *Dedicated to H.R.H. The Prince of
Wales.* New and Cheaper Edition, Revised, with numerous Illustrations. Post
8vo, 3s. 6d.

MACKAY.

Elements of Modern Geography. By the Rev. ALEXANDER
MACKAY, LL.D., F.R.G.S. 55th Thousand, Revised to the present time. Crown
8vo, pp. 300, 3s.

The Intermediate Geography. Intended as an Intermediate
Book between the Author's 'Outlines of Geography' and 'Elements of Geography.' Eighteenth Edition, Revised. Fcap. 8vo, pp. 238, 2s.

Outlines of Modern Geography. 191st Thousand, Revised to
the present time. Fcap. 8vo, pp. 128, 1s.

Elements of Physiography. New Edition. Rewritten and
Enlarged. With numerous Illustrations. Crown 8vo.   [*In the press.*

MACKENZIE. Studies in Roman Law. **With** Comparative
Views of **the** Laws of France, England, and Scotland. By Lord MACKENZIE,
one of the Judges of the Court of Session in Scotland. Sixth Edition, Edited
by **JOHN** KIRKPATRICK, M.A., LL.B., Advocate, Professor of History in the
University of Edinburgh. 8vo, 12s.

MACPHERSON. Glimpses of Church and **Social** Life in the
Highlands in Olden Times. By ALEXANDER MACPHERSON, F.S.A. Scot. With
6 Photogravure Portraits and other full-page Illustrations. Small 4to, 25s.

M'PHERSON. Golf and Golfers. Past and Present. By **J.**
GORDON M'PHERSON, Ph.D., F.R.S.E. With an Introduction by the Right Hon.
A. J. BALFOUR, and a Portrait of the Author. Fcap. 8vo, 1s. 6d.

MACRAE. **A** Handbook of Deer-Stalking. By ALEXANDER
MACRAE, **late** Forester to Lord Henry Bentinck. With Introduction **by** Horatio
Ross, Esq. **Fcap. 8vo,** with 2 Photographs from Life. 3s. 6d.

MAIN. Three Hundred English Sonnets. Chosen and Edited
by **DAVID M.** MAIN. New Edition. Fcap. 8vo, 3s. 6d.

MAIR. A Digest of Laws and Decisions, Ecclesiastical and
Civil, relating to the Constitution, Practice, and Affairs of the Church of Scot-
land. With Notes and Forms of Procedure. By the Rev. WILLIAM MAIR, D.D.,
Minister of the Parish of Earlston. New Edition. Revised. Crown 8vo, 9s. net.

MARCHMONT AND THE HUMES OF POLWARTH. By
One of their Descendants. With numerous Portraits and other Illustrations.
Crown 4to, 21s. net.

MARSHMAN. History of India. **From the** Earliest Period to
the present time. By JOHN CLARK MARSHMAN, C.S.I. Third and Cheaper
Edition. Post 8vo, with Map, 6s.

MARTIN.
> **The** Æneid of Virgil. Books I.-VI. Translated **by** Sir THEO-
> DORE MARTIN, K.C.B. Post 8vo, 7s. 6d.
> Goethe's Faust. Part I. Translated into English Verse.
> Second Edition, crown 8vo, 6s. Ninth Edition, fcap. 8vo, 3s. 6d.
> Goethe's Faust. Part II. Translated into English Verse.
> Second Edition, Revised. Fcap. 8vo, 6s.
> The Works of Horace. Translated into English Verse, with
> Life and Notes. 2 vols. New Edition. Crown 8vo, 21s.
> Poems and Ballads of Heinrich Heine. Done into English
> Verse. Third Edition. Small crown 8vo, 5s.
> The Song of the Bell, and other Translations from Schiller,
> Goethe, Uhland, and Others. Crown 8vo, 7s. 6d.
> Madonna Pia: A Tragedy; and Three Other Dramas. Crown
> 8vo, 7s. 6d.
> Catullus. With Life and Notes. Second Edition, Revised
> and Corrected. Post 8vo, 7s. 6d.
> The 'Vita Nuova' of Dante. Translated, with an Introduction
> and Notes. Third Edition. Small crown 8vo, 5s.
> Aladdin: A Dramatic Poem. By ADAM OEHLENSCHLAEGER.
> Fcap. 8vo, **5s.**
> Correggio: **A** Tragedy. By OEHLENSCHLAEGER. With Notes.
> Fcap. 8vo, **3s.**

MARTIN. On some of Shakespeare's Female Characters. By
HELENA FAUCIT, Lady MARTIN. Dedicated by permission to Her Most Gracious
Majesty the Queen. Fifth Edition. With a Portrait by Lehmann. Demy
8vo, 7s. 6d.

MARWICK. Observations on the Law and Practice in regard
to Municipal Elections and the Conduct of the Business of Town Councils and
Commissioners of Police in Scotland. By Sir JAMES D. MARWICK, LL.D.,
Town-Clerk of Glasgow. Royal 8vo, 30s.

MATHESON.
Can the Old Faith Live with the New? or, The Problem of
Evolution and Revelation. By the Rev. GEORGE MATHESON, D.D. Third Edition. Crown 8vo, 7s. 6d.
The Psalmist and the Scientist; or, Modern Value of the Religious Sentiment. Third Edition. Crown 8vo, 5s.
Spiritual Development of St Paul. Third Edition. Cr. 8vo, 5s.
The Distinctive Messages of the Old Religions. Second Edition. Crown 8vo, 5s.
Sacred Songs. New and Cheaper Edition. Crown 8vo, 2s. 6d.

MATHIESON. The Supremacy and Sufficiency of Jesus Christ
our Lord, as set forth in the Epistle to the Hebrews. By J. E. MATHIESON,
Superintendent of Mildmay Conference Hall, 1880 to 1890. Second Edition.
Crown 8vo, 3s. 6d.

MAURICE. The Balance of Military Power in Europe. An
Examination of the War Resources of Great Britain and the Continental States.
By Colonel MAURICE, R.A., Professor of Military Art and History at the Royal
Staff College. Crown 8vo, with a Map, 6s.

MAXWELL.
A Duke of Britain. A Romance of the Fourth Century.
By Sir HERBERT MAXWELL, Bart., M.P., F.S.A., &c., Author of 'Passages in
the Life of Sir Lucian Elphin.' Fourth Edition. Crown 8vo, 6s.
Life and Times of the Rt. Hon. William Henry Smith, M.P.
With Portraits and numerous Illustrations by Herbert Railton, G. L. Seymour,
and Others. 2 vols. demy 8vo, 25s.
POPULAR EDITION. With a Portrait and other Illustrations. Crown 8vo, 3s. 6d.
Scottish Land-Names: Their Origin and Meaning. Being
the Rhind Lectures in Archæology for 1893. Post 8vo, 6s.
Meridiana: Noontide Essays. Post 8vo, 7s. 6d.
Post Meridiana: Afternoon Essays. Post 8vo, 6s.
Dumfries and Galloway. Being one of the Volumes of the
County Histories of Scotland. With Four Maps. Demy 8vo, 7s. 6d. net.

MELDRUM.
The Story of Margrédel: Being a Fireside History of a Fifeshire Family. By D. STORRAR MELDRUM. Cheap Edition. Crown 8vo, 3s. 6d.
Grey Mantle and Gold Fringe. Crown 8vo, 6s.

MERZ. A History of European Thought in the Nineteenth Century. By JOHN THEODORE MERZ. Vol. I., post 8vo, 10s. 6d. net.

MICHIE.
The Larch: Being a Practical Treatise on its Culture and
General Management. By CHRISTOPHER Y. MICHIE, Forester, Cullen House.
Crown 8vo, with Illustrations. New and Cheaper Edition, Enlarged, 5s.
The Practice of Forestry. Crown 8vo, with Illustrations. 6s.

MIDDLETON. The Story of Alastair Bhan Comyn; or, The
Tragedy of Dunphail. A Tale of Tradition and Romance. By the Lady MIDDLETON. Square 8vo, 10s. Cheaper Edition, 5s.

MIDDLETON. Latin Verse Unseens. By G. MIDDLETON, M.A.,
Lecturer in Latin, Aberdeen University; late Scholar of Emmanuel College, Cambridge; Joint-Editor of 'Student's Companion to Latin Authors.' In 1 vol.
crown 8vo. [In the press.

MILLER. The Dream of Mr H——, the Herbalist. By HUGH
MILLER, F.R.S.E., late H.M. Geological Survey, Author of 'Landscape Geology.'
With a Photogravure Frontispiece. Crown 8vo, 2s. 6d.

MILLS. Greek Verse Unseens. By T. R. MILLS, M.A., late
Lecturer in Greek, Aberdeen University; formerly Scholar of Wadham College,
Oxford; Joint-Editor of 'Student's Companion to Latin Authors.' In 1 vol.
crown 8vo. [In the press.

MINTO.

A Manual of English Prose Literature, Biographical and Critical: designed mainly to show Characteristics of Style. By W. MINTO, M.A., Hon. LL.D. of St Andrews; Professor of Logic in the University of Aberdeen. Third Edition, Revised. Crown 8vo, 7s. 6d.

Characteristics of English Poets, from Chaucer **to Shirley.** New Edition, Revised. Crown 8vo, 7s. 6d.

Plain Principles of Prose Composition. Crown 8vo, **1s. 6d.**

The Literature of the Georgian Era. Edited, with a Biographical Introduction, by Professor KNIGHT, St Andrews. Post 8vo, 6s.

MOIR. Life of Mansie Wauch, Tailor in Dalkeith. By D. M. MOIR. With CRUIKSHANK's Illustrations. Cheaper Edition. Crown 8vo, 2s. 6d. Another Edition, without Illustrations, fcap. 8vo, 1s. 6d.

MOLE. For **the Sake** of **a** Slandered Woman. By MARION MOLE. Fcap. 8vo, 2s. 6d. net.

MOMERIE.

Defects of Modern Christianity, and other Sermons. By Rev. ALFRED WILLIAMS MOMERIE, M.A., D.Sc., LL.D. Fifth Edition. Crown 8vo, 5s.

The Basis of Religion. Being an Examination of Natural Religion. Third Edition. Crown 8vo, 2s. **6d.**

The Origin of Evil, **and** other **Sermons. Eighth** Edition, Enlarged. Crown 8vo, 5s.

Personality. The Beginning and End of Metaphysics, and a Necessary Assumption in all Positive Philosophy. Fifth Edition, Revised. Crown 8vo, 3s.

Agnosticism. Fourth Edition, Revised. Crown 8vo, 5s.

Preaching and Hearing; and other Sermons. Fourth Edition, Enlarged. Crown 8vo, 5s.

Belief in God. Third **Edition. Crown 8vo, 3s.**

Inspiration; and other **Sermons. Second Edition, Enlarged.** Crown 8vo, **5s.**

Church and **Creed.** Third Edition. Crown **8vo,** 4s. 6d.

The Future **of Religion,** and other Essays. Second Edition. Crown 8vo, 3s. 6d.

The English Church **and** the Romish **Schism.** Second Edition. Crown 8vo, 2s. 6d.

MONCREIFF.

The Provost-Marshal. **A Romance of the** Middle Shires. **By** the Hon. FREDERICK MONCREIFF. **Crown 8vo, 6s.**

The X Jewel. A Romance **of the** Days of James VI. **Crown** 8vo, 6s.

MONTAGUE. Military Topography. Illustrated by Practical Examples of a Practical Subject. By Major-General W. E. MONTAGUE, C.B., P.S.C., late Garrison Instructor Intelligence Department, Author of 'Campaigning in South Africa.' With Forty-one Diagrams. Crown 8vo, 5s.

MONTALEMBERT. Memoir of Count de Montalembert. **A** Chapter of Recent French History. By Mrs OLIPHANT, Author of the 'Life **of** Edward **Irving,' &c.** 2 vols. crown 8vo, £1, 4s.

MORISON.

Doorside **Ditties.** By JEANIE MORISON. **With a Frontis-**piece. Crown 8vo, 3s. 6d.

Æolus. A Romance in Lyrics. **Crown 8vo, 3s.**

There as Here. Crown 8vo, 3s.
*** *A limited impression on hand-made paper, bound in vellum, 7s. 6d.*

Selections from Poems. Crown 8vo, 4s. 6d.

Sordello. An Outline Analysis of **Mr** Browning's **Poem.** Crown 8vo, 3s.

MORISON.

Of " Fifine at the Fair," "Christmas Eve and Easter Day,' and other of Mr Browning's Poems. Crown 8vo, 3s.

The Purpose of the Ages. Crown 8vo, 9s.

Gordon : An Our-day Idyll. Crown 8vo, 3s.

Saint Isadora, and other Poems. Crown 8vo, 1s. 6d.

Snatches of Song. Paper, 1s. 6d. ; cloth, 3s.

Pontius Pilate. Paper, 1s. 6d. ; cloth, 3s.

Mill o' Forres. Crown 8vo, 1s.

Ane Booke of Ballades. Fcap. 4to, 1s.

MUNRO. The Lost Pibroch, and other Sheiling Stories. By Neil Munro. Crown 8vo, 6s.

MUNRO.

Rambles and Studies in Bosnia-Herzegovina and Dalmatia. With an Account of the Proceedings of the Congress of Archæologists and Anthropologists held at Sarajevo in 1894. By Robert Munro, M.A., M.D., F.R.S.E., Author of 'The Lake-Dwellings of Europe,' &c. With numerous Illustrations. Demy 8vo, 12s. 6d. net.

Prehistoric Problems. With numerous Illustrations. Demy 8vo, 10s. net.

MUNRO. On Valuation of Property. By William Munro, M.A., Her Majesty's Assessor of Railways and Canals for Scotland. Second Edition, Revised and Enlarged. 8vo, 3s. 6d.

MURDOCH. Manual of the Law of Insolvency and Bankruptcy : Comprehending a Summary of the Law of Insolvency, Notour Bankruptcy, Composition - Contracts, Trust - Deeds, Cessios, and Sequestrations ; and the Winding-up of Joint-Stock Companies in Scotland ; with Annotations on the various Insolvency and Bankruptcy Statutes ; and with Forms of Procedure applicable to these Subjects. By James Murdoch, Member of the Faculty of Procurators in Glasgow. Fifth Edition, Revised and Enlarged. 8vo, 12s. net.

MURRAY. A Popular Manual of Finance. By Sydney J. Murray. In 1 vol. crown 8vo. *[In the press.*

MY TRIVIAL LIFE AND MISFORTUNE : A Gossip with no Plot in Particular. By A Plain Woman. Cheap Edition. Crown 8vo, 3s. 6d.

By the Same Author.

POOR NELLIE. Cheap Edition. Crown 8vo, 3s. 6d.

MY WEATHER - WISE COMPANION. Presented by B. T. Fcap. 8vo, 1s. net.

NAPIER. The Construction of the Wonderful Canon of Logarithms. By John Napier of Merchiston. Translated, with Notes, and a Catalogue of Napier's Works, by William Rae Macdonald. Small 4to, 15s. *A few large-paper copies on Whatman paper*, 30s.

NEAVES. Songs and Verses, Social and Scientific. By An Old Contributor to 'Maga.' By the Hon. Lord Neaves. Fifth Edition. Fcap. 8vo, 4s.

NICHOLSON.

A Manual of Zoology, for the Use of Students. With a General Introduction on the Principles of Zoology. By Henry Alleyne Nicholson, M.D., D.Sc., F.L.S., F.G.S., Regius Professor of Natural History in the University of Aberdeen. Seventh Edition, Rewritten and Enlarged. Post 8vo, pp. 956, with 555 Engravings on Wood, 18s.

Text-Book of Zoology, for Junior Students. Fifth Edition, Rewritten and Enlarged. Crown 8vo, with 358 Engravings on Wood, 10s. 6d.

Introductory Text-Book of Zoology, for the Use of Junior Classes. New Edition, Revised and Enlarged. *[In the press.*

NICHOLSON.

A Manual of Palæontology, for the Use of Students. With a
General Introduction on the Principles of Palæontology. By Professor H.
ALLEYNE NICHOLSON and RICHARD LYDEKKER, B.A. Third Edition, entirely
Rewritten and greatly Enlarged. 2 vols. 8vo, £3, 3s.

The Ancient Life-History of the Earth. An Outline of the
Principles and Leading Facts of Palæontological Science. Crown 8vo, with 276
Engravings, 10s. 6d.

On the "Tabulate Corals" of the Palæozoic Period, with
Critical Descriptions of Illustrative Species. Illustrated with 15 Lithographed
Plates and numerous Engravings. Super-royal 8vo, 21s.

Synopsis of the Classification of the Animal Kingdom. 8vo,
with 106 Illustrations, 6s.

On the Structure and Affinities of the Genus Monticulipora
and **its Sub-Genera**, with Critical Descriptions of Illustrative Species. Illustrated
with **numerous Engravings on** Wood and Lithographed Plates. Super-royal
8vo, 18s.

NICHOLSON.

Thoth. A Romance. By JOSEPH SHIELD NICHOLSON, M.A.,
D.Sc., Professor of Commercial and Political Economy and Mercantile Law in
the University of Edinburgh. Third Edition. Crown 8vo, 4s. 6d.

A Dreamer of Dreams. A Modern Romance. Second Edition. Crown 8vo, 6s.

NICOLSON AND MURE. A Handbook to the Local Govern-
ment (Scotland) Act, 1889. With Introduction, Explanatory Notes, and Index.
By J. BADENACH NICOLSON, Advocate, Counsel to the Scotch Education
Department, and W. J. MURE, Advocate, Legal Secretary to the Lord Advocate
for Scotland. Ninth Reprint. 8vo, 5s.

OLIPHANT.

Masollam : A Problem of the **Period. A Novel. By LAURENCE**
OLIPHANT. 3 vols. post 8vo, 25s. 6d.

Scientific Religion ; or, Higher Possibilities of Life and
Practice through the Operation of Natural Forces. Second Edition. 8vo, 16s.

Altiora Peto. Cheap Edition. Crown 8vo, boards, 2s. 6d. ;
cloth, 3s. 6d. Illustrated Edition. Crown 8vo, cloth, 6s.

Piccadilly. With Illustrations by Richard Doyle. New Edition, 3s. 6d. Cheap Edition, boards, 2s. 6d.

Traits and Travesties ; Social and Political. Post 8vo, 10s. **6d.**

Episodes in a Life **of** Adventure ; or, Moss from a Rolling
Stone. Cheaper Edition. Post 8vo, 3s. 6d.

Haifa : Life in Modern Palestine. Second Edition. **8vo, 7s. 6d.**

The Land of Gilead. With Excursions in the **Lebanon.**
With Illustrations and Maps. Demy 8vo, 21s.

Memoir **of** the Life of Laurence Oliphant, and of Alice
Oliphant, **his Wife.** By Mrs **M. O.** W. OLIPHANT. Seventh Edition. 2 vols.
post 8vo, **with** Portraits. 21s.
POPULAR EDITION. With a New Preface. Post 8vo, with Portraits. 7s. 6d.

OLIPHANT.

Annals **of** a Publishing House. William Blackwood and his
Sons ; including a History of their Magazine and Friends. By Mrs OLIPHANT.
With Four Portraits. Demy 8vo. [*Vols. I. and II. in the press.*]

Who was Lost and is Found. Second Edition. Crown
8vo, 6s.

Miss Marjoribanks. New Edition. Crown **8vo, 3s. 6d.**

OLIPHANT.

The Perpetual Curate, and The Rector. New Edition. Crown
8vo, 3s. 6d.

Salem Chapel, and The Doctor's Family. New Edition.
Crown 8vo, 3s. 6d.

Katie Stewart, and other Stories. New Edition. Crown 8vo,
cloth, 3s. 6d.

Katie Stewart. Illustrated boards, 2s. 6d.

Valentine and his Brother. New Edition. Crown 8vo, 3s. 6d.

Sons and Daughters. Crown 8vo, 3s. 6d.

Two Stories of the Seen and the Unseen. The Open Door
—Old Lady Mary. Paper covers, 1s.

OLIPHANT. Notes of a Pilgrimage to Jerusalem and the Holy
Land. By F. R. OLIPHANT. Crown 8vo, 3s. 6d.

OSWALD. By Fell and Fjord; or, Scenes and Studies in Iceland. By E. J. OSWALD. Post 8vo, with Illustrations. 7s. 6d.

PAGE.

Introductory Text-Book of Geology. By DAVID PAGE, LL.D.,
Professor of Geology in the Durham University of Physical Science, Newcastle.
With Engravings and Glossarial Index. New Edition. Revised by Professor
LAPWORTH of Mason Science College, Birmingham. [In preparation.

Advanced Text-Book of Geology, Descriptive and Industrial.
With Engravings, and Glossary of Scientific Terms. New Edition. Revised by
Professor LAPWORTH. [In preparation.

Introductory Text-Book of Physical Geography. With Sketch-
Maps and Illustrations. Edited by Professor LAPWORTH, LL.D., F.G.S., &c.,
Mason Science College, Birmingham. Thirteenth Edition, Revised and Enlarged.
2s. 6d.

Advanced Text-Book of Physical Geography. Third Edition.
Revised and Enlarged by Professor LAPWORTH. With Engravings. 5s.

PATON.

Spindrift. By Sir J. NOEL PATON. Fcap., cloth, 5s.

Poems by a Painter. Fcap., cloth, 5s.

PATON. Body and Soul. A Romance in Transcendental Path-
ology. By FREDERICK NOEL PATON. Third Edition. Crown 8vo, 1s.

PATRICK. The Apology of Origen in Reply to Celsus. A
Chapter in the History of Apologetics. By the Rev. J. PATRICK, D.D. Post 8vo,
7s. 6d.

PAUL. History of the Royal Company of Archers, the Queen's
Body-Guard for Scotland. By JAMES BALFOUR PAUL, Advocate of the Scottish
Bar. Crown 4to, with Portraits and other Illustrations. £2, 2s.

PEILE. Lawn Tennis as a Game of Skill. By Lieut.-Col. S. C.
F. PEILE, B.S.C. Revised Edition, with new Scoring Rules. Fcap. 8vo, cloth, 1s.

PETTIGREW. The Handy Book of Bees, and their Profitable
Management. By A. PETTIGREW. Fifth Edition, Enlarged, with Engravings.
Crown 8vo, 3s. 6d.

PFLEIDERER. Philosophy and Development of Religion.
Being the Edinburgh Gifford Lectures for 1894. By OTTO PFLEIDERER, D.D.
Professor of Theology at Berlin University. In 2 vols, post 8vo, 15s. net.

PHILLIPS. The Knight's Tale. By F. EMILY PHILLIPS, Author
of 'The Education of Antonia.' Crown 8vo, 3s. 6d.

PHILOSOPHICAL CLASSICS FOR ENGLISH READERS.
Edited by WILLIAM KNIGHT, LL.D., Professor of Moral Philosophy, University
of St Andrews. In crown 8vo volumes, with Portraits, price 3s. 6d.
[For List of Volumes, see page 2.

POLLARD. **A** Study in Municipal Government : The Corpora-
tion of **Berlin.** By JAMES POLLARD, C.A., Chairman of the Edinburgh Public
Health Committee, and Secretary of the Edinburgh Chamber of Commerce.
Second Edition, Revised. Crown 8vo, 3s. 6d.

POLLOK. The Course of Time : A Poem. By ROBERT POLLOK,
A.M. Cottage Edition, 32mo, 8d. The Same, cloth, gilt **edges,** 1s. 6d. Another
Edition, with Illustrations by Birket Foster and others, **fcap.,** cloth, 3s. 6d., or
with edges gilt, 4s.

PORT ROYAL LOGIC. Translated from the French ; **with**
Introduction, Notes, and Appendix. By THOMAS SPENCER BAYNES, LL.D., Professor in the University of St Andrews. Tenth Edition, 12mo, 4s.

POTTS AND DARNELL.
Aditus Faciliores : An Easy Latin Construing Book, **with**
Complete Vocabulary By A. W. POTTS, M.A., LL.D., and the Rev. C. DARNELL,
M.A., Head-Master of Cargilfield Preparatory School Edinburgh. Tenth Edition,
fcap. 8vo, 3s. 6d.
Aditus Faciliores Graeci. An Easy Greek Construing Book,
with **Complete Vocabulary.** Fifth Edition, Revised. Fcap. 8vo, 3s.

POTTS. School Sermons. By the late ALEXANDER WM. POTTS,
LL.D., First Head-Master of Fettes College. With a Memoir and Portrait.
Crown 8vo, 7s. 6d.

PRINGLE. The Live Stock of the Farm. By ROBERT O.
PRINGLE. Third Edition. Revised and Edited **by** JAMES MACDONALD. Crown
8vo, 7s. 6d.

PRYDE. Pleasant Memories of a Busy Life. By DAVID PRYDE,
M.A., LL.D., Author of ' Highways of Literature,' 'Great Men in European History,' 'Biographical Outlines of English Literature,' &c. With a Mezzotint Portrait. Post 8vo, 6s.

PUBLIC GENERAL STATUTES AFFECTING SCOTLAND
from 1707 to 1847, with Chronological Table and Index. 3 vols. large 8vo, £3, 3s.

PUBLIC GENERAL STATUTES AFFECTING SCOTLAND,
COLLECTION OF. Published Annually, with General Index.

RAMSAY. Scotland and Scotsmen in the Eighteenth Century.
Edited from the MSS. of JOHN RAMSAY, Esq. of Ochtertyre, by ALEXANDER
ALLARDYCE, **Author** of 'Memoir of Admiral Lord Keith, K.B.,' &c. 2 vols.
8vo, 31s. 6d.

RANKIN.
A Handbook of the Church **of** Scotland. By JAMES RANKIN,
D.D., Minister of Muthill ; Author of 'Character Studies in the Old Testament,'
&c. An entirely New **and** much Enlarged Edition. Crown 8vo, with 2 Maps,
7s. 6d.
The First Saints. Post 8vo, **7s.** 6d.
The Creed in Scotland. An Exposition of the Apostles'
Creed. With Extracts from Archbishop Hamilton's Catechism of 1552, John
Calvin's Catechism of 1556, and a Catena of Ancient Latin and other Hymns.
Post 8vo, 7s. 6d.
The Worthy Communicant. A Guide to the Devout Obser-
vance of the Lord's Supper. Limp cloth, 1s. 3d.
The Young Churchman. Lessons on the Creed, the Com-
mandments, the Means of Grace, and the Church. Limp cloth, 1s. 3d.
First Communion Lessons. 25th Edition. Paper Cover, 2d.

RANKINE. A Hero of the Dark Continent. Memoir of Rev.
Wm. Affleck Scott, M.A., M.B., C.M., Church of Scotland Missionary at Blantyre,
British Central Africa. By W. HENRY RANKINE, B.D., Minister at St Boswells.
With a Portrait and other Illustrations. Crown 8vo, 5s.

RECORDS OF THE TERCENTENARY FESTIVAL OF THE
UNIVERSITY OF EDINBURGH. Celebrated in April 1884. Published under
the Sanction of the Senatus Academicus. Large 4to, £2, 12s. 6d.

ROBERTSON. The Early Religion of Israel. As set forth by
Biblical Writers and Modern Critical Historians. Being the Baird Lecture for
1888-89. By JAMES ROBERTSON, D.D., Professor of Oriental Languages in the
University of Glasgow. Fourth Edition. Crown 8vo, 10s. 6d.

ROBERTSON.
Orellana, and other Poems. By J. LOGIE ROBERTSON,
M.A. Fcap. 8vo. Printed on hand-made paper. 6s.
A History of English Literature. For Secondary Schools.
With an Introduction by Professor MASSON, Edinburgh University. Cr. 8vo, 3s.
English Verse for Junior Classes. In Two Parts. Part I.—
Chaucer to Coleridge. Part II.—Nineteenth Century Poets. Crown 8vo, each
1s. 6d. net.
Outlines of English Literature for Young Scholars. With
Illustrative Specimens. In 1 vol. crown 8vo.   [*In the press.*

ROBINSON. Wild Traits in Tame Animals. Being some
Familiar Studies in Evolution. By LOUIS ROBINSON, M.D. With Illustrations
by STEPHEN J. DADD. In 1 vol. crown 8vo.   [*In the press.*

RODGER. Aberdeen Doctors at Home and Abroad. The Story
of a Medical School. By ELLA HILL BURTON RODGER. Demy 8vo, 10s. 6d.

ROSCOE. Rambles with a Fishing-Rod. By E. S. ROSCOE.
Crown 8vo, 4s. 6d.

ROSS AND SOMERVILLE. Beggars on Horseback : A Riding
Tour in North Wales. By MARTIN Ross and E. Œ. SOMERVILLE. With Illustrations by E. Œ. SOMERVILLE. Crown 8vo, 3s. 6d.

RUTLAND.
Notes of an Irish Tour in 1846. By the DUKE OF RUTLAND,
G.C.B. (Lord JOHN MANNERS). New Edition. Crown 8vo, 2s. 6d.
Correspondence between the Right Honble. William Pitt
and Charles Duke of Rutland, Lord-Lieutenant of Ireland, 1781-1787. With
Introductory Note by JOHN DUKE OF RUTLAND. 8vo, 7s. 6d.

RUTLAND.
Gems of German Poetry. Translated by the DUCHESS OF
RUTLAND (Lady JOHN MANNERS).   [*New Edition in preparation.*
Impressions of Bad-Homburg. Comprising a Short Account
of the Women's Associations of Germany under the Red Cross. Crown 8vo, 1s. 6d.
Some Personal Recollections of the Later Years of the Earl
of Beaconsfield, K.G. Sixth Edition. 6d.
Employment of Women in the Public Service. 6d.
Some of the Advantages of Easily Accessible Reading and
Recreation Rooms and Free Libraries. With Remarks on Starting and Main-
taining them. Second Edition. Crown 8vo, 1s.
A Sequel to Rich Men's Dwellings, and other Occasional
Papers. Crown 8vo, 2s. 6d.
Encouraging Experiences of Reading and Recreation Rooms,
Aims of Guilds, Nottingham Social Guide, Existing Institutions, &c., &c.
Crown 8vo, 1s.

SAINTSBURY. The Flourishing of Romance and the Rise of
Allegory (12th and 13th Centuries). By GEORGE SAINTSBURY, M.A., Professor of
Rhetoric and English Literature in Edinburgh University. Being the first vol-
ume issued of "PERIODS OF EUROPEAN LITERATURE." Edited by Professor
SAINTSBURY. Crown 8vo, 5s. net.

SALMON. Songs of a Heart's Surrender, **and** other Verse.
By ARTHUR L. SALMON. Fcap. 8vo, 2s.

SCHEFFEL. The Trumpeter. A Romance of the Rhine. By
JOSEPH VICTOR VON SCHEFFEL. Translated from the Two Hundredth German
Edition by JESSIE BECK and LOUISA LORIMER. With an Introduction by Sir
THEODORE MARTIN, K.C.B. Long 8vo, 3s. 6d.

SCHILLER. Wallenstein. A Dramatic Poem. By FRIEDRICH
VON SCHILLER. Translated by C. G. N. LOCKHART. Fcap. 8vo, 7s. 6d.

SCOTT. Tom Cringle's Log. By MICHAEL SCOTT. **New** Edition.
With 19 Full-page Illustrations. Crown 8vo, 3s. 6d.

SCOUGAL. Prisons and their Inmates; or, Scenes **from a**
Silent World. By FRANCIS SCOUGAL. Crown 8vo, boards, 2s.

SELKIRK. Poems. By J. B. SELKIRK, Author of 'Ethics **and**
Æsthetics of Modern Poetry,' 'Bible Truths with Shakespearian Parallels,' &c.
New and Enlarged Edition. **Crown** 8vo, printed on antique paper, 6s.

SELLAR'S Manual of the Acts relating to Education in Scot-
land. By J. EDWARD GRAHAM, B.A. Oxon., Advocate. Ninth Edition. Demy
8vo, 12s. 6d.

SETH.

Scottish Philosophy. A Comparison of the Scottish and
German Answers to Hume. Balfour Philosophical Lectures, University of
Edinburgh. By ANDREW SETH, LL.D., Professor of Logic and Metaphysics in
Edinburgh University. Second Edition. **Crown** 8vo, 5s.

Hegelianism and Personality. Balfour Philosophical Lectures.
Second Series. Second Edition. Crown 8vo, 5s.

Man's Place in the Cosmos, and **other** Essays. Post 8vo,
7s. 6d. net.

SETH. A Study of Ethical Principles. By JAMES SETH, M.A.,
Professor of Philosophy in Cornell University, U.S.A. Second Edition, Revised.
Post 8vo, 10s. 6d. net.

SHADWELL. The Life of Colin Campbell, Lord Clyde. Illustrated by Extracts from his Diary and Correspondence. By Lieutenant-General
SHADWELL, C.B. With Portrait, Maps, and Plans. 2 vols. 8vo, 36s.

SHAND.

The Life of General Sir Edward Bruce Hamley, K.C.B.,
K.C.M.G. By ALEX. INNES SHAND, Author of 'Kilcarra,' 'Against Time,' &c.
With two Photogravure Portraits and other Illustrations. Cheaper Edition, with
a Statement by Mr Edward Hamley. 2 vols. demy 8vo, 10s. 6d.

Half a Century; or, Changes in Men and Manners. Second
Edition. 8vo, 12s. 6d.

Letters from the West of Ireland. Reprinted from the
'Times.' Crown 8vo, 5s.

SHARPE. Letters from and to Charles Kirkpatrick Sharpe.
Edited by ALEXANDER ALLARDYCE, Author of 'Memoir of Admiral Lord Keith,
K.B.,' &c. With a Memoir by the Rev. W. K. R. BEDFORD. In 2 vols. 8vo.
Illustrated with Etchings and other Engravings. £2, 12s. 6d.

SIM. Margaret Sim's Cookery. With an Introduction by L. B.
WALFORD, Author of 'Mr Smith: A Part of his Life,' &c. **Crown** 8vo, 5s.

SIMPSON. The Wild Rabbit in a New Aspect; **or,** Rabbit-
Warrens **that Pay.** A book for Landowners, Sportsmen, Land Agents, Farmers,
Gamekeepers, **and** Allotment Holders. A Record of Recent Experiments con-
ducted on the Estate of the Right Hon. the Earl of Wharncliffe at Wortley Hall.
By J. SIMPSON. Second Edition, Enlarged. Small **crown** 8vo, 5s.

SINCLAIR. Audrey Craven. By MAY SINCLAIR. Crown
8vo, 6s.

SKELTON.

The Table-Talk of Shirley. By JOHN SKELTON, Advocate,
C.B., LL.D., Author of 'The Essays of Shirley.' With a Frontispiece. Sixth
Edition, Revised and Enlarged. Post 8vo, 7s. 6d.

SKELTON.

The Table-Talk of Shirley. Second Series. Summers and Winters at Balmawhapple. With Illustrations. Two Volumes. Second Edition. Post 8vo, 10s. net.

Maitland of Lethington ; and the Scotland of Mary Stuart. A History. Limited Edition, with Portraits. Demy 8vo, 2 vols., 28s. net.

The Handbook of Public Health. A Complete Edition of the Public Health and other Sanitary Acts relating to Scotland. Annotated, and with the Rules, Instructions, and Decisions of the Board of Supervision brought up to date with relative forms. Second Edition. With Introduction, containing the Administration of the Public Health Act in Counties. 8vo, 8s. 6d.

The Local Government (Scotland) Act in Relation to Public Health. A Handy Guide for County and District Councillors, Medical Officers, Sanitary Inspectors, and Members of Parochial Boards. Second Edition. With a new Preface on appointment of Sanitary Officers. Crown 8vo, 2s.

SKRINE. Columba: A Drama. By JOHN HUNTLEY SKRINE Warden of Glenalmond ; Author of 'A Memory of Edward Thring.' Fcap. 4to, 6s

SMITH.

Thorndale ; or, The Conflict of Opinions. By WILLIAM SMITH, Author of 'A Discourse on Ethics,' &c. New Edition. Crown 8vo, 10s. 6d.

Gravenhurst ; or, Thoughts on Good and Evil. Second Edition. With Memoir and Portrait of the Author. Crown 8vo, 8s.

The Story of William and Lucy Smith. Edited by GEORGE MERRIAM. Large post 8vo, 12s. 6d.

SMITH. Memoir of the Families of M'Combie and Thoms, originally M'Intosh and M'Thomas. Compiled from History and Tradition. By WILLIAM M'COMBIE SMITH. With Illustrations. 8vo, 7s. 6d.

SMITH. Greek Testament Lessons for Colleges, Schools, and Private Students, consisting chiefly of the Sermon on the Mount and the Parables of our Lord. With Notes and Essays. By the Rev. J. HUNTER SMITH, M.A., King Edward's School, Birmingham. Crown 8vo, 6s.

SMITH. The Secretary for Scotland. Being a Statement of the Powers and Duties of the new Scottish Office. With a Short Historical Introduction, and numerous references to important Administrative Documents. By W. C. SMITH, LL.B., Advocate. 8vo, 6s.

"SON OF THE MARSHES, A."

From Spring to Fall ; or, When Life Stirs. By "A SON OF THE MARSHES." Cheap Uniform Edition. Crown 8vo, 3s. 6d.

Within an Hour of London Town: Among Wild Birds and their Haunts. Edited by J. A. OWEN. Cheap Uniform Edition. Crown 8vo, 3s. 6d.

With the Woodlanders and by the Tide. Cheap Uniform Edition. Crown 8vo, 3s. 6d.

On Surrey Hills. Cheap Uniform Edition. Crown 8vo, 3s. 6d.

Annals of a Fishing Village. Cheap Uniform Edition. Crown 8vo, 3s. 6d.

SORLEY. The Ethics of Naturalism. Being the Shaw Fellowship Lectures, 1884. By W. R. SORLEY, M.A., Fellow of Trinity College, Cambridge, Professor of Moral Philosophy in the University of Aberdeen. Crown 8vo, 6s.

SPROTT. The Worship and Offices of the Church of Scotland. By GEORGE W. SPROTT, D.D., Minister of North Berwick. Crown 8vo, 6s.

STATISTICAL ACCOUNT OF SCOTLAND. Complete, with Index. 15 vols. 8vo, £16, 16s.

STEEVENS. The Land of the Dollar. By G. W. STEEVENS, Author of 'Naval Policy,' &c. Crown 8vo, 6s.

STEPHENS.

The **Book of** the Farm ; detailing **the** Labours of the Farmer, Farm-Steward, Ploughman, Shepherd, Hedger, Farm-Labourer, Field-Worker, and Cattle-man. Illustrated with numerous Portraits of Animals and Engravings of Implements, and Plans of Farm Buildings. Fourth Edition. Revised, and in great part Re-written, by JAMES MACDONALD, F.R.S.E., Secretary Highland and Agricultural Society of Scotland. Complete in Six Divisional Volumes, bound in cloth, each 10s. 6d., or handsomely bound, in 3 volumes, with leather back and gilt top, £3, 3s.

** Also being issued in 20 monthly Parts, **price** 2s. **6d. net each.**

[*Part I. ready.*

Catechism of Practical Agriculture. 22d Thousand. **Revised** by JAMES MACDONALD, F.R.S.E. With numerous Illustrations. Crown 8vo, 1s.

The Book of Farm Implements and Machines. By J. **SLIGHT** and R. SCOTT BURN, Engineers. Edited by HENRY STEPHENS. Large 8vo, £2, 2s.

STEVENSON. British Fungi. (Hymenomycetes.) By Rev. JOHN STEVENSON, Author of 'Mycologia Scotica,' Hon. Sec. Cryptogamic Society of Scotland. Vols. I. and **II.**, post 8vo, with Illustrations, price 12s. 6d. net each.

STEWART. Advice to Purchasers of Horses. By JOHN STEWART, **V.S.** New Edition. 2s. 6d.

STODDART. Angling Songs. **By** THOMAS TOD STODDART. New Edition, with a Memoir by ANNA **M. STODDART.** Crown 8vo, 7s. 6d.

STODDART.

John Stuart Blackie : A Biography. **By ANNA** M. STODDART. With 3 Plates. Third Edition. 2 vols. demy 8vo, 21s.

POPULAR EDITION, with Portrait. Crown 8vo, 6s.

Sir Philip Sidney : Servant of God. Illustrated **by MARGARET** L. HUGGINS. With a New Portrait of Sir Philip Sidney. **Small 4to, with a** specially designed Cover. 5s.

STORMONTH.

Dictionary of the English Language, Pronouncing, Etymological, and Explanatory. By the Rev. JAMES STORMONTH. Revised by the Rev. P. H. PHELP. Library Edition. New and Cheaper Edition, with Supplement. Imperial 8vo, handsomely bound in half morocco, 18s. net.

Etymological and Pronouncing Dictionary of the English Language. Including a very Copious Selection of Scientific Terms. For use in Schools and Colleges, and as a Book of General Reference. The Pronunciation carefully revised by the Rev. P. H. PHELP, M.A. Cantab. Thirteenth Edition, with Supplement. Crown 8vo, pp. 800. 7s. 6d.

The School Dictionary. New Edition, Revised.

[*In preparation.*

STORY. The Apostolic Ministry in the Scottish Church (The Baird Lecture for 1897). By ROBERT HERBERT STORY, D.D. (Edin.), F.S.A. Scot., Professor of Ecclesiastical History in the University of Glasgow ; Principal Clerk of the General Assembly ; and Chaplain to the Queen. Crown 8vo, 7s. 6d.

STORY.

Nero ; A Historical Play. **By W. W. STORY,** Author of 'Roba di Roma.' Fcap. 8vo, 6s.

Vallombrosa. Post 8vo, **5s.**

Poems. 2 vols., 7s. 6d.

Fiammetta. A Summer Idyl. Crown 8vo, **7s.** 6d.

Conversations in a Studio. **2** vols. crown 8vo, 12s. 6d.

Excursions in Art and Letters. Crown **8vo, 7s.** 6d.

A Poet's Portfolio : Later Readings. 18mo, **3s.** 6d.

STRACHEY. Talk at a Country House. Fact and Fiction. By Sir EDWARD STRACHEY, Bart. With a Portrait of the Author. Crown 8vo, 4s. 6d. net.

STURGIS. Little Comedies, Old and New. By JULIAN STURGIS.
Crown 8vo, 7s. 6d.

SUTHERLAND. Handbook of Hardy Herbaceous and Alpine
Flowers, for General Garden Decoration. Containing Descriptions of upwards
of 1000 Species of Ornamental Hardy Perennial and Alpine Plants; along with
Concise and Plain Instructions for their Propagation and Culture. By WILLIAM
SUTHERLAND, Landscape Gardener; formerly Manager of the Herbaceous Depart-
ment at Kew. Crown 8vo, 7s. 6d.

TAYLOR. The Story of my Life. By the late Colonel
MEADOWS TAYLOR, Author of 'The Confessions of a Thug,' &c., &c. Edited by
his Daughter. New and Cheaper Edition, being the Fourth. Crown 8vo, 6s.

THOMAS. The Woodland Life. By EDWARD THOMAS. With a
Frontispiece. In 1 vol. square 8vo.   [*In the press.*

THOMSON.
The Diversions of a Prime Minister. By Basil Thomson.
With a Map, numerous Illustrations by J. W. Cawston and others, and Repro-
ductions of Rare Plates from Early Voyages of Sixteenth and Seventeenth Centuries. Small demy 8vo, 15s.

South Sea Yarns. With 10 Full-page Illustrations. Cheaper
Edition. Crown 8vo, 3s. 6d.

THOMSON.
Handy Book of the Flower-Garden : Being Practical Direc-
tions for the Propagation, Culture, and Arrangement of Plants in Flower-
Gardens **all** the year round. With Engraved Plans. By DAVID THOMSON,
Gardener to his Grace the Duke of Buccleuch, K.T., at Drumlanrig. Fourth
and Cheaper Edition. Crown 8vo, 5s.

The Handy Book of Fruit-Culture under Glass : Being a
series of Elaborate Practical Treatises on the Cultivation and Forcing of Pines,
Vines, Peaches, Figs, Melons, Strawberries, and Cucumbers. With Engravings
of Hothouses, &c. Second Edition, Revised and Enlarged. Crown 8vo, 7s. 6d.

THOMSON. A Practical Treatise on the Cultivation of the
Grape Vine. By WILLIAM THOMSON, Tweed Vineyards. Tenth Edition. 8vo, 5s.

THOMSON. Cookery for the Sick and Convalescent. With
Directions for the Preparation of Poultices, Fomentations, &c. By BARBARA
THOMSON. Fcap. 8vo, 1s. 6d.

THORBURN. Asiatic Neighbours. By S. S. THORBURN, Bengal
Civil Service, Author of 'Bannú; or, Our Afghan Frontier,' 'David Leslie :
A Story of the Afghan Frontier,' 'Musalmans and Money-Lenders in the Pan-
jab.' With Two Maps. Demy 8vo, 10s. 6d. net.

THORNTON. Opposites. A Series of Essays on the Unpopular
Sides of Popular Questions. By LEWIS THORNTON. 8vo, 12s. 6d.

**TRANSACTIONS OF THE HIGHLAND AND AGRICUL-
TURAL SOCIETY OF** SCOTLAND. Published annually, price 5s.

TRAVERS.
Mona Maclean, Medical Student. A Novel. By GRAHAM
TRAVERS. Twelfth Edition. Crown 8vo, 6s.

Fellow Travellers. Fourth Edition. Crown 8vo, 6s.

TRYON. Life of Vice-Admiral Sir George Tryon, K.C.B. By
Rear-Admiral C. C. PENROSE FITZGERALD. With Two Portraits and numerous
Illustrations. Second Edition. Demy 8vo, 21s.

TULLOCH.
Rational Theology and Christian Philosophy in England in
the Seventeenth Century. By JOHN TULLOCH, D.D., Principal of St Mary's College in the University of St Andrews, and one of her Majesty's Chaplains in
Ordinary in Scotland. Second Edition. 2 vols. 8vo, 16s.

Modern Theories in Philosophy and Religion. 8vo, 15s.

TULLOCH.

Luther, and other Leaders of the Reformation. **Third Edition, Enlarged.** Crown 8vo, 3s. 6d.

Memoir of Principal Tulloch, **D.D.,** LL.D. By Mrs OLIPHANT, Author of '**Life** of Edward Irving.' **Third** and Cheaper Edition. 8vo, with Portrait, **7s.** 6d.

TWEEDIE. The Arabian Horse: **His** Country and People. By Major-General W. TWEEDIE, C.S.I., Bengal Staff Corps; for many years H.B.M.'s Consul-General, Baghdad, and Political Resident for **the** Government of India in Turkish Arabia. In one vol. royal 4to, with Seven Coloured Plates and other Illustrations, and a Map of the Country. Price £3, 3s. **net.**

TYLER. The **Whence** and the Whither of Man. A Brief **History** of his Origin and Development through Conformity to Environment. **The** Morse Lectures of 1895. By JOHN M. TYLER, Professor of Biology, Amherst **College, U.S.A.** Post 8vo, 6s. **net.**

VEITCH.

Memoir of John Veitch, LL.D., Professor of Logic and Rhetoric, University of Glasgow. By MARY R. **L.** BRYCE. With Portrait and 3 Photogravure Plates. Demy 8vo, 7s. 6d.

Border Essays. By JOHN VEITCH, **LL.D., Professor of** Logic **and Rhetoric,** University of Glasgow. Crown 8vo, 4s. 6d. **net.**

The History and Poetry of the Scottish **Border : their** Main **Features and** Relations. New and Enlarged Edition. **2 vols. demy 8vo,** 16s.

Institutes of Logic. Post 8vo, 12s. 6d.

The Feeling for Nature in Scottish Poetry. From the Earliest Times to the Present Day. 2 vols. fcap. 8vo, in roxburghe binding, 15s.

Merlin and other Poems. Fcap. 8vo, 4s. 6d.

Knowing and Being. Essays in Philosophy. **First Series.** Crown 8vo, 5s.

Dualism and Monism ; and other Essays. Essays in **Philosophy.** Second Series. With an Introduction by R. M. Wenley. Crown 8vo, 4s. 6d. net.

VIRGIL. The Æneid of Virgil. Translated **in** English Blank Verse by G. K. RICKARDS, M.A., and Lord RAVENSWORTH. 2 vols. fcap. 8vo, 10s.

WACE. Christianity **and Agnosticism.** Reviews of some Recent Attacks on the Christian **Faith. By HENRY** WACE, D.D., Principal of King's College, London ; **Preacher of Lincoln's Inn ;** Chaplain to the Queen. Second Edition. Post 8vo, **10s. 6d. net.**

WADDELL. An Old Kirk Chronicle : Being a History of **Auld**hame, Tyninghame, and Whitekirk, in East Lothian. From Session Records, 1615 to 1850. By Rev. P. HATELY WADDELL, B.D., Minister of the United Parish. Small Paper Edition, 200 Copies. Price £1. Large Paper Edition, 50 **Copies.** Price £1, 10s.

WALDO. The Ban of **the Gubbe.** By CEDRIC DANE WALDO. Crown 8vo, 2s. 6d.

WALFORD. Four Biographies from 'Blackwood': Jane Taylor, Hannah **More,** Elizabeth Fry, Mary Somerville. **By L.** B. WALFORD. Crown 8vo, 5s.

WARREN'S (SAMUEL) WORKS :—

Diary of a Late Physician. Cloth, 2s. 6d. ; boards, 2s.

Ten Thousand A-Year. Cloth, 3s. 6d. ; boards, 2s. 6d.

Now and Then. The Lily and the **Bee.** Intellectual and Moral Development of the Present **Age.** 4s. 6d.

Essays : Critical, Imaginative, and Juridical. **5s.**

WENLEY.

Socrates and Christ : **A** Study **in the Philosophy of Religion.**
By R. M. WENLEY, M.A., D.Sc., D.Phil., Professor of Philosophy in the University of Michigan, U.S.A. Crown 8vo, 6s.

Aspects of Pessimism. Crown **8vo, 6s.**

WHITE.

The Eighteen **Christian Centuries. By the Rev.** JAMES
WHITE. Seventh Edition. Post 8vo, with Index, 6s.

History of France, **from the Earliest Times. Sixth** Thousand.
Post 8vo, with Index, 6s.

WHITE.

Archæological **Sketches in** Scotland—Kintyre and Knapdale.
By Colonel **T. P.** WHITE, R.E., of the Ordnance Survey. With numerous Illustrations. 2 vols. folio, £4, 4s. Vol. I., Kintyre, sold separately, £2, 2s.

The Ordnance **Survey of** the United Kingdom. A Popular
Account. Crown 8vo, 5s.

WILLIAMSON. **The** Horticultural Handbook and Exhibitor's
Guide. A Treatise on Cultivating, Exhibiting, and Judging Plants, Flowers, **Fruits, and** Vegetables. By W. WILLIAMSON, Gardener. Revised by MALCOLM DUNN, Gardener to his Grace the Duke of Buccleuch and Queensberry, Dalkeith Park. New **and** Cheaper Edition, enlarged. Crown 8vo, paper cover, 2s. ; cloth, **2s. 6d.**

WILLIAMSON. Poems of Nature **and Life. By** DAVID R.
WILLIAMSON, Minister of Kirkmaiden. Fcap. 8vo, 3s.

WILLS. Behind an Eastern Veil. **A Plain Tale of Events**
occurring in the Experience of a Lady who **had a unique opportunity of** observing the Inner Life of Ladies of the Upper **Class in Persia.** By C. J. WILLS, Author of 'In the Land of the Lion and Sun,' 'Persia as it is,' &c., &c. Cheaper Edition. Demy 8vo, 5s.

WILSON.

Works of Professor Wilson. Edited by his Son-in-Law,
Professor FERRIER. 12 vols. crown 8vo, £2, 8s.

Christopher in his Sporting-Jacket. **2 vols., 8s.**

Isle of Palms, City of the Plague, **and** other Poems. 4s.

Lights and Shadows of Scottish Life, and other Tales. 4s.

Essays, Critical and Imaginative. 4 vols., 16s.

The Noctes Ambrosianæ. **4 vols., 16s.**

Homer **and his** Translators, and the Greek Drama. **Crown**
8vo, 4s.

WORSLEY.

Poems and Translations. By PHILIP STANHOPE WORSLEY,
M.A. Edited by EDWARD WORSLEY. Second Edition, Enlarged. Fcap. 8vo, 6s.

Homer's Odyssey. Translated into English Verse in the
Spenserian Stanza. By P. S. Worsley. New and Cheaper Edition. Post 8vo, 7s. 6d. net.

Homer's Iliad. Translated by P. S. Worsley and Prof. Con-
ington. 2 vols. crown 8vo, 21s.

YATE. England and Russia Face to Face in Asia. A Record of
Travel with the Afghan Boundary Commission. By Captain A. C. YATE, Bombay Staff Corps. 8vo, with Maps and Illustrations, 21s.

YATE. Northern Afghanistan ; or, Letters from the Afghan
Boundary Commission. By Major C. E. YATE, C.S.I., C.M.G., Bombay Staff Corps, F.R.G.S. 8vo, with Maps, 18s.

YULE. Fortification : For the use of Officers in the Army, and
Readers of Military History. By Colonel YULE, Bengal Engineers. 8vo, with Numerous Illustrations, 10s.